Φ

TWENTIETH-CENTURY HOUSES
Frank Lloyd Wright Fallingwater Bear Run, Pennsylvania 1935
Alvar Aalto Villa Mairea Noormarkku 1937–9
Charles and Ray Eames Eames House Pacific Palisades, California 1949

FRANK LLOYD WRIGHT
Unity Temple Oak Park, Illinois 1908
Barnsdall (Hollyhock) House Los Angeles 1921
Johnson Wax Administration Building and Research Tower Racine 1936, 1944

ARTS & CRAFTS HOUSES I
Philip Webb Red House Bexleyheath, Kent 1859
William Richard Lethaby Melsetter House Orkney, Scotland 1898
Sir Edwin Lutyens Goddards Abinger Common, Surrey 1900

ARTS & CRAFTS HOUSES II
Charles Rennie Mackintosh Hill House Helensburgh, Scotland 1903
C.F.A. Voysey The Homestead Frinton-on-Sea, Essex 1905–6
Greene and Greene Gamble House Pasadena, California 1907–8

ARTS & CRAFTS MASTERPIECES
Edward Prior St Andrew's Church Roker, Sunderland 1905
Charles Rennie Mackintosh Glasgow School of Art Glasgow 1897–1909
Bernard Maybeck First Church of Christ, Scientist, Berkeley California 1910

PLACES OF WORSHIP
Sir Christopher Wren St Paul's Cathedral London 1675–1710
Jože Plečnik Church of the Sacred Heart Prague 1922–33
Tadao Ando Church on the Water Hokkaido 1988 **Church of the Light** Osaka 1989

TWENTIETH-CENTURY MUSEUMS I
Ludwig Mies van der Rohe New National Gallery, Berlin 1962–8
Louis I. Kahn Kimbell Art Museum Fort Worth, Texas 1972
Richard Meier Museum für Kunsthandwerk Frankfurt am Main 1985

TWENTIETH-CENTURY MUSEUMS II
Arata Isozaki The Museum of Modern Art, Gunma Gunma Prefecture, Japan 1971–4
James Stirling, Michael Wilford and Associates Clore Gallery London 1987
Tate Gallery, Liverpool 1988
James Ingo Freed United States Holocaust Memorial Museum
Washington, DC 1993

CONTEMPORARY CALIFORNIA HOUSES
Frank Gehry Schnabel House Brentwood, California 1990
Eric Owen Moss Lawson-Westen House Brentwood, California 1993
Franklin D. Israel Drager House Berkeley, California 1994

LOST MASTERPIECES
Joseph Paxton Crystal Palace London 1851
Ferdinand Dutert Palais des Machines Paris 1889
McKim Mead and White Pennsylvania Station New York 1905–10

TWENTIETH-CENTURY CLASSICS
Walter Gropius Bauhaus, Dessau 1925–6
Le Corbusier Unité d'Habitation Marseilles 1945–52
Louis I. Kahn Salk Institute La Jolla, California 1959–65

CITY ICONS
Antoni Gaudí Expiatory Church of the Sagrada Família Barcelona 1882–
Warren and Wetmore Grand Central Terminal New York City 1903–13
Jørn Utzon Sydney Opera House Sydney 1957–73

PIONEERING BRITISH 'HIGH-TECH'

Introduction by James S. Russell

Encountering the Willis Faber & Dumas Building unsuspectingly for the first time is disconcerting. One does not see the building itself, only the buildings across the street reflected in its sinuous, shiny surface; a surface that undulates along the street front to an indeterminate end. Instead of the deferential gesture it was designed to be, this exterior seems more an architectural abrogation, giving up any presence it might have asserted in favour of the image of the rather ordinary streetscape that surrounds it. It would seem to have little in common with the crenellated complexity of James Stirling's and James Gowan's Leicester University Engineering Building and the gantry-festooned bravura that is Richard Rogers' Lloyd's Building. While these projects have divergent concerns, they tackle rather similar questions, such as: Is the architect a humanist, a sociologist, or a behavioural engineer? Is design supposed to change people's lives or simply celebrate them? What is the appropriate expression of a public (even if commercial) building? In offering individual answers, these buildings opened a debate on deep dilemmas in the practice of architecture, ones that continue to concern us today.

Foster's building is, at first glance, the most anomalous of these three buildings. When one looks at the slick, machined surfaces one does not think of a humanist architect behind the design, certainly not in comparison with contemporary figures such as Herman Hertzberger or Aldo van Eyck, who were thought in the 1960s and 1970s to most deeply express idealistic notions of how architecture could support comity. However, Willis Faber shows Foster as prescient about the evolving social ecosystem of the workplace. While all three of these buildings brilliantly respond to their programme, Foster's intention was little less than to create an architecture suitable to dramatically redefined ways of working. He is, in that sense, the perfect functionalist, the one among this group closest to the most emphatic ideals of the 1920s Modern Movement.

Almost twenty-five years after its completion, the Willis Faber & Dumas Building incorporates all the key design elements that business today is just discovering to be important. While Willis Faber & Dumas was not the only company attempting to replace the traditional pyramid hierarchies of the workplace, in which information (at best) flows only up or down, its strategy has proven more durable than most. Far more so than in the 1970s, the metaphor for work today is the network, with currents of information flowing in many directions. The openness, spontaneity of interaction (encouraged by the iconic waterfall of escalators) and the flexibility of the Willis Faber & Dumas Building's open plan are all

currently sought-after values in the workplace – seen, for example, in the use of escalators in the Pittsburgh headquarters of Alcoa and the light-drenched internal 'street' of the British Airways headquarters near Heathrow Airport, London – to name just two recently completed examples. The pool, sunny cafeteria, and grassed-over roof garden were widely regarded as frills when installed at Willis Faber, but, as retaining valued people in a business environment with a shortage of skills has become critical, many of the amenities pioneered there are now regularly found in the million-square-foot campuses popping up along the freeways in Silicon Valley. Businesses today use similar amenities (from fitness centres and tennis courts to coffee bars and gourmet cafeterias) to attract or retain the best and brightest talent.

Foster's insightfulness into the sociology of the workplace at the Willis Faber & Dumas Building may come as a surprise since the building is so expressively suppressed – most of its tremendous technological refinement and innovation is hidden. That which is not visible is rendered so discreetly (the minimalist curtain-wall fittings, for example) as to attract little notice. Compared to the drama of the entrance sequence, the exterior is an elegant bore, coming alive only at night, when the innards of this garden-topped 'machine for working' are presented for the delectation of passers-by.

Foster proclaims himself as anti-style, and the Willis Faber & Dumas Building makes a convincing case. The same could never be said of Richard Rogers. Rogers' motivations seem much more complex than Foster's. The work of the Richard Rogers Partnership is besotted with the expressive potential of technology, yet Lloyd's remade the workplace in a way that is arguably even more profound than Foster's accomplishments. The acrobatic use of technology in the Lloyd's Building actually obscures the truth of this observation, as does Lloyd's of London's reluctance to open the building to the public.

Accommodating change and growth had been a serious issue at Lloyd's for many years before Rogers was brought in to design a new building, as Kenneth Powell's text makes clear. The idea of the 'Room' – a single space within which all the underwriters could work and interact – began to fall victim to the sheer number of underwriters and the increased speed and technological demands of the process. In theory, all of the underwriters would like to be able to see each other, perhaps over a vast clear space; yet Lloyd's was so inextricably a part of the cramped plan of the medieval City of London that building a single-level space – a twenty-first-century bourse – could never seriously be contemplated. Rogers solved the problem by extruding the Room vertically, wrapping a spectacular top-lit atrium with its several new levels. While a vertical solution was obvious, it would not obviously work. Rogers proportioned the atrium and the lofty ceilings to maximize visibility across and between floors. The escalators and glass-enclosed external elevators speed movement between floors, which also has the effect of easing accessibility to the entire extent of the Room. This is in truth a city within the City. Inevitably such an arrangement disturbed a wide variety of hierarchical relationships that had long been established; indeed, it is unclear at Lloyd's what the hierarchy is. One is nearest the greatest number of other people if one is near the atrium and on the centre level, but there is no emblematic architectural symbolism of this hierarchy; it had to become established by use.

The building was erected at a time of wrenching transformations in the financial businesses. Transformations that affected traders' lives (which, in the end, rocked Lloyd's) were the vastly increased risks associated with seismic political change throughout the world and a volatile, information-technology-intensive global economy. Arguably, the building became a lightening rod for the discontent engendered by these changes. The genius of the scheme, however, has allowed it to gracefully accept enormous technological change, at least, in the form of ubiquitous computer terminals with their unprecedented wiring needs and the vastly increased loads they put on the cooling system. No similar structure in New York, for example, could accept change of such speed or dimension without hugely expensive alteration. There is no equivalent to the scale of Lloyd's Room elsewhere. Instead the trading floors that have everywhere sprouted up are generally hacked out of standard office buildings, which means jamming transfer trusses in, reconfiguring elevator cores, and pushing ceilings between floor beams to achieve enough height to accommodate raised floors. Though the financial/insurance/ investment businesses are now as information-technology intensive as any on earth, they paradoxically desire to place their traders, however umbilically-linked to computer screens, in vast rooms, so that everyone can see everyone else, and react with exceptional speed to business or political developments worldwide. The New York Stock Exchange needs a solution as brilliantly synthetic as Lloyd's but as yet has not proved brave enough to emulate it.

The functional brilliance of Lloyd's has been missed by many critics simply because they are so taken with the spectacle of the exterior, in which every element of the services, elevators and stairs has been lovingly if not obsessively articulated. This is an aspect of

Rogers' work that owes something to the liberating influence of Stirling. Strip away the technological exhibitionism of Lloyd's and you get Louis Kahn's Richards Medical Building in Philadelphia of 1961, in which the simple geometry of the 'served' laboratories are readily adapted through the external 'servant' shafts that deliver the mechanical services. (The relationship is much clearer in plan than from the indecipherably hyperactive exterior.) Indeed, it is much easier to see the relationship of Richards with Lloyd's than it is to see Richards as a model for Leicester University Engineering Building, even though the Stirling/Gowan and Kahn buildings share a typology. Which is only to suggest the profoundly different attitude that Stirling brings to architecture – an attitude arguably more influential than that of either Foster or Rogers, even though Leicester is the oldest building in this anthology.

John McKean's text describes the dilemma facing architecture after the 1950s – one that Stirling brought to the noisy surface of architectural debate. While, as McKean assures us, this highly idiosyncratic design goes to great lengths to assure us of a glove-like fit with the programme, we should remember that a heroic redefinition of the lab-building paradigm in the style of Kahn is not something that Stirling attempts. In fact, to accept the Leicester University Engineering Building primarily as a functionalist success would be to miss most of what the building is about. It 'quotes' vernacular industrial construction; it juxtaposes deadpan use of off-the-shelf technology (the patent glazing) with a bravura purpose-built workshop roofing system and exhibitionistic atrium glazing. Classrooms and labs pinwheel around the circulation core, which itself takes visitors for a very rich and varied journey. No geometry goes unarticulated. Though not a biological laboratory, many of the metaphors are anatomical: distinctly expressed parts are united using fluid, membrane-like spaces or knuckle-like hinges in what is palpably an assemblage rather than a unity.

In short, Rogers puts spectacular aesthetic effects to functional ends, while Stirling at Leicester was able to take the look of functionalism to spectacular aesthetic ends. With the gantries, sawtooth roofs, exposed spiralling exit stairs and lovingly detailed smokestack, Stirling and Gowan brought to the surface a question that has raised hackles ever since: is it wrong to use an imagery of industrialism for clearly formalist ends?

Critics have often come out against Stirling and such soulmates as Robert Venturi (forget for a minute that the expression that came out of the analysis is entirely different). By contrast, Rogers and Foster take the 'responsible' course of the 1920s functionalists, creating buildings that may very well have changed the lives of their occupants; certainly they hoped to alter for the better the fortunes

of their client companies. Stirling, the subversive, takes the lives of his users at face value. For him architecture is about finding a suitable expression for what people do, not transforming what they do. The question this begs is whether such aestheticizing of functionalism trivializes architecture. Certainly many critics think so – with Stirling having been described as a talented but perhaps misguided Postmodernist, whose facility with architectural form disguised a lack of a transcendent, Kahnian ideology.

McKean states how Stirling, in 1956, criticized American functionalist practice as 'anonymous; hiding a mechanical [perhaps he means mechanistic] disposition of elements'. There, functionalism concerned 'industrial process', he argued, while in Europe it remained an 'essentially humanist method of designing to specific use'. It is not hard to read into this passage a criticism of the approach Foster would later take on the Willis Faber & Dumas Building, not to mention numerous other projects. (There is much in Willis Faber that recalls the seminal 1960s work of Ezra Ehrenkrantz and the Educational Facilities Laboratories for the School Construction Systems Development programme in California, which, as Stirling observed, attempted a construction-easing integration of systems and structure that could be readily standardized. It worked. American construction methods are far more rigidly standardized than those of either Europe or Asia.)

Much has been made of the exhibitionism of technology at Lloyd's (especially the mechanical systems, the expression of which has never been of interest to Foster and only intermittently to Stirling). However, Rogers can be seen as liberated from the straitjacket of puritanical functionalist modernism by Stirling's richly tactile and less ideology-driven work. Indeed, at the time of writing, Stirling's 'humanistic' method has largely prevailed. Few architects today enslave themselves to systems, to the simplistic power of such diagrammatic organizing devices as Kahn's 'servant and served'. Stirling and Gowan ransacked history and memory to make an assemblage of images. They, among others, allowed architects to become artists again, expressively embellishing the programme in whatever way their muse took them. This method has given us today's pluralism of aesthetics, a world in which Frank Gehry, Steven Holl, Daniel Libeskind, Gunther Behnisch and Tadao Ando can coexist ideologically, not to mention a Britain that has nurtured such diverse talents as those of Nicholas Grimshaw, Jan Kaplicky and Amanda Levete of Future Systems, David Chipperfield and Allsop & Störmer.

James Stirling and James Gowan

Leicester University
Engineering Building
Leicester 1959–63

John McKean

Photography
Jeremy Cockayne, Richard Einzig/Arcaid;
cover detail also by Jeremy Cockayne
Drawings
John Hewitt

We are no longer in the period of *'towards an architecture'. It is architecture or nothing. And if it is architecture, it is architecture continually redefined – not in words but in forms.*

John Summerson, 1959.

1

1 The Leicester University Engineering Building, photographed on completion in 1963.
2, 3 All Saints, the central London church by William Butterfield, begun in 1849, completed externally in 1853. Garish brick, powerfully facetted shapes, picturesque composition, functional arguments, tight and asymmetrical planning on far too small a site. 'Mr Butterfield always seems to build *con amore* when there are extraordinary difficulties,' commented *The Ecclesiologist*, XV, 1854, p59.

2

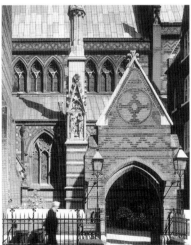

3

The art critic

The Leicester University Engineering Building, 1959–63, by James Stirling and James Gowan was the first building in Britain after Modernism. In architecture, this building is the great symbol of that sense of revulsion and liberation which permeated English art and letters in these years, the years of 'pop' and of 'angry young men'. It mirrors astonishingly accurately the place of All Saints, Margaret Street, the London church by William Butterfield 110 years earlier.

John Summerson, resurrecting Butterfield in his classic 1945 essay subtitled 'The Glory of Ugliness', began: 'People of taste screw up their faces at the architecture of William Butterfield'. Certainly Stirling & Gowan elicited a parallel response at Leicester. Nikolaus Pevsner used it to epitomise the enemy of good (ie Modernist) taste in his talk 'The Anti-pioneers' on BBC radio at the end of 1966. Pevsner's fury led him so to screw up his face that he talked of it as incorporating 'lecture theatres jutting out. These are of exposed concrete; the rest is faced with blue engineering bricks …'.

But there is neither blue brick nor raw concrete; on the contrary, it is quite different on the eye from Stirling & Gowan's earlier essays in the 'Brutalist' vernacular. As Stirling commented, 'it is clear that when Professor Pevsner approaches a building which he thinks he should not like, he closes his eyes'. The lecture theatres certainly jut out, but they, like the remaining structure, are covered with brick-red tiles. Red tiles and bricks which remind us, again, of Butterfield's garish, clashing brick church – as well as the more obvious po-faced, literally 'red-brick university', as that generation of newer British universities was known.

The extreme of literalness can generate an extravagant rhetoric. At Leicester, Stirling & Gowan straight-facedly demonstrate a direct fit to their programme. It is a low-cost building, in two distinct parts: first, a collection of fixed elements, each clearly articulated at the front (including the requirement for a water tank far above the ground for use in the hydraulic labs below); second, behind and almost filling its tight footprint, a general shed of workshops. Over these sheds, industrial roof-lighting aims north – which just happens to be at 45 degrees to the plan geometry. In front, at first floor level, rise two differently sized lecture theatres. Above the smaller are stacked four identical labs, above the larger rises a tiny, six storey tower of offices served by the one and only lift the building could afford. The vertical circulation spaces between the two towers diminish towards the top as the traffic decreases.

All so logical! Which says nothing about the scintillating crystal waterfall between the chamfered towers, about the faceted cylindrical glass escape stair, about why the aerodynamics lab is cantilevered rhetorically three floors above the service road … nothing about overall appearance, the forms in such dynamic equilibrium – 'if you removed the top floor the building would overturn', as Stirling remarked later. This hoover on the hearthrug, this exercise in 'bloody-minded elan and sheer zing' (to quote Reyner Banham) made its neighbours look effete.

Banham recalled how, when he first saw its images, 'for the last time, one knew at once, here was a building that was going to have that kind of impact.' As his words suggest, it was a first – something instantly recognisable as extraordinary and important; but there was also a sense of finality, of a story that could continue no further. Today its novelty remains refreshing, though we would be less inclined to follow critics of 30 years ago in stressing sadomasochistic qualities or in praising its ugliness.

Leicester University Engineering Building stands up as a masterpiece of the primitive, in the sense of denying precedent and bluntly facing off smooth intellectual Modernism. Its expressionism 'is often exaggerated – in its coarse but honest originality', to quote a contemporary on Butterfield's All Saints. Rough but suave, painful but beautiful, it takes Modernist conceits of the 1920s (like entering up a great ramp under the belly of a lecture theatre) but forms them in a hard-edged, English industrial language which makes even Corbusier seem soft.

It is a tiny building, its three-dimensional organisation tight as a clenched fist – just like the masterly planning of All Saints. We have no need here to argue how much at Leicester is Gowan's, but it is certainly not Stirling's alone, as overseas critics too often presume. One might fruitfully look at Stirling's buildings of 1975–85 alongside Alexander Thomson's of 1855–65: great, quixotic and strong. But Stirling and Gowan's Engineering Building is quite different; the unprecedented little masterpiece yet also swan song of a youthful design team, which thereafter fragmented, it stands alone, twinned with Butterfield's youthful and also never-repeated All Saints. Each, bursting out of its chosen camouflage – the one 'Gothic' the other 'industrial' – amazes with an intense power.

'But that treats this building as a "phenomenon",' objects James Gowan. 'You talk about it as if it's an "image", an "idea".' The Leicester University Engineering Building both

4

5

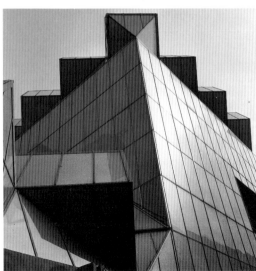

6

7

shows a rational development of ideas and it has precedents in Stirling & Gowan's experience; but it is essentially programme driven. Gowan unashamedly repeats the word 'functional'.

The functionalist

The available site at first appeared far too small. Some of the building's engineering workshops – heat engines, hydraulics and structures – contain very heavy machinery while others need large hydraulic testing tanks built into their floors. To create sufficient pressure for experiments in the hydraulics sump, the large water tank was required at a minimum head of 100 feet. All this demanded that these workshops be at ground level, with the other teaching workshops surrounding them.

The client considered flexibility to be essential and the rearrangement of workshop spaces likely. So the whole workshop building became an anonymous shed, within which all subdivisions, being non-structural, could be changed without touching the skin. This workshop tablecloth folds up and over the higher strip along the southwest boundary, where ancillary and service accommodation – boiler house, transformer station and maintenance – had to be fitted underneath. The aerodynamics and electrical workshop laboratories, being less heavily serviced, could be raised to this upper level.

It was stressed that because of the rapid obsolescence rate of equipment, its replacement would be an almost continuous process. Throughout the building, therefore, there are facilities for gantry haulage of heavy equipment. To allow direct access for machinery, the strip of higher workshops overhangs the service road, from which they can be lifted directly off lorries through floor openings. Exactly similarly, a removable panel stacks above one below, on each floor of the research laboratory block, overhanging the eastern entrance below.

The engineering department particularly requested that all these teaching workshops should be daylit by a north-light roof only. It proved impossible to arrange the building on a north–south axis, because of its restrictive site. To obtain precise north light, therefore, the roof is turned to run diagonally across the plan. The whole of the teaching workshop block is covered with 'plyglass' used as both roof and wall cladding, above a storey-height brick plinth. Plyglass is a fibreglass sandwich between two sheets of clear glass, with an additional aluminium layer in the sandwich on the south

8

9

10

11

faces of the glazed roof.

These heavy workshops inevitably cover more than two-thirds of the available site. Having added a small amount of parking at the front and a service road with its parking at the back, there was no alternative but to stack the remaining accommodation on the small amount of site left.

The principal approach, from the northeast, leads towards the tower. From the car-park to the right, the main entrance is on the axis with the tower. Alternatively, directly facing the approach, there is a secondary entrance by ramp to the podium terrace overlooking the park. The front building, its lozenge-shape at ground floor dictated by the angled site boundary, contains entrances, cloakrooms and lavatories. The lavatories are ventilated by a snorkel projecting from the podium at the apex of the terrace. By-laws allow low-level discharge of fumes if a specified horizontal distance from the nearest window is maintained.

Above the podium are two lecture halls, seating 100 and 200 students respectively. On top of the smaller one, the four levels of research laboratories contain heavy equipment. This part of the building has deep structural floors, between whose diagrid beams are cut the service runs for the floor above. Experiments with such equipment may misfire, necessitating the rapid extraction of fumes, and to avoid the expense of air-conditioning, the windows project out to form a venturi section, so that opening these horizontal louvres creates an immediate cross-ventilation.

Above the larger lecture theatre, the glazed staff offices are arranged beneath the required high-level water tank. Between these taller blocks are circulation shafts: stairs (one of which only needs to service the research labs block), a lift and, flanking the main stair, three large pipes for the drop from the hydraulics tank.

This planning solution and the section are largely based on the movement of 200 to 300 students and staff. A density graph shows a tapering pyramid with 200 people at ground level falling to about 30 on the fifth floor and then four for each of the upper three levels of staff rooms. In accordance with the lower occupancy, the circulation floors decrease in area towards the top, so the glass skin containing this decreasing circulation steps in and cuts back as it rises up the tower, to pass eventually (by now only 10 feet wide) over the top next to the hydraulics tank.

The whole building is faced in three materials: red brick, tiles and glass. The client particularly requested a building not primarily of fairfaced concrete. All planes of in-situ con-

13

12

crete, whether ceiling, wall, floor or terrace, are therefore veneered in red tile. Where the in-situ concrete is used as a skeletal frame, the planes are faced in a skin of brick. Only patent glazing was sufficiently flexible for the direct sheathing and cladding methods used.

The lecture theatres, their cantilevers stabilised by the weight of the floors above, are plenum-ventilated and lined with fibrous plaster. Their steep rake allows a clear view of the top of the lecturer's demonstration bench. A second entrance to the back of the large lecture theatre was required for latecomers, thus a spiral stair rises from the podium terrace.

The chamfered corners of the research laboratories and the splay of the podium are necessitated by the angled building line. These setbacks and the need for north lights established a second geometry for the whole building, at 45 degrees to the norm.

It couldn't be more straightforward.

The tactics

'I find that when making a presentation of a project to a client, we must never talk about aesthetics and explanations must always be in terms of common sense, function and logic,' commented Stirling. 'If you mention the word "beauty" their hair would stand on end and you'd probably lose the commission.'

Boundaries were certainly to be carefully observed. I have heard Stirling at the Architectural Association in London talk of the Cambridge History Faculty Library as if it were entirely an exercise in the logistics of rainwater removal. *British Buildings 1960–1964*, edited by Kenneth Frampton and others, dedicated 'to Colin Frederick Rowe', and the first book to feature the Leicester building speaks in precisely this dead-pan tone.[2]

Architectural Design, where from 1953 Theo Crosby could give Stirling & Gowan's generation a voice, was *the* 1950s journal for students and the profession's young intellectuals. It was packed with punctiliously professional articles – on expansion joints, window-frame details and panel sections; perhaps on the psychology of repose and the influence of colour; on the lumen and the decibel. But who ever mentioned the word 'beauty'? (*AD*'s articles on theories of functionalism, for example, stood out, of course – carefully distanced by subject, like Peter Smithson on Stephenson's Rocket, or even just by the colour of the paper they were printed on.)

The very Ingleish postwar landscape

When the architects of this postwar trained generation stuck their heads over the parapet around 1950, they saw a landscape which appeared without character, safe, bland – lacking in rhetorical power. This may seem an odd image in the wake of the most progressive and reformist government Britain ever elected.[3] One caricature sees it as prefabricated and repetitive ad infinitum; technologically sane, sociologically committed, but drained of artistic power. Here Hertfordshire schools stand out. Another sees the *welfstadt* housing – the best housing in postwar Europe – being formed by woolly Marxist architects in timid and mediocre Stalinist imagery, much actually borrowed from the gentle Modernism of Sweden's welfare state. Here the 'people's detailing' of shallow pitches and picturesque brick forms, of clapboard panels and timber window frames of the London County Council stand out.[4]

If there were any admirable British architects, they were Wells Coates, uncompromising and unfashionable before the war, and Berthold Lubetkin, then on the point of retiring from architecture to farm pigs; even the quality of Leslie Martin's rigorous Festival Hall in London could hardly be seen through its context of Festival of Britain whimsy.[5] *The Architectural Review* was identified with both these enemy strands: the empirical picturesque and the anonymous functionalist – a bizarre symbiosis. Pevsner, now on its editorial staff, personified the duality: calling for an International Style that was expressionless, while praising the English virtue of compromise and the careless grace of the picturesque tradition.[6] His colleague, J M Richards, similarly had argued in *Circle* for anonymity: 'The architect-artist is a pest who should be eradicated' – Gowan paraphrases Richards' point rather crudely, but this is probably what his generation heard.[7]

Richards, who had followed Pevsner's classic Modernist paperback *Pioneers of the Modern Movement* (1936) with his own *Modern Architecture* (1940),[8] ended the war eulogising English suburbia.[9] It was a betrayal. 'To consult the Genius of the Place in All': Pope's dictum oft repeated amidst *The Architectural Review*'s newly invented 'Townscape', seemed a surrender to all that was provincial and second-rate in English culture. This 'New Empiricism' (as *The Architectural Review* dubbed it) seemed trivial. Empirical trust in precedent rather than principle appeared weak and whimsical – and very English.[10] When, 30 years later, *The Architects' Journal* in a long, condescending

12 'The nocturnal transformation: glowing with its own internal and strictly functional illumination, it assumes a mantle of light and mystery that no other architectural spectacle in the world can offer.' P R Banham, *The New Statesman*, 14 February 1964.

13 Client group, with Edward Parkes second from left, and Gowan at far right, snapped on site by Stirling.

14 Leicester's Victoria Park, seen from the prow of Leicester University Engineering Building.

14

review, found a new Stirling building neither quaint enough nor sincerely functionalist enough, the architect was goaded to reply, with a certain droll economy, 'I didn't much like your article. Snide, mean and very Ingleish.'[11] It is exactly in this sense, with Pevsner's 1955 Reith Lectures *The Englishness of English Art* in their ears, and in 'the bitter knowledge of the sweet taste of the Festival of Britain whimsy' that a new generation united in the 1950s in looking beyond little England.

They felt not only homogeneity as a war-marked group, but also quite different from those trained as architects before or as it began – the generation of Cleeve Barr and Anthony and Oliver Cox, of Denys Lasdun and Peter Moro. That generation, who had rallied round the AA's *Focus*[12] before the war, and many of whom now were in the middle ranks of the LCC housing department, were conducting their own institutional revolution. In 1958 they forced a special General Meeting on the Royal Institute of British Architects, which instigated a revolutionary takeover of this 'cozy club for elderly private practitioners'. The same year, the same new technocratic officer class ran a RIBA conference in Oxford on education, which proposed a rigorous, professional, university-level education for all architects.

That generation of technicians of the people, however, whether LCC communists or *Architectural Review* empiricists, was already one revolution too late, and they became the enemy of the young. Thus 'combat was joined between a barely middle-aged architectural establishment armed with a major magazine, and a generation of battle-hardened and unusually mature students'.[13] Sickened by its brave little gaieties, they felt that 'the style of the Festival of Britain seemed at best sentimental, at worst effete'. It lacked seriousness; it was bland; and it was parochial. 'Modern architecture,' Robert Maxwell concluded, ' had been sold short in Britain.'

'We are ashamed,' wrote Alison and Peter Smithson in 1954, 'that we cannot realise the potential of the Twentieth Century; ashamed that philosophers and physicists must think us fools, and painters think us irrelevant. Our generation must try and produce evidence that men are at work.'

What shaped these rising forces, some of whose individuals I am already naming? Mapping the location of these groups onto this territory, we certainly see them coalesce geographically. In fact we are now all in quite a small corner of London, with a remarkably small collection of people certain in their beliefs – just as revolutionaries in their tight cells of furious debate. Moreover, aided by their growing influence through teaching and writing – for Colin Rowe, James Stirling and Peter Smithson were the mid-1950s student heroes – they were certain that they represented the vanguard of architectural thought of the moment.

The cultural formation:
scouring the horizon for Stirling's world
The first shape to form out of the mist seemed to have originated in prewar Liverpool. There, three brilliant and precocious teenagers, Colin Rowe, Robert Maxwell and Thomas Stevens, went up together as architecture students. The outbreak of war shattered continuity; but Rowe, though called up into the paratroopers, 'mildly broke his back' (to quote Stevens[14]) on his tenth trial jump and it ended his war. After hospitalisation, Rowe returned to Liverpool to complete his architectural training. When the postwar veterans returned, now with Stirling among them, they found Rowe – who for some had been their fellow student in an earlier life – about to return as their tutor. There was immediate collusion and an inspiring education. Rowe, meanwhile, had studied with Rudolf Wittkower and published his pivotal essay, 'The Mathematics of the Ideal Villa', comparing the geometries of Palladio and Le Corbusier, in *The Architectural Review* in March 1947, and arrived back in Liverpool in 1948.

'There was furious debate … some staff resigned and a few students went off to other schools. I was left,' said Stirling, 'with a deep conviction of the moral rightness of the new architecture … We oscillated backwards and forwards, between the antique and the just arrived "Modern Movement" – which for me was the foreign version only – as taught by Colin Rowe' – which meant Giuseppe Terragni but not Walter Gropius. Rowe, Stevens continued, created 'a very formalistic but very rebellious group', many of whom, at the start of the 1950s, had filtered down to London. There Maxwell chanced to meet Alan Colquhoun. Mentioning his friend Stevens, Maxwell was trounced to find Colquhoun claiming him as a friend since schooldays. For Stevens, as Banham put it, 'knew everybody and a few others'.[15] 'The closest these architects came to a polemical movement,' wrote a historian of Modern architecture, 'was the continual passage through Sam Stevens' Thayer Street flat.'[16] Stevens adds another link to the serious study of history at the Courtauld Institute, where he and Banham, like Rowe, were tutored by Rudolf Wittkower. Wittkower's seminal study *Architectural Principles*[17] was published by the Courtauld in 1949. So at Stevens' flat could be found Banham's 'old

Marylebone High Street network', almost exclusively architects, many of whom had first met there: Maxwell, Colquhoun, Stirling, Colin St John Wilson and many others; with Banham less obvious and Kenneth Frampton edging in. Stirling, who stayed here for a while, described it as an architectural finishing school.

Scanning the horizon, we can pick out another form; at first it seems to show a similar physiognomy but becomes unbalanced by some extraordinary protuberances. We are at Banham's flat in Primrose Hill in London, where by chance (and introduced, of course, by mutual friend Stevens) the occupant of the adjoining flat is Wilson. The group here embraces Stirling, Maxwell and Peter Carter, then enlarges to include the other dedicatees of Banham's Courtauld thesis, his dissection of heroic Modernism, *Theory and Design in the First Machine Age*. Finally published in 1960, it began: 'to Alison and Peter Smithson, James Stirling, C A St John Wilson, Peter Carter, Colin Rowe and Alan Colquhoun, for a constant view of the mainstream of modern architecture flowing on'.

But chez Banham, you would also find all sorts of people, young artists inventing 'Pop', like Richard Hamilton, John McHale, Lawrence Alloway and certainly among them his neighbour, sculptor Bill Turnbull – as Stevens says, 'Sunday morning coffee at Banham's was almost a religious rite.' As the image of that group dissolves, however, another seems to grow out of it. This gels at the Institute of Contemporary Arts around the name of the Independent Group, to be formally reconvened in 1954 by McHale, and Alloway, with Peter and Alison Smithson, sculptor Edouardo Paolozzi, photographer Nigel Henderson, Banham, Turnbull and Hamilton. On a slightly wider orbit are others including architects Stirling, Wilson and John Voelcker.

The 'This is Tomorrow' 1956 exhibition at the Whitechapel Gallery in east London began here, with this group where Pop Art originated. Hamilton, McHale and Voelcker made one construction, Paolozzi, Henderson and the Smithsons a 'habitat'; Stirling, with Michael Pine and Richard Matthews, contributed a large, papier-mache free-form object based on photographs of soap bubbles. It was an exhibition of form, containing, to quote an ironic outsider, 'Futurist blasphemy, Dada idiocy, some of the puritanism of De Stijl and several brands of surrealism'.[18] In other words, it more accurately might have been called 'this was yesterday'; but, here, a recent history was being critically revisited and reused by a new, angry generation.

The IG, however, ranged widely. Here Wilson gave his first ever lecture; it was on proportion systems, which explains another prevailing mood, and Stirling called it 'bloody good'.[19] Here, also, structural engineer Frank Newby co-chaired with Stirling a discussion on Pier Luigi Nervi.

If that shifting group defies shape description, on the opposite flank a more rigorously precise form becomes discernible. We are in the French pub in Soho on Saturday mornings, in what looks an almost exclusively architectural group. And if Banham was the Sunday scribe and intellectual focus, on Saturday Joseph Rykwert seems to become *éminence grise*, amidst the now recognisable shapes of Colquhoun, Stirling, Wilson, Newby (who first met Stirling here in 1954), Stevens and others, occasionally including Paolozzi, Cedric Price, Douglas Stephen and Theo Crosby.

Yet another, equally sharply drawn shape emerges – perhaps really one of those above, moving on – which Gowan calls 'the NW1 group'.[20] Here David Gray, Kit Evans and John Miller, AA graduates of the mid 1950s, now join Stirling, Colquhoun, Newby and others. On one occasion when Gowan was showing pictures to this group, Paolozzi followed with his own slides. They would take it in turns to show their work; but if they had no current work – if they were spending all of every day churning out working drawings for a commercial office, as Stirling and Gowan, Gray and then Colquhoun and Miller were for Lyons Israel & Ellis – they showed slides of what interested them. Stirling mentions 'all things vernacular from the very small – farms, barns and village housing – to the very large – warehouses, industrial structures, railway sheds', as well as bombed-out churches, English baroque and much else. Gowan's list we shall see shortly.

The sociology: Lucky Jim and other stories

Beyond spilling their obsession with architecture into endless words and images, they tried to make buildings, and certainly needed to make a living. There was little work in the early 1950s; they scraped assistantships at the LCC, with firms like Yorke Rosenberg & Mardall or Lyons Israel & Ellis – Lawrence Israel and Tom Ellis' office, which was growing on the reputation for sharply competent education buildings. Their obsession with architecture gained space in teaching, and they entered competitions. Throughout the 1950s, from Coventry Cathedral to Sydney Opera House, the young architects were incessantly entering competitions which their architecture could never win.[21]

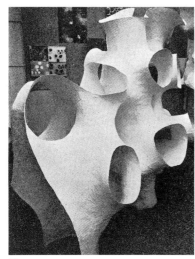

15

16

17

18 The Skylon, the 1951 exhibition marker, on which Newby and Gowan assisted engineer and architect respectively.

19 'Whenever anyone said it's a ridiculous fire stair,' Gowan comments on the spiral glazed stair at Leicester, 'I'd see the image of Eiffel standing on his one at the tower.'

20, 21 A table designed and made by Stirling for his Liverpool bedsit, then exhibited in 1951 at the ICA.

22, 23 Stirling's Sheffield entry (with Cordingley), 1953. Elevation shows the clear geometry (rhythm of A:A:A:B:A:A:B:A:C:A:C and back again: A:C:A:B:A:A:B:A:A:A:A), and up-axonometric, drawn years later by Leon Krier, shows the entrance hall. 'Several of the ideas which appear here,' Stirling said in 1965, 'are put together in projects which came after – eg the approach ramp to

entrance lobbies, the sloping undercut to lecture theatres, and the free-form glazing wall wrapping round the space of the principal receiving area'.

24 LCC housing at Roehampton Alton West, showing the five Corbusian Unité blocks.

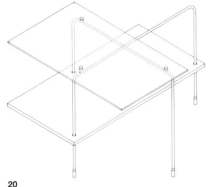

20

21

18

19

What of the world outside? In 1951, after six years in power, the Labour Party had achieved its highest ever vote in a UK general election – 48.8 per cent. But, though polling a nearly one per cent majority, due to the vagaries of the constituency system Churchill's Conservatives regained power which they then held until 1964.

The 1950s had opened with the Korean war dragging Britain into increasing rearmament, and the darkening shadow of potential atomic and nuclear destruction. 'Nobody, I fancy, feels "happy" about the age in which we live or the future which even the living may know before they die', wrote W H Auden. 'At all times in history men have felt anxious about their own fate or the fate of their class or community, but there has seldom been a time, I believe, when the present and the future of the whole human endeavour on this earth have seemed questionable to so many people'.[22] But architects, by their very *raison d'être*, have to be more positive. 'The angry young despair', the mantle of ennui taken on from Cyril Connolly of the 1940s by Kingsley Amis in the 1950s, must be alien to them.

Those angry young men can burst out with resentment: 'I suppose people of our generation aren't able to die for good causes any longer … There aren't any good causes left. If the big bang does come, and we all get killed off it won't be in aid of the old-fashioned grand design … About as pointless and inglorious as stepping in front of a bus …'. But Stirling *was* that older generation, he was at D-day 'when', as Jimmy Porter's speech from John Osborne's *Look Back in Anger* continues, 'we were still kids'.

Young architects were also angry but, unlike the new despairing young, they had fought – often when teenagers themselves. They still fought; maybe Brutalism was, as was said, 'violent, aggressive' – Peter Smithson's blunt chin and his blunt phrases, Alison sharp and brooking no cant. Banham in only a couple of lines said 'bloody-mindedness', 'fortiter in re', 'je m'en foutisme', 'suaviter in modo'. (*Architectural Review* readers could take European languages, if not the architecture.) Such phrases might indeed embrace Stirling and perhaps even Gowan. Meanwhile, Stirling had become interested in Butterfield, Street and Scott. 'Was it to do with finding a genuine Brutalism?' he mused.[23] To the Smithsons and Banham, however, Brutalism, far from a newly fashionable rugged vernacular, was involved in developing a sense of 'another ordinariness'. In this sense, Stirling was absolutely right to deny the label Brutalist for himself.

The era of 'postwar Britain' had its back broken at this moment in the mid 1950s. This image was reflected in William Golding's *Lord of the Flies* and Kingsley Amis' *Lucky Jim*, both sensationally appearing in 1954, and then in Osborne's *Look Back in Anger*, on the Royal Court stage two years later. Its political confirmation was the 1956 invasions of Egypt by Britain and France after nationalisation of the Suez Canal on 26 July, and of Hungary by the USSR. It was the end of the heroic image of the Soviet Union and, perhaps, of 'Great' Britain.

In the years up to the Leicester commission, Britain seemed to become a cynical world, at the sleazy end of the Supermac era, with its unreal promises of happiness shaped like a TV screen, holidays abroad for everyone, and the anodyne slogan 'you've never had it so good' (which Prime Minister Macmillan actually said in 1957). The younger generation, depressed and jaded, had little drive. While 'angry young men' dominated the theatre, sharpest were the provincial sounds of the so called 'red-brick' novelists – 'red-brick' designating those universities which, lacking the prestige of England's ancient institutions, were usually nineteenth-century foundations. Often, like Leicester, they had been collegiate to London University and were gaining their independence just at this moment.

The architects, of course, flatly rejected the provincial context so important to 'angry young men-ist' culture. But the architects were red-brick at heart if not by their own education. Scholarship boys by and large, they sympathised with the red-brick's natural role as breeding ground of radical change. If not involved in their social and intellectual protest, at least they could respond to the intellectual new brooms devising, for example, how a new university department of engineering might be set up from scratch.

The critical idea: about architecture

Modern architecture, finally institutionalised in Britain, could only now begin to have its myths investigated by a younger generation. Having been neglected for an (admittedly short) generation, the source material of the 1920s and 1930s was exhumed. Mies van der Rohe and Le Corbusier, from what was becoming clearer as 'the heroic period',[24] were studied; but so were Frank Lloyd Wright, Futurism and Hugo Häring. So, for example, Banham's doctorate under Pevsner (but deeply undermining Pevsner's position on Modernism) detailed how the 1920s and 1930s had had little to do with functionalism – Rowe and Stevens had long spotted that.

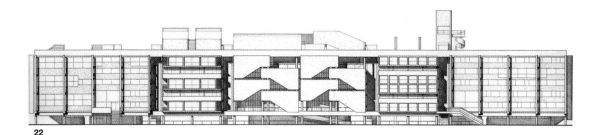

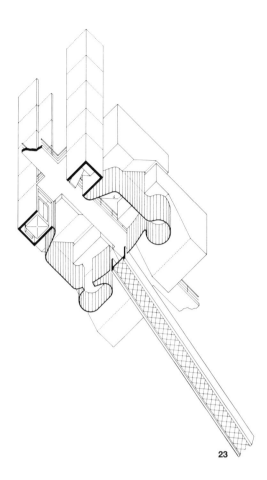

'The difference,' Stevens adds, 'is that we didn't *disapprove*.' But they noted, as Rowe put it later, that the architect allied to mechanisation, and the architect as agent of social welfare, of social revolution, were two incompatible Modernist fantasies.

From the functionalist impasse – that a schedule of accommodation doesn't tell you how to design a building – there needed to be another set of tools beyond organisation or artistic whim. The Renaissance historian Wittkower had, to his astonishment, found himself sucked into this vacuum. Wittkower sought to show how the architecture of Alberti and particularly of Palladio had intellectual meaning, and indeed was primarily symbolic rather than abstract. Colin Rowe had made his striking Corbusier–Palladio comparisons; John Voelcker (a central member of the IG) and Andrew Derbyshire were designing 'Palladian' power stations for Farmer & Darke. 'The general impact of Professor Wittkower's book on a whole generation of postwar architectural students is one of the phenomena of our time', Banham wrote in an important article entitled 'The New Brutalism' in the December 1955 *Architectural Review*. In the following months, James Gowan's tiny 'Palladian' house on the Isle of Wight was designed; with its H-plan symmetry, its horizontal bay rhythms of 1:2:1, room plan shapes of 1:1 and 1:1.5 or 1:2.5 and its height-to-width ratios of 3:4. 'It was not until the 1950s,' Gowan wrote, 'that we recognised fully the classical armature in Le Corbusier's work.' [25]

Three typical comments from 1956/7: 'The two main English vices', scorned Stevens, are 'picturesque muddle-headedness in planning combined with a casual formal confusion'. Rowe continued, decrying 'the insufferable tedium of Townscape … the provincial quality of "Englishness" lately so much valued'. Moreover, Rykwert railed against 'the attitude of the technocrats and administrators of architecture, of zones and curtain-wallers – very much the majority attitude'; but, equally, he turned his anger on 'the callow, anti-social arrivisme of *Lucky Jim* (which he saw 'reflected in the lower reaches of Brutalism').

Rykwert, writing in 1957, saw the dangers of the prevalent crude functionalism most sharply: 'Because of the permissive nature of technical data, designers who claim to stick as closely to the bare functional requirements as possible have produced results which are surprisingly like their commercial confrères who only aim to streamline casings for industrial products … What is even worse, speculators, administrators and technicians whom we architects have converted to such slogans as "form follows function" or "truth to materials" find now that they can dictate to us … We have come to the end of a non-figurative architecture'.

Leicester University Engineering Building was the first building in Britain to face and surmount this challenge; our first, therefore, after Modernism.

The new pedagogy

Never has there been such a generation of verbal architects turned academics. Naturally Rowe and Stevens would land in academia, later followed by the more maverick Banham, by Frampton and then Rykwert.[26] Looking back from the mid 1990s, never has such a talented looking group been so easily sidelined from architectural production; with now a great clutch of emeritus professorships between them but having designed pitifully little: Colquhoun, Maxwell, Smithson, Gowan and even Wilson – but never Stirling.

If they were intellectuals who could also design buildings, and on occasion very fine buildings, Stirling remained an artist, a moulder of form and imagery, who could also read and think. It is exactly right that Stirling was much more influenced by Saxl and Wittkower's *British Art and the Mediterranean* than by *Architectural Principles* which so bowled over his contemporaries, including Gowan. For this atlas-like book was simply a folio of wonderful images, making astonishingly novel visual cross-references. As Stirling added, 'This large book was the one that none of us students could ever fit on our bookshelves, it just lay on the floor and got *looked at*'[27] (my emphasis on the visual; Stirling's on the droll matter-of-factness, an abiding characteristic which will become obvious later).

Biography: early lives and times

James Gowan, born in Glasgow in 1926, had the first part of his architectural training in the Glasgow School of Art's old-fashioned, technical course, before joining the RAF in 1942 where he served as a radar instructor until 1946. James Stirling (1926–92), though also born in Glasgow, was a Liverpudlian; he began at Liverpool Art School in 1942, but within months was a paratrooper. Taking part in the 1944 D-day landings with the the Sixth Airborne Division, he narrowly missed death in hand to hand fighting.[28]

After the war, still under 20 but with three years of war service, Stirling arrived at Liverpool School of Architecture, where he spent five years, with half the penultimate year on exchange in USA. Gowan, meanwhile, hoping to complete

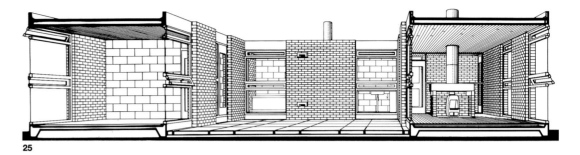

25

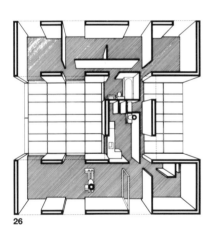

26

25, 26 James Gowan, house at Cowes, Isle of Wight. This little house was brought into the partnership in 1956 already at sketch design approval. Palladian in layout, with plan bays 1:1.5:1, room shapes 1:1, 1:1.5 or 1:2.5, and height-to-width ratio of 3:4. Stirling's publication of the house in these two drawings emphasises different qualities. At the time, *The Architects' Journal*, 24 August 1958, noted its transparent formality: 'Standing in a bedroom you look across the courtyard into the living room through the window that corresponds exactly to your own and beyond it into the garden through the far window ...'

28 Axonometrics of two of the house studies (A above, B below) generated by Gowan within the partnership in 1956. Highly articulated spaces spin out from a free-form service and circulation core; their memory is apparent in the designing of Leicester.

his training in London after the war, was warned off the AA by students and recommended to Kingston. During this time and after qualifying, Gowan assisted Brian O'Rorke before moving to Powell & Moya. There, for the 1951 Festival of Britain, he worked on the Skylon while Frank Newby was assisting Felix Samuely with its structure. In this year at the ICA Stirling exhibited a table he had brought down to London from Liverpool; and he began to produce the series of theoretical designs and competition entries which sustained his development through the early 1950s. Or, as Stirling (typically) puts it: 'When I did competitions, it was not because I was seriously trying to get into practice. I was working off a surplus of ideas which had accrued in the first years out of school'.

In 1952, as the LCC's Alton East estate at Roehampton, with its 'people's detailing' became public, Colin St John Wilson persuaded *The Observer* to publish a short article against compromise and the Picturesque. It was mocked by Hugh Casson whom *The Observer* then invited to write on architecture. The next year, the Smithsons, with Nigel Henderson and Paolozzi, installed 'A Parallel of Life and Art' at the ICA. In the autumn, when Crosby joined *Architectural Design* and shortly thereafter Banham (recommended to them by Anthony Blunt at the Courtauld) reached *The Architectural Review*, this generation's conversations began to become public. 'After my first piece was published,' Banham said with a wry smile, 'I'd a stern crit from Sandy Wilson and Peter Carter.' When Pevsner shortly afterwards declared in *The Architectural Review* (April 1954) that the Picturesque and the Modern Movement have 'fundamentals in common', it elicited uproar. A letter published under the name of Alan Colquhoun but involving much heated debate in its composition, was published in reply.

In 1953, Stirling entered the Sheffield University Competition, as did the Smithsons. Stirling's entry (done with Alan Cordingley), can be seen as what Rowe has called his 'initiatory monument'. It is a 'virtual' slab block whose horizontal circulation is 'a spine or driving axle onto which rooms are connected like mechanical assembly', while 'the vertical circulation articulates the different types of accommodation', to quote Stirling. Such concerns reach fulfilment at Leicester. Look at the approach ramp from the ground to the first floor foyer, the foyer itself with its curved glazed skin under the sloping lecture theatres, and the twin towers of lift and stairs to which it leads. Perhaps it is most clear in the 'up view' axonometric,[29] where the startling resemblance with Leicester is immediately apparent.

After short, unfruitful employment with James Cubitt and then with Gollins, Melvin & Ward, Stirling joined Lyons Israel & Ellis in 1953 as senior assistant, where Gowan arrived from Stevenage New Town Corporation the following year. In November 1954 the postwar restraint on private building ended; with this lifting of the need for building licences, architecture in any serious sense was finally, in Summerson's phrase, 'no longer an illegal profession'. But at Lyons Israel & Ellis, 'it was a nine to five, heads down job, and we whacked out the drawings', says Gowan, adding 'Stirling learned a lot in three years!'.

1955 began with Crosby's editorial in January's *Architectural Design* talking of 'a re-evaluation of those advanced buildings of the twenties and thirties – lessons of the formal use of proportion and a respect for the sensuous use of each material ...' and ended with Banham's discussion of Wittkower and Brutalism in December's *Architectural Review*. The same year, Stirling, as part of the British Mars Group CIAM-10 contingent, prepared a village housing project for the CIAM-10 meeting in Aix-en-Provence, as did both the Smithsons and William Howell and John Partridge. Howell and Partridge, meanwhile, with Killick and Stanley Amis revealed a sea change in the LCC with their Corbusian slab blocks at Roehampton Alton West, while at Bentham Road, equally rigorous LCC housing came from Wilson, Carter and Colquhoun. Stirling became a visiting critic at the AA and, in September, wrote about Le Corbusier's not yet complete Maisons Jaoul in *The Architectural Review*. In pointed contrast with Corbusier's Villa Stein at Garches, he warmed to their brutal honesty as a vote of no-confidence in 'the white architecture of the thirties'.[30] At this point he was recommended to the father of an AA student, and commissioned to design a series of flats at Ham Common; on the strength of this, he and Gowan left Lyons Israel & Ellis to form their own partnership.

When Stirling & Gowan set off from Lyons Israel & Ellis, with the chalk and cheese of Ham Common and the Isle of Wight house, it was said they were an unlikely couple. Today, Gowan muses: 'it was a strange partnership'.[31] How did it come about?

The partnership: Stirling & Gowan

At Ham Common, Stirling had an awkwardly long and narrow back-garden plot; it was an extremely tricky formal task to shoehorn the required 30 dwellings onto the site while

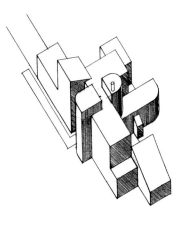

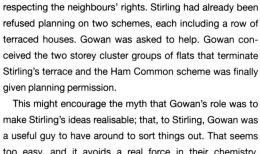

27

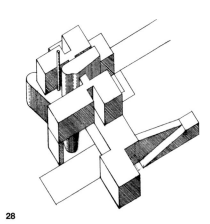

28

29

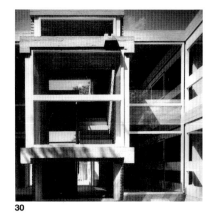

30

respecting the neighbours' rights. Stirling had already been refused planning on two schemes, each including a row of terraced houses. Gowan was asked to help. Gowan conceived the two storey cluster groups of flats that terminate Stirling's terrace and the Ham Common scheme was finally given planning permission.

This might encourage the myth that Gowan's role was to make Stirling's ideas realisable; that, to Stirling, Gowan was a useful guy to have around to sort things out. That seems too easy, and it avoids a real force in their chemistry. Certainly Stirling & Gowan had different agendas. But in the few years from 1955 to the completion of Leicester University Engineering Building, each had a partner who could, and would, stand up to the other.

Although Stirling & Gowan repudiated the label Brutalist, they were clearly using both the formal, classical organising ideas, and – until Leicester – the banal, as-found materials. A highly skilled formal authority is clear from the start. The entrance lobbies and stairs in the cluster blocks at Ham Common, influenced by De Stijl (according to them both), have an architectural sensibility whose echo is still seen at Leicester. Instead of being broken by a first floor slab, the glazed side walls continue upwards, with a bridge across between them. The notion suggested at Ham Common that circulation is 'the dynamic and motivating element of a building', to quote Stirling, had already been clear in his Sheffield competition entry.

Stirling & Gowan worked together for just three years before their first chance came to put up a major building, at Leicester, which their partnership could not outlive. In 1956, they began a series of housing studies which were developed as theoretical exercises to establish a working method for the newly formed partnership. 'We agreed the free right to share drawings,' Gowan explains, 'to take one from the other's board and carry on with it. And we developed a rule as to how we'd end an argument. How was that? It would be decided by what suits the building!'

Architectural practice and ideas can rarely have had such an intensity as in these housing studies they did together. The calculated vulnerability of two strong-minded and extremely individualistic men sharing and developing each other's drawings is a remarkable test. In these cluster studies (and the architects' use of the word is much closer to De Stijl than to the Team-10 'sociological' usage at that moment), 'it was considered desirable to express separately the existence of each functioning space within the terms of

the main discipline'. As Stirling says, 'results tended to be cluster assemblies'.

'The intention was to find a set of formal values,' Stirling continues. 'After discussion on the components, sketch ideas were evolved, exchanged and exchanged again. The product did not appear to become less personal by this process.' But perhaps the method simply reinforced a predilection in both men for such highly articulated architecture? The plans, with service and circulation in central, free-form space, which spills vertically, and to which functional elements are linked (even in House B adding a ramp to a first floor entry), clearly are remembered in mental processes at Leicester. Gowan filled notebooks with such studies: 'I'd work on these houses perhaps over a weekend; we'd then go through them together and decide which to go for. The more romantic ones, which I'd go for, he hated. Then, when they got tighter, it had appeal to him'.

Stirling's comment on these studies at this point interestingly changes tack: 'We decided that a more spontaneous, less intellectual use of materials, which directly solved each problem as it occurred, was likely to result in greater vitality. Thus the fabric might be an amalgam of different materials each chosen for a specific purpose'. It is a glimpse, once more, of their differing preoccupations as they move from Brutalism towards Leicester. Geometry is still clearly a controlling issue; living rooms are double cubes, and so on, even if it is not explicitly stated. Interestingly, in Stirling's publication of the Isle of Wight house, he obscures its proportion, showing perspectives instead of plan or section; whereas Gowan's makes a point of emphasising it. These differing perceptions reappear at Leicester.

By 1957, fees from Ham Common had run out and they both began to teach in London, Gowan at the AA, Stirling at Regent Street Polytechnic. At the same time, infill housing in Preston became their largest real project thus far. This intricate, low-rise housing was a job passed on to them by Lyons Israel & Ellis, who kept the prestigious part – the tower blocks designed by Colquhoun – for themselves.

In 1958, Stirling & Gowan were invited to enter a competition for a new Cambridge college to be called 'Churchill'. Leslie Martin – who the following year would recommend them for Leicester – was on the jury, which then chose theirs as one of four for a second stage; thus although they didn't win, the scheme was worked through in much detail. They proposed a rigorous formality, laid on the blank site without compromise – 'the Blenheim of the Welfare State', as Rowe

31

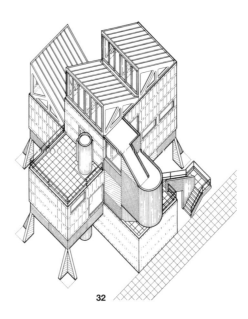

32

33

34

commented, nicely picking up a Churchillian undertone. The building consists of a vast but low square wall of student rooms; formally quartered, two of which have square rectangular courts of more accommodation, two have specialised collegiate pavilions.

There is also a little library which, freestanding within the vast court, seems more like the earlier house studies, in its formal order and the articulation of its elements. This – whose three-dimensional assembly like that of the housing studies, is devised by Gowan – is clearly en route to Leicester. We also see here all the fascination with castles, their use of battered earthworks and their crenellations, which lived on in Gowan's post-Stirling work,[32] as well as the unyielding geometric precision.

They then built a school hall in London, engineered by Frank Newby. Tiny monopitch pavilions rotated to make one square, behind battered embankments it was almost a microcosm of Churchill – except that it was built. Finally, in 1959 just before being offered Leicester, they produced a sketch project for 48 student rooms for an existing Cambridge college which, unlike Churchill, had a sensitive, difficult site. The solution marked a new turn in their formal vocabulary. Particularly in its sweep, as a two-sided curving wall, the protective back castellated with service towers, and the fragile scintillating, facetted glazed front, it breaks from their earlier geometries. 'The college members,' Stirling notes, 'would have seen reflected in the glass a shattered cubist image of the trees in the garden.' Its sweeping enclosure of the landscape with such a plastic wall obviously prefigures Stirling's later essay at Oxford. Sadly, it divided the college fifty-fifty, and therefore got no further. But then they were offered Leicester.

The psychology

Assistants were already involved on a part-time basis before Stirling & Gowan began Leicester; the Preston housing and the Camberwell school hall were still on site. But for Leicester, first David Walsby and then Michael Wilford, assisting with the working drawings, were supplemented by two students.

The effect on working practice was obvious. Gowan muses: 'The productive relationship was weakened by others coming in. Stirling was happy to delegate, but I wanted to work it all out myself'. Of course both partners were totally absorbed with the architecture; but while Stirling, in Gowan's view, 'was obsessed by the finished shape; tire-

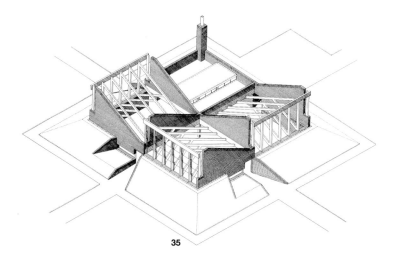

35

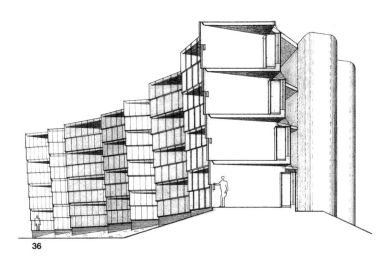

36

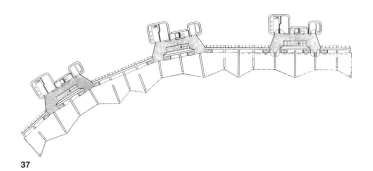

37

somely fastidious in details of what it looked like, giving great care and attention to appearance', Gowan's own obsession seems more in the link between formal idea and practical realisation.

If others could be delegated to work out the details, 'how do you maintain work at the same level?' Gowan ponders: 'You make a list, I suppose … With four people you can … Two can have a row on the floor for minutes, and it is sorted out, but … the difference became obvious; and we never devised a new working relationship. What do you do when you've got 20 staff? Stirling and I always said the ideal would be six people. We never got there'.

The intensity between the partners overwhelmed their new assistants. 'Stirling and Gowan occupied drawing boards located in the left and right hand windows,' explains Michael Wilford, 'and I worked in a centre window between them on a higher drawing board, desperately trying to keep my head down and avoid the verbal salvos they fired at each other … it was dynamite.' 'The uneasy partnership occasionally broke into open warfare,' Malcolm Higgs recalls, 'as it did just before the tender drawings for Leicester went out: the whole design was recast at incredible speed and intense silence over a weekend.' 'We worked in silent concentration,' Wilford adds, 'punctuated only by Stirling and Gowan's passionate arguments on design.'

'The style of today is unlikely to last, because phases of so excessively high a pitch of stimulation can't last'. This is how the equally overwhelmed Pevsner ends his broadcast discussion of the Leicester University Engineering Building. 'We cannot, in the long run, live our day to day lives in the midst of explosions'. It might more accurately be an epitaph to the partnership. With Leicester more or less complete and autonomous, they divorced.

In the office, the partners were inscrutable to others. Discussion seen by assistants was only on the work in hand. 'Always sharp and to the point,' says Wilford; 'without jokes or light-hearted banter.' More to the point it was not about ideas – other than in their concrete resolution in the job. Leon Krier, the next most original talent to work with Stirling, was struck by the lack of debate in the office: 'the why of choosing a concept would never be freely discussed'. In the office of Stirling & Gowan, 'debates were never abstract'. Behind all this is the constant sense that for each architect there was always another world.

Wilford sees the Gowan–Stirling relationship as similar to his own much later relationship with Stirling – always retain-

ing the measured distance. I suspect it was rather different. Certainly there was distance; Stirling and Gowan rarely met socially. Certainly Gowan, like Wilford, had another life; whereas Stirling, in the words of a later associate, 'lived and breathed architecture'. But there clearly is a Gowan architecture. He rarely lectured, published little, and was intensely private. 'In many people's opinion [Gowan is] the most intelligent living member of his formidable generation.'[33]

So it is not only unavoidable to look at differences between Stirling and Gowan, but it is perhaps essential, as it offers a clue to this explosive creative chemistry of their partnership.[34] Each is a man of few and carefully chosen words. Stirling never a joiner; Gowan always a loner. When each, nearly 20 years later, was asked for a statement about themselves as architect, both responses are fascinating and revealing; Gowan's more unexpected and more remarkably open than Stirling's.[35] At that same time, when each was asked by me to contribute to a book of drawings about architecture,[36] both submitted images of Leicester. Stirling sent the intricate, cutaway axonometric without the stair glazing; Gowan the early, very ordered, calm, almost orthogonal perspective – very different images.

Each took on no public role as theorist or critic; each preferred specific things to general ideas. Both taught – and elicited fierce loyalties – but rarely lectured.

It is too easy to polarise them, such as: Gowan loves simplicity – order, proportion, unimposed calm, 'he eschews restless intervention of one space on another',[37] while Stirling loves complexity. Of course there is Vanbrugh as much as Palladio in the Churchill College scheme, but it is Gowan as much as Stirling who enthuses on castles, pavilions and railway hoppers: 'We had a lot in common; in the immediate panorama we shared views. I had more misgivings, he had certainty (he was beholden to Corb – it was almost religious)'.

Stirling's other world – which only impinged on the office when Louis Kahn phoned, when his article appeared in *The Architectural Review*, or when Colin St John Wilson dropped by – is clear already. It is in his circles of conversation, formalising into teaching and writing, but never in his whole career intruding into the office … other than when Gowan, not accepting that icebergs are to be circumnavigated, heads straight on.

Clearly Gowan's stubborn, almost reckless independence was attractive to the students Andrew Anderson, Malcolm

38, 39 Railway hoppers: two
among many Gowan
photographs of powerfully
shaped solids, with secondary
exo-skeletons but without
windows, and far from an
anonymous 'Functional
Tradition'.

40 Turner's supremely cool
Palm House at Kew, West
London, photographed by
Gowan in the 1950s.
41, 42 Stirling & Gowan's
own solid geometry at
Leicester University
Engineering Building.

38

39

40

Higgs and, a year behind them, Quinlan Terry, for whom Gowan had been their third year unit master – 'that trio of religious cranks from the AA', as another contemporary called them. Higgs, talking of his student work in 1958/9 described their 'strong dislike of modern architecture; the notion of originality which obsessed the then critics of architecture, was a discredited idea among us'. But their drawings spoke even more clearly: as absurdly extreme as Peter Cook's amazing science fictions,[38] and though Anderson's medieval monastic thesis project even appeared in Archigram, they rarely were as inspired. They shocked by their bloody-minded traditionalism. Of Higgs and Anderson's fourth year housing project (neat planning of split-level flats without access decks, but using 10 storey traditional construction and steeply pitched roofs) Anderson commented: 'It can speak for itself. I can remember a number of usually sane and rational people getting worked up as a result'. Simultaneously, Higgs and Terry were working three days a week on Leicester. They had been hired by Gowan. Terry moves out of this story to work with, and later succeed, Raymond Erith, a fine revivalist *pasticheur* for whom the greatest architect of all time was Palladio. Gowan's later work also makes his rather different reverence for Palladio yet clearer.

Gowan's reputation is for efficiency and thoroughness, for modesty, penetrating judgement, and wit. But is it really true that while Gowan resented the then current tyranny of Le Corbusier, it was under his influence that Stirling began to dare to question it? That sounds too simple. What was Gowan looking at – what were the images he would show, to his AA students, or to 'the NW1 group' that night Paolozzi was there? We find Owen Williams' 'Drys' building for Boots at Beeston, Nottingham; brick kilns; railway hoppers, oast houses – all these powerfully formed industrial objects. They are windowless, tall, bold structures, shaped with a particularity, contrasting with the repetitive, visually anonymous industrial tradition in J M Richards and Eric de Maré's *Architectural Review*. However, he also looked at castles like Restormel in Cornwall, at crenellated walls and earth works; and the far from anonymous nineteenth-century high culture of Clifton suspension bridge, Kew Palm House, and Eiffel's spiral escape stair on his tower.

Did Gowan find Leicester absurdly complicated? Certainly he was against a tower dominating the park (which inevitably opened the way for its more monstrous neighbours – first Lasdun's and then Arup Associates' even more appalling tower which landed between them); but he was overruled by client and partner together. Stirling scorned playing safe. That may, as critics are happy to psychologize, have been born of his escaping death by inches in violent mortal combat; it certainly became a stubborn assertiveness. But, of course, the courage of one's convictions is only sane when the convictions have value. Gowan describes Stirling as more intuitive than himself – Stirling trusted his intuition.

One assistant saw, at Leicester, Gowan's 'patience, dedication and ingenuity trying to make sense out of what seemed to be unworkable designs';[39] but again that is far too simplistic. The designs were Stirling & Gowan's; if Stirling worried with the chamfer's formation, Gowan worried with the geometry's realisation. Gowan, whose interest is in proportion and the almost mesmeric simplicity of Palladio, holds onto the ordering – the underlying three-dimensional 10 foot grid module, saying 'you can't relate dynamic volumes on loose dimensional arrangements.' Stirling, whose interest is in neo-plastic interlocking volumes, who (in Colin St John Wilson's words) 'abominated monotony above all else', and who is easily bored, creates complexity of image, with the chamfers, the diagonals hitting the eye, the visual dynamic.

Both Gowan and Stirling clearly shared the design at Leicester, bringing to it their differing perspectives and skills. This amalgam was what, in the end, gives Leicester University Engineering Building its extraordinary vigour: a quality lacking from the next few, equally assertive but comparatively barren, achievements of each alone – the Schreiber House, the History Faculty Library.

Right back to Ham Common, Gowan talks of the designing as a layering of fragments to build an indivisible, coherent whole: 'one did a bit, the other did a bit; the first developed that, the second took it on …' 'Stirling did the elevation of a little block I designed,' he says, the words revealing exactly what is sensed reappearing at Leicester. With the three-dimensional assembly of the elements, Gowan leads, blocking up the form over the armature of a clear geometric grid. Stirling then takes his bold chisel to this, the order is deformed, enriched, overlaid with other issues in the more subtle final shaping – 'he was always obsessed with the finished shape', as Gowan notes. And so, as we might expect, the early, massing drawings which survive tend to be Gowan's; the immense energy in holding onto the desired surface shaping to be Stirling's.

41

42

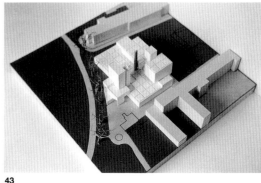

43

43 Model, viewed from
the north, of the earliest
sketch scheme to survive
from late 1959.

44, 45 The context from the
east and from the north, with
the park in front, the University
around – Martin's planned
development off to the right,
and Victorian terraced
Leicester beyond (45).

46 Axonometric, as from the
north, dated 25 February 1960,
which first shows the final
building's recognisable *parti*.

47 The next variant, probably
drawn March 1960, reverses
the towers and also the lecture
theatres while concealing the
cross route. The half bay
overhang at the back now
rests on diagonal struts.

44

45

The job history

In July 1959, Stirling & Gowan were appointed at Leicester. Shortly thereafter, paying an unexpected visit to their office, the Vice-Chancellor was surprised to enter one room, with simply Mr Stirling and Mr Gowan. Within the Building Committee, their client was essentially Edward Parkes, an academic engineer of the same generation as his architects, who had been invited from Cambridge to devise a new department at Leicester. His unusual proposal was for a unitary engineering department of about 200 students, whose life would be centred in the teaching workshops. The traditionally central role of formal lectures would be played down, though they would remain essential; there would be alcoves for group work in the laboratories and individual tutorial teaching in the staff rooms. His team of specialist staff would inevitably not be appointed until the building was coming out of the ground.

University College Leicester, becoming an independent university in 1957, appointed Leslie Martin to co-ordinate a master plan for its nine acre site on the edge of Victoria Park. Martin devised a formal, rectilinear spiral for future science buildings, but an awkward corner, really an appendix to the campus, and tight behind earlier neo-Georgian pastiche blocks, was left over. Here would be the department of engineering. Martin recommended to the client that it be designed by Stirling & Gowan. Being on a corner outside the development plan for the whole university, it could, as Martin has put it, 'stand on its own feet'.

The architects found themselves with a rather unwanted, tight site on the edge of the campus; surrounded on three sides by mediocre, long, brick blocks; but on the fourth, forming the edge of the great, flat expanse of Victoria Park. They also found themselves with certain unbending, clear client requirements. Having landed their first job complex enough to extend their talents, such pressures were just what they needed to exploit. Moreover, they were outside the master plan, and there was no existing Modernist language for them to work within. It was, as Leslie Martin says, a unique site for which he felt sure the architects whom he recommended would produce a unique building. Nor, unlike many of their contemporaries, were Stirling & Gowan concerned to build fragments of possible futures.[40] They would leave the future to find its own way; they aimed, in Gowan's memorable phrase of that moment, to find 'a style for the job'.

The brief was just that: a few laconic sheets of foolscap. It simply suggested a schedule of accommodation; other conditions have already been mentioned – flexibility and access for machine replacement in workshops, no exposed concrete surfaces, and so on. Planners might object to high-rise, but they too had to bow down before the irremovable programme: this building needed that head of water. (Actually, the Building Committee had only demanded a 60ft drop; Gowan mischievously adds today: 'they got 100 feet and of course were more than happy'.)

Observations on design development: a narrative

Development of the brief was completed by September 1959 and design work began in earnest. In an early proposal – the earliest to survive, its model recorded and, revealingly, published only by Gowan – the site is carpeted with a rectangular grid of six by ten square bays. The workshops are mostly single-storey, but some bays are lifted up and at this point the research laboratories hang rather awkwardly on top. Specialist spaces, squeezed up above the gridded footprint, are bunched into a taller block at the front of the site, over lecture theatres. Already final forms can be discerned: a tower at the park edge on top of the expressed lecture theatre, that theatre itself hanging above a single storey solid podium sliced off acutely by the diagonal site boundary. A cross axis from the entrance/stair hub through the workshops to the back is reflected in the cut-out upper floor above; the higher workshop block vestigially overhangs the back service road. (On this first model, the existing building which restricts the site at the back is omitted; Stirling & Gowan's proposal anticipated the development of that site in a further phase which would bridge a link to their building.)

Before the end of 1959, at least two sketch proposals and three such models had been presented to the client.[41] In the axonometric sketch dated 25 February 1960, the form has reached the recognisably 'aircraft-carrier' gestalt of the final building. The six by ten 20ft square bays are unchanged (and will remain unchanged into the actual building, though half a bay becomes cantilevered), and the form is virtually finalised with the higher row of workshops and chimneys in place. The research laboratories are pulled to the front, replacing the offices; while an office tower surmounts the second lecture theatre. Recognisable elements of the developing scheme include: the exhaust pipe/totem pole at the point of 'arrival' (not the entrance); the clear cut of the cross route (which will eventually disappear); and, most obviously now, the system of north-lights running diagonal to the grid.

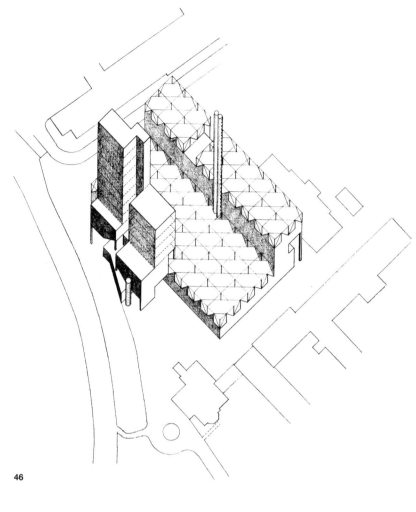

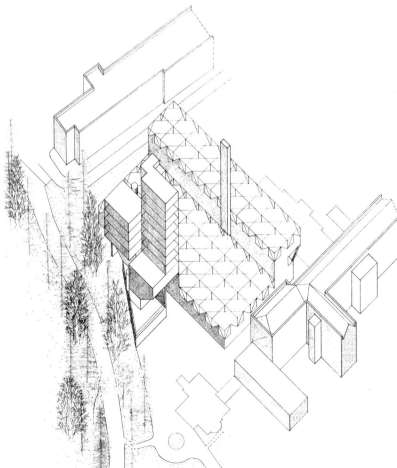

So we have reached a *parti* which is essentially as the final building: the ladder of undifferentiated offices (seven floors topped by the water tank) and a smaller pile of research laboratories are each as repetitive vertically as the workshops are repetitive horizontally. Each block sits on a clearly articulated lecture theatre, under which the public spaces meet in a central core at the crossing of the three orthogonal circulation axes. The strategy is clear. In Stirling's words: 'architects don't have the specialist knowledge to query the brief; in this situation it is essential to propose a generalised solution … There is no attempt visually to relate any of the rooms to each other when the activity which takes place in them is different … The only expressed units of accommodation are those we understood at the level of our own experience and felt reasonably confident would not change – lecture theatres, staircases, etc'.

Very soon, the towers were swapped, and the final massing became recognisable in another sketch axonometric probably done in March 1960. The general arrangement is unchanged. But the lecture theatres are now reversed, more clearly to signal entrances under their brooding vast lintels, an effect which will be further dramatised when the nearest corner of the lecture theatre becomes cantilevered out. The office block in fact becomes an entrance arch at ground level, where its structure continues down to the ground, through or past the lecture hall. The whole building appears to have a solid plinth, integral with the windowless triangular prow under the larger lecture theatre. (The snorkel on this podium has temporarily vanished round the corner.) On top of this unbroken surrounding wall, the workshop roof is unchanged; and at the back the higher workshops are now cantilevered and strutted very much as we will know them.

Though the sawtooth profile and exposed structure of the workshop roof adds a lively froth to the soberly defensive wall below, it conceals its diagonal thrust. The silhouette on the elevations suggests an almost conventional north-light profile: only in axonometric can it be seen as something quite different.

In March 1960, the University approved the initial design. Stirling, appointed visiting critic at Yale University in 1960, was missing for four crucial months during the design process; Gowan presented the final scheme to the building committee alone.

The next, and second from last scheme, is fascinating in that while its overall form is very nearly finalised, some crucial elements are quite different from what was actually built.

This, rather calm and stately scheme, is finalised early in the summer of 1960.[42] For the first time, the four storey block of research labs, hanging in the air over the smaller lecture theatre, has its eastern corner sliced away. If that cutoff was initially derived from observing a site boundary, this line is immediately exploded by the lecture hall underneath which is now dramatically turned through 90 degrees, to project its rear towards the park.

Suddenly a quite new dialectic with the other block is set up, and a much more subtle sense of dynamic balance hovers between them. The simpler notion of the project 'having a tower' (as remains in the written descriptions) is undermined by our much more ambiguous perceptions, as we begin to see a grouping of miniature city elements.

The scale of the elements and therefore of the whole complex, remains quite different from that of the final building. The front blocks are clad in large areas of plate glass; the taller tower fully glazed, the squatter tower wrapped in even bands of glass and brick. The workshop tablecloth seems to be formed of vast, simple trusses, still clearly marking a 20 foot rhythm around the perimeter. Its structure is essentially as in the earlier axonometric studies; that is, trusses spanning both ways with the grid, against which the concertina roof runs within this depth, on the 45 degree diagonal.

The design of the central circulation space, the pinwheel to which all the elements link, was considerably advanced by Stirling's winning the argument with the fire officer about the escape stair. Having shown convincingly that there could be no fire risk in the absence of any combustible materials in this area, fire doors between stairs and landings are omitted; the three vertical tubes of stair, lift and services each stand independently and are bridged and linked to rooms simply as needed, the whole being enclosed in glass. At the same time the glass spiral below the lecture theatre was accepted.[43]

Now the projecting lozenge alters its meaning: being pulled apart with a steep ramp cut up its side to a new, higher entrance, it suggests an inhabitable upper plateau. We feel a new sensibility of 'building the site', of stacking up inhabitable layers and forms. This is encouraged by the eye-level perspective now replacing the bird's-eye axo (and model's) viewpoint; it is unified with a handrail which wraps up and round to the podium and reappears round the clifftop balconies above – all reinforced by the image of people drawn leaning on the rails on all these levels, looking back towards the park.

48, 49 Sketches by Michael Wilford. The 'rather calm and stately scheme' (shown in both 51 and 52) was superseded by this later version. Only in axonometric could Wilford explain the surface shape.

50 Gowan's perspective of the penultimate scheme, early summer 1960. The big bay rhythms reflected in plate glass office windows, in vast simple workshop trusses still concealing their diagonal but exposing their top chords.

51, 52 Elevations of the penultimate scheme as it moved from the glazing of fig 50 to that of fig 57 (overleaf).

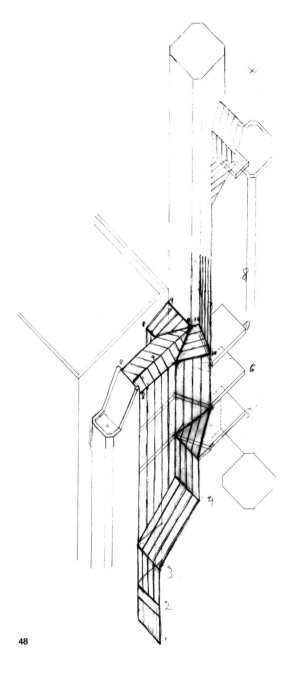

48

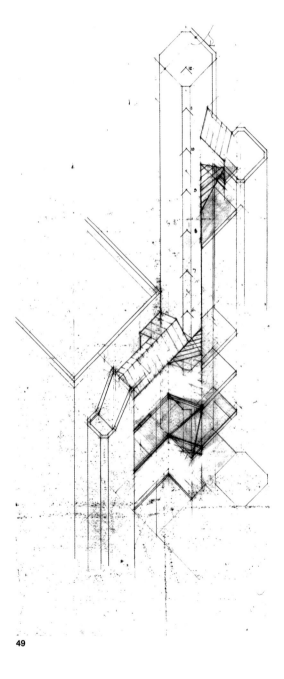

49

Perhaps it was the cut-off corner on the research labs which suggested the similar splaying of the tower. Perhaps it was just a sense in the air – many buildings of the moment suddenly chamfer corners gratuitously; the Smithsons' Economist complex does it most elegantly. Clearly what the chamfer does here is reinforce the sense of a wrapped-round skin of glass. These cut-off blocks, however, had to transfer their loads down through the rectilinear geometry of the ground plan.

As drawings follow one another, we can see the detail being worked through and refined, until we reach a full set of ⅛in working drawings (which, though all are dated 9 September 1960, in important aspects show much earlier intentions). The envelope – the towers whose detailed forming was Stirling's concern and the workshops whose roofing Gowan continually developed – should have reached its final development in this completed scheme.

Certainly the sketch perspective shows the towers approaching their final form.[44] There had been considerable debate about the contrast in image between the plate glass towers and the patent glazed sheds, with the implication that it reflected showpiece intellectual work at the front and lower grade industrial work at the back. It seems that Edward Parkes, the client, felt the factory aesthetic inappropriate for a school, though fine for workshops. Stirling, straight-faced as ever, was happy to emulate the 'traditional prewar industrial estate, with the office block up front, the workshop behind'. Gowan knew it just could never be afforded.

'We had a long argument in the office; it was a major row,' comments Gowan on what was the most famous exception to their usual practice of battling out design decisions in private. 'Stirling felt that pictorially it would be let down by patent glazing, against the sheen of plate glass. He was prepared to let the cost rocket. I said it was a madness,' Gowan expands, calling on the quantity surveyor as his chief witness. In effect the reality of the limited budget finally settled the issue; patent glazing was applied to tower and workshops alike.

It may seem easy for Gowan to add today 'I thought that pictorially it would work very well; I had a picture in my mind of Kew, giving it a consistency …'; nevertheless, his stubbornness was to great visual effect. No-one had ever had the effrontery to wrap an office tower in patent glazing. Generally considered by architects as a low-quality industrial cladding, it would now have its finest hour. In fact the

50

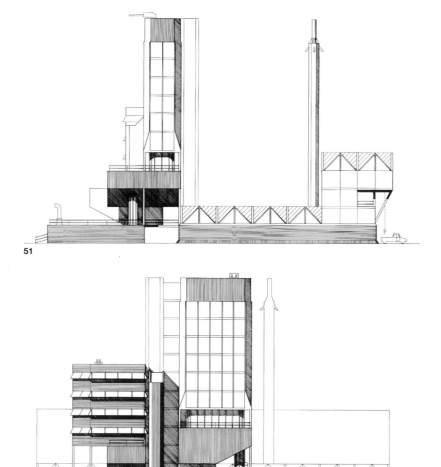

51

52

tower glazing in the '9 September' drawings is still only halfway towards the final building; here its long wall divides into ten panels of vertical sliding sashes of light amber tinted glass. On the actual building that wall has sixteen strips of clear patent glazing, with top-hung vents every third row. The visual effect is very different. Similarly, the research laboratory tower is now equally transformed, but to quite different ends. No longer oscillating ambiguously between equal areas of plate glass and brick, narrower bands of window stand as almost solid, prismatic strips on the outside of a solid brick cube. The argument, as we know, was for quick through-ventilation, and that certainly worked effectively.[45] Like the building's offices, the research laboratory block's glazing is still only halfway to the final design. The off-white prisms on the front wall divide into four, just as the earlier plate glass windows. On the actual building it divides into 12 clear panes.

The late decision to use these tiny panes is critical to the overall effect of scintillating crystal, but also fundamental to the mirage of scale which the final building catches perfectly – the tiny balanced skyscrapers. Once built, the yin and yang of the towers – this dialectic of the sleek mesh and the spiky rings – will be even more obvious at night, the one tall, slim translucent with darker bands marking the floors, the other simply four, larger, lower, crystalline rings.

In the 9 September fully worked-out drawings, the cascading glass enclosure of the pinwheel is still not in its final, articulated form. At the front, however, the lozenge podium has developed its final shape, although the snorkel has not yet reappeared. The point is snubbed off at 45 degrees, and the metal handrail replaced. To make the use of the tile-on-concrete veneer so obvious that only a Pevsner could miss it, this podium edge becomes two, long, chunky red tiled converging cubes which don't quite touch, held in the air on tiny metal pins.[46]

Other formal detailed refinements, many of them working through the overlay of the two grids, continue up to the last minute; two cylindrical chimneys are replaced by one octagonal one, into which the two boiler flues enter above roof level; the cylindrical glazed stair into the lecture theatre, its punning visual shadow, similarly becomes octagonal.

Signifier and signified

Stirling famously said that every building should have at least two ideas. At Leicester they are the idea of functional parody and of shapely paradigm. Does that need decoding?

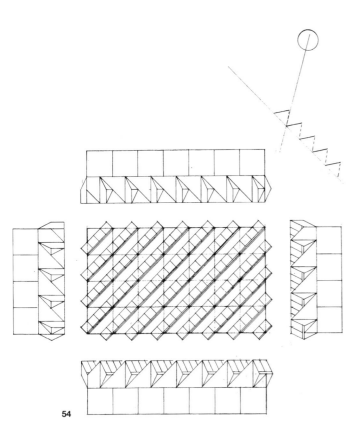

54

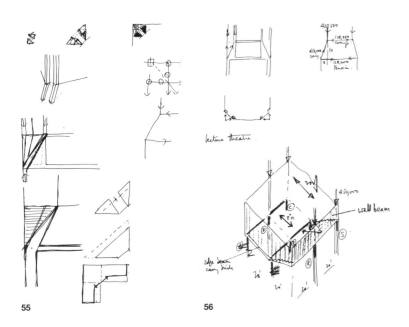

55   56

53

The progressive engineer

In April 1960, Stirling & Gowan engaged Frank Newby as structural engineer, who had recently become senior partner of F J Samuely & Partners following Samuely's premature death. Although the architects' friend and contemporary, Newby had much wider experience. Having joined Samuely in 1949, he recalls, 'within two years I had been introduced to steel folded plates and to star beams … my engineering training, apart from logic, had been discarded'.[47] By 1960 – when he introduced both a star beam (ie one with more than two ends) and a folded plate roof at Leicester – his wide experience included all the structures for Tom Ellis including the years Gowan and Stirling were there. But Leicester was not just the architects' first project in the spotlight, it was also Newby's first since Samuely's death. 'I was young too,' he muses; 'it was a test for me as well.'[48]

He began work on the office tower at the end of May. There, Stirling's having chamfered the corners of the tower implied a structural octagon which now needed a connecting shape to transfer these loads back to the corners of the original rectangle, without interfering in the spaces beneath. For this, one of the building's most elegant details was developed: a great canted joint in each corner. The shaping was Stirling's,[49] but Newby made it possible. Newby tied the corners together underneath, with a horizontal double Y, the star beam, all to be cast of in-situ concrete.

Like all great structural solutions, it has an apparent simplicity and the feel of common sense, a logic which can be demonstrated in miniature, modelled with everyday material – the octagonal net holding up slab floors, the storey deep canted wedges transferring the loads back to the rectangle, and the star tension member holding it all steady. Looking up at the building, one senses its rightness. Yet it remains tall, elegant, fragile – and, of course, broken; contradicted by the great, partly cantilevering, hall below. The tall entrance columns, only 12 inches wide and appearing miraculously slender, are, in Newby's words, 'just stalks'; the stiffness, the solidity of the building is all in its being tied back to the solid towers of lift and stairs.

Stirling felt strongly that structure should not dominate architecture. In his typical way, when asked about its role as form-giver, he replied: 'Structure is something which holds a building up and stops it falling down. An architecture over-concerned with structure is superficial'. 'Although the structure was dealt with at a fairly late stage,' Newby adds, 'there was a great deal of inspired discussion on possible solutions which led to the removal of the outside supporting column of the large lecture theatre so that it cantilevered from the tower building, and to the introduction of raking columns for the workshop block.'[50]

Newby is too modest. In his sketch of 28 May we can see him saying to Stirling: what about removing these columns? You can if you wish. 'I like that,' Newby imitates Stirling's laconic tone of voice in reply. ('Jim didn't say a great deal,' he adds.) Into June 1960, we find Newby sketching various proposals for the back of the lecture theatre – as a cantilevering wall-beam or lattice wall-truss. On 25 July, Newby was doodling with a two-way grid for the research laboratory block. He sketched it diagonally, checked it approximately and got Stirling's approval straight away. The resulting diagrid structure, with vertical columns round its perimeter at 10 foot centres, neatly transfers the loads from its oddly shaped plan down to the 20 foot square grid below.

Newby says: 'I took the mass and said let's look at how to structure it'. But on occasion it had more powerful formal implications than that might suggest. With the higher workshop strip, he realized immediately that the architects' cantilever was much greater than its support could allow. Remarkably in-tune with the building's form-making, he proposed a series of great raking struts, like shelf-brackets, springing from the first floor where they are tied back to the floor slab. Stirling worked closely with Newby on these raking struts, and this development struck his imagination.[51]

The tale of the workshop roof

'I would talk to Jim about the tower,' Newby smiles, 'and then go over and talk to James about the workshop. Oh yes, it was divided between them.' Before Newby did go over and became involved, Gowan continued developing the workshop roof towards its final form. A balsa model of the '9 September' scheme (made before Newby came in) shows the east/west concertina roof fitting within the depth of the trusses, just as before. But now, instead of a grid of two-way spanning trusses within which the roof sits at 45 degrees, Gowan's proposed structure is simplified to rows of Warren trusses running north–south, diagonally on plan and at right angles to the corrugated roof above which their precast concrete top chords are exposed. Were these trusses to sit on the perimeter wall, there would be a continuous series of little flat triangles all around the edge, patching the gap between the two geometries. It was most inelegant. However, if the trusses were raised above the enclosing

53 Gowan's model of a workshop roof proposal shown to Newby when he first began work on it.

54 A workshop roof diagram and its elevational implications from the same time.

55, 56 Sketches by Frank Newby in May and June 1960. The engineer is developing ideas for discussing with Stirling, means of constructing the octagon to rectangle junction of the office tower frame (56), and proposals for how to hang the lecture theatre corner as a cantilever.

57 Axonometric showing the design developing: glazing changes both the scale of the tower and new, narrow prismatic bands on research laboratories.

58 The *parti* of the building clearly explained by the architects in isometric circulation building.

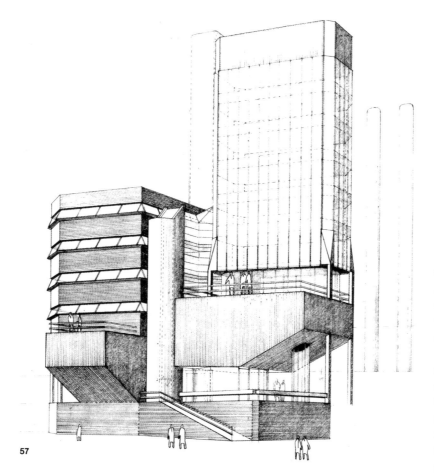

57

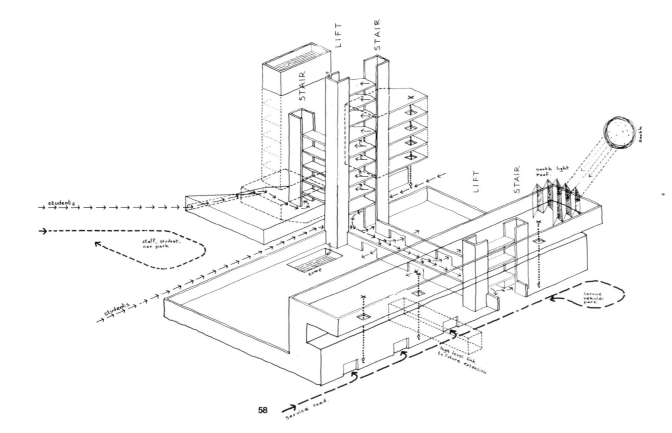

58

wall, to sit on triangular struts above the ring beam and internal columns, these triangles could slope down neatly to the wall head. It is this structural development which produces the building's most spectacular formal development: the diamond end units of the prisms which now identify the roof.

Gowan produced the roof on his own. Despite its much more insistent diagonal than before, he was keen to keep it as a skin, tightly articulated around the edge. Gowan refers to Edward Reynolds' Fourth year AA project scheme submission for the SPD Depot Building. This project, its engineering tutored by Newby, stuck in the imagination of the time; its facetted roof geometry set boldly at an angle to the plan grid. But Gowan notes that 'in modelling the perimeter, I was antagonistic to the Reynolds thing … The notion in my mind was the bat's wing: membrane and bones. Not my favourite animal, but taut'.

For the architects, the exposed structure was crucial: a very visible row of top chords of the trusses between which the furrowed roof-lights threaded. [52] 'I had only one model in my mind,' Gowan says; ' a pre-First World War factory off the North Circular Road. Clearly it was not the simplest way to do a roof. I knew there would be some resistance to it – but I had this model! Engineers want the easy route. Newby could see a mile off that this would involve him in hellish botheration.' 'Hang on!' interrupts Newby; 'like all architects, they said "all problems are solvable". But I had to raise the immense flashing problems at the nodes.' 'So', Gowan continues, 'he argued that it was novel and not practical; then I raised my trump card – the factory on the North Circular. He said he knew why it was an external structure (to do with protection from corrosive fumes inside), and that there was no such reasoning here … in fact one had one's hands full, and there was not much we could do. Stirling and I were disappointed there was no exposed top chord'.

Responding to the awesome difficulty of making watertight the many intersections where the envelope and structural systems met at right angles, Newby quickly suggested that the trusses be rotated through 90 degrees to align with the roof corrugations. He first considered that the patent-glazing tablecloth might be draped between these trusses, with a parallel secondary support for the gutters running between them, but he moved on quickly to suggest that, if the trusses were inclined, they could be seen as a folded plate framework, and the glazing might then be fixed directly to the structure. Between Gowan and Newby, the geometrical comprehension, structural ingenuity and clarity of devel-

60

59–61 Photographs taken shortly after the building's completion: The main entrance arch, under the tower of offices, by day and night. The unearthly glow from the milky prisms offset by the carefully spot-lit entrance hall and spiral escape stair vanishing up into the lecture theatre's hull.

61

62

63

64

65

66

67

68

opment of this roof was a major achievement. According to Gowan, 'it was a terrible effort'.

But all was not structural functionalism. Having arrived at the astonishingly powerful visual form of diamonds and their edge closers through earlier structural explorations, this was not going to be abandoned now. Even though this form no longer derives from the making and support of the roof, the formal fantasy is not to be let slip. Now holding to that shape, instead of the row of parallel trusses, there was an asymmetrically shaped folded plate. Loads are transferred on a folding plate along the valleys and ridges, here being brought down to the ring beam on the points of the diamonds. But as the ends are staggered these loads are asymmetrical and need careful stiffening. For each end diamond one additional strut is necessary. To the roof fabricated up from steel square sections and angles, as this was 'an odd man out', Newby smiles, 'I made it a tube'.

Finally, it went to tender. The contract figure of £447,500 was negotiated with contractors already working for the university. The price was within the UGC's tight cost limits; expensive tiled and plyglass claddings offset by standard cheap concrete paving in the workshops and mill finish aluminium patent glazing.[53]

As full-time assistant in the office, David Walmsby, who was helping build Preston at the same time, left the office over the summer, though he drew up for Gowan a full set of ⅛in scale record drawings. (These, though dated 6 September, were already outdated when he brought them back to the office.) By then, with final approvals from planning and from the University, they had engaged Michael Wilford to work on Leicester in August 1960. Quinlan Terry had been working with them on a part-time basis since 1959, Kit Evans made the early models when Stirling was in the States; Malcolm Higgs joined at the end of 1960, exactly as site work began. Terry and Higgs were AA students working half the week in the office. Wilford, who already had considerable office experience, was now with them full-time, though doing his diploma as an evening student at the hard-nosed Northern Polytechnic. Between the areas which concentrated the attention of the separate partners, Wilford would plug the design gaps. He drew a complete set of ½in working drawings, in fact all the details from glazing system to joinery and tile cladding throughout.

There was a great deal of development work, and by the end there were produced 300 working drawings, a lot of the details ready barely weeks ahead of the contractors. 'There

62 Cleaning the glazing at Leicester above the workshop roof.

63, 65 Construction of in-situ concrete lecture theatre and office tower frame.

64, 66, 72, 73 Workshop roofing construction.

67, 68 Workshop edge: the lower encircled with fairfaced brick, the upper to be clad in plyglass.

69, 70 Completed workshop roof by day and night.

71 Fourth year AA student project by Edward Reynolds, 1957, elevation and roof plan. An experimental, formally integrated, clear and subtle design, its warehouse roof exploiting the geometric tablecloth; its offices bunched into a corner tower. Newby tutored its engineering; Gowan, on the AA staff, closely watched it develop, though he did not tutor Reynolds who also knew Stirling.

69

70

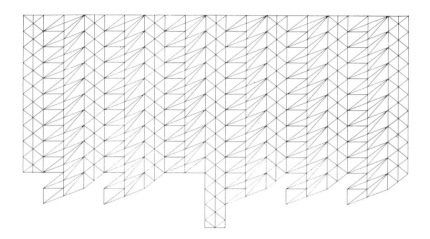

71

72

73

was rigorous testing,' Wilford adds; Higgs was sent to Holland to find high quality cladding tiles to colour match their bricks. They made up huge sample concrete slabs to which tiles were fixed and then tested under different conditions. Tiles had never been used in this way before, wrapping all exposed surfaces including soffits; the detailing and testing ensured that here, unlike some other buildings which soon followed, there were no problems of tiles falling off. The crucial point of the detailing was that tiles were not fixed to render, but directly to very accurately cast structural concrete. It was formed against a serrated rubber matting, with horizontal corrugations up to an inch deep, giving a grooved key for the tiles with dove-tailed backs which were laid vertically. As the engineer notes, 'there were no problems at all'.[54]

They tested the jointing and the glazing systems; they made mock-ups of the 10 foot high workshop roof-lights and their diamond end bays. All laboratory joinery, the benches and cupboards, was designed by Gowan. 'We got by with very little correspondence, few telephone calls, and a secretary, attending two afternoons a week, coped with administration', says Wilford. Stirling adds: 'as always in my experience, the contractor was led protesting through the operation. We visited the site sometimes once or even twice a week and, in varying degrees, had to become surveyors, administrators, site agents, etc; all for five per cent!' The winter was exceptionally hard, and the site was shut for three months. It was handed over in the autumn of 1963, though the interiors were still incomplete when it was reviewed early in 1964; and Richard Einzig's photographs of the period cannot hide odd scaffold poles and ladders.[55]

True functionalism

The language of Stirling & Gowan found its ideal vehicle at Leicester. This 'new institution of a scientific and educational type' (to quote them) perfectly suited their dead-pan concern with programmatic analysis, economy and logic. The brief was built up of easily identifiable components; the site was tightly confined. All could be exploited to an extreme without ever breaking the straight-faced line. If its formal richness might, for an instant, seem to have flown free of the programme, it could immediately be shown to be giving that same programme a clear expression.

'An architect should exhibit his skill in turning the difficulties which occur in raising an elevation from a convenient plan into so many picturesque beauties; and this constitutes the great difference between the principles of classic and

pointed architecture. In the former he would be compelled to devise expedients to conceal these irregularities; in the latter he has only to beautify them.' Pugin, who so influenced Butterfield, used these words in 1841. It is unlikely if a better description of Leicester could be found than the neat adjective 'pointed;' but even so, the argument remains timeless.

Stirling in 1956 criticised contemporary functionalism in the USA as anonymous; hiding a mechanical disposition of elements. There, functionalism concerned 'industrial process', he argued; while in Europe it remained an 'essentially humanist method of designing to a specific use'. Similarly, 'the true picturesque derives from the sternest utility', wrote Horatio Greenough, just as Butterfield's All Saints was beginning to astonish High Victorian Londoners.

The sternest utility, however, can be a motor deliberately used to create extremely difficult design situations, which then demand ingenuity of solution. Where functionalism solves problems, Leicester rhetorically exploits them – '*con amore*'; and, in Rowe's phrase, it achieves 'an amalgam of austerity of principle and licentiousness of imagination'.

We know there is no such thing as simple 'honest expression of function'. We also know how something which appears like that is immensely persuasive. 'The eye grasps intuitively how it works; it speaks straight', wrote The *Architectural Review*'s critic of Leicester. 'It is the grand old myth of functionalism come true for once', added Banham, his ambiguity being slightly more aware. Certainly Leicester's forms are neither anonymous nor gratuitous and fanciful; but neither are they a conceptually transparent glove round the programme. Lecture theatre can be read as 'function', taken almost as a ready-made fragment might be collaged by Picasso onto a sculpture. Circulation space, as a poured crystal residue around the three vertical shafts, is equally clearly articulated. But what is that great roof of milky diamond furrows? That smooth box with rings of barbs round it? That tower covered in a net of patent glazing? The public areas can be read directly – entrance arch, lecture theatre. But the more private areas, if equally memorable shapes, are in more arcane, inexplicable languages. These are surely formal more than functional devices.

'No doubt there is a certain architectural quality in the composition of stable masses; particularly where they are asymmetrical,' Stirling responds, without so much as a glimmer of a smile. For his discussion of function is in other terms: 'I have a rather ad hoc and expedient attitude to structure, particularly as a design element, and usually man-

74

77 Outside the research laboratories and workshop block.

74, 75 Details of rainwater spout and open horizontal louvres.

76 Recent overall view showing recladding.

75

76

78

79

80

age to prevent it from intruding on the architectural solution. I am more concerned with sociological, environmental and organisational problems which I regard as being more important to the evolution of design'.

'I think at a subjective level it's right,' Gowan adds today about Leicester. ' I think in functionalism, there's a splendid moment when it works and it looks good, you get a resonance, as it were: it just looks wonderful. Material functionalism just isn't good enough. Modern architecture is eloquent when it works vigorously, transparently, invitingly …'

'Material functionalism' in the sense used by its 1950's adherents, is perhaps most clearly defined by Durand. One should, he said: 'not cling to that in architecture which gives pleasure, seeing that by attending solely to achieving its true purpose, it is impossible for it not to give pleasure, and that by seeking to give pleasure it can become ridiculous.'[56]

Stirling & Gowan saw through the thinness in this. Yet, while recognising the functionalist fallacy – that architectural quality will inevitably appear if one forms a mould of spaces determined solely by their uses – this formulation still held an attraction as generator for creative development.

By 1960, functionalism had become a rather embarrassing notion; so its adherents were thrilled when they saw Leicester rejuvenating it. But what they didn't see was Leicester toppling their functionalism as firmly as Banham's thesis had toppled Pevsner's, or Wittkower's had toppled the connoisseur's view of the Renaissance.

In their formative ideas, both Gowan and Stirling acknowledged a key influence in De Stijl. Gowan refers to a pinwheel house of 1923 by Van Doesburg and Van Eesteren, with qualities which Stirling & Gowan had already explored in their house in the Chilterns in 1955, where the rooms are cubes spun at half levels off a central stair, and Gowan clearly sees this as an exercise on the way to Leicester. 'The New Architecture,' Van Doesburg wrote, 'is formless and yet exactly defined. It does not have an a priori schema, a mould into which it would pour the functional spaces.'[57]

Such an idea obviously resonated with Stirling & Gowan, as did the image of Van Doesburg and Van Eesteren's dynamic project – its rooms spinning off a glazed central shaft. But if this was an important artistic icon of an earlier age, it was not yet itself a sophisticated architecture. Stirling & Gowan therefore took this 'Heroic Period functionalism' and exploited it; collaged it onto their own architecture. In this way too, Leicester was the first building in Britain after Modernism.

Other early masters worked harder than the De Stijl group with the notion of functionalism. Hugo Häring, for example, had aimed 'to examine things and allow them to discover their own images. It goes against the grain with us to bestow a form on them from the outside'. Commenting on this in 1960, Colin St John Wilson, showed how, in the spirit of particularity, functional analysis implied that formal solutions would be discovered en route, in the design process itself. 'This was not an approach calculated to make life easy for either architect or public', Wilson added, 'it is the lore of the Lone Ranger'. The resonance with Leicester, being designed by Wilson's friend just at that moment, needs no forcing.

Actually, Stirling & Gowan didn't want to take functionalism further; nor did they did want to develop the alternative, expressive functionalist tradition of Häring, Aalto or Scharoun. In fact, while Stirling claims 'the expression (articulation) of the most important accommodation is something we have always been concerned with', their interior spaces at Leicester have the minimum of functional articulation. They 'remain abstract in form and archaic in character'.[58] In this sense, therefore, the building is a masterpiece of the primitive, with the architects collaging this early modern flavour into their other concerns.

By playing the game absolutely straight – quite without any patronising, knowing winks: even the 'brick' doors in the podium are, of course, logical – the complex, three-dimensional forms are all the more powerful. There is an apparent air of nineteenth-century, common-sense, ad-hoc straightforwardness, like that of the Leicester industrial buildings to which Stirling refers, or at least to Paxton and Turner's glasshouses.

There is a studied casualness – look at how the podium hand rails meet at the prow. There is also a sense of its being produced as it went along, with the glass cascade appearing almost improvised or accidental; far from being high-tech glass engineering, it is craftsmanlike, with the cutting of bars to length on site – as Banham said, 'it's all bolts, nuts and raggedy flashings left as found'. But 'improvised and accidental' does not just display a Brutalist approach to constructed surface, it is part of the process of development of formal invention. Both here and, as we have seen, with the workshop roofs, quite unexpected formal and perceptual conditions appear and are embraced. Stirling & Gowan's openness to happy accident can run alongside an obsessive aesthetic determination.

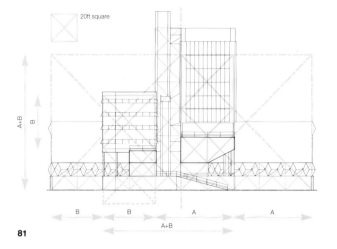

20ft square

82

83

The architects' concerns

Leicester, said Stirling, was the culmination of 'six or seven years' designing articulated buildings'. As we have seen, different functional areas therefore formed different shapes, are constructed in different ways and have different visual characteristics internally. 'The choice of structure was a later decision in the design sequence', while the appearance of rooms was determined by their functions.

Criticising 'the excessive circulation and compromised room usage inherent in the *plan libre*,' Stirling aimed to 'allow rooms to become private spaces again … having an ideal shape according to their use and be at their most functional without compromise'. So Stirling & Gowan express the elements as clear, primary volumetric statements, held together by that most powerful negative form, the evanescent circulation; 'the skeleton', as Stirling put it simply, 'onto which the various rooms are hung'. And hung, need he add, for the most powerful plastic effect. (Louis I Kahn's contemporary 'server' and 'served' tale with the Richards Medical Research Building is quite different, and not to be confused by obvious visual links in the buildings.[59])

Of course the forms must be structurally stable – even if dynamically; so the extent of a cantilever, in physical fact, is dictated by the weight of what is holding the other end down. They must also be visually stable: so the geometric ordering – the unifying 10 foot module in three dimensions – is an essential base. A glance at Leicester's plan makes this explicit, while the elevations respond to similar analysis. In an almost hilarious example of po-faced functionalism, taking the '100ft water head' literally, in early schemes the 10ft cube module simply stacked up 10 floors on which sat the tank, making an exactly double-square elevation. Gowan has a sketch which is nothing but an assembly of 10ft and 20ft squares. The large lecture theatre is square on plan, the small is double square. Volumetrically, the large is half a 4-module cube, its back half truncated; the smaller, with the same section but halved in width, is a double 2-module cube, its back half similarly sliced off. Identical on plan to the small hall, the office tower has a proportion of 1:2; the research labs 3:4. Were this not all clear enough, the point is intimated as you arrive to meet a 3:4:5 triangle sticking its tongue out at you. Extreme geometric formation can run alongside the most reasonable of planning arguments.

'But,' Stirling continues, 'the planning of spaces and rooms was secondary to the creation of a circulation system.' Circulation, therefore, is like some invisible muscle; it is minimal, taut, fit, powerful. Starting in the double height entry hall, stairs and lift rise with platforms of varying shapes and diminishing size, linking to the rooms on each floor. To this, as it were existenz-minimum movement diagram, Stirling & Gowan add a facetted membrane, made up of glazed scales which articulate each shift in the modelling of the calculated circulation volume. Inside this tiny kaleidoscope of prisms, the perceived quality can be vertiginous, as in a hall of mirrors. The experience is far from the architecture promenade of Heroic Period Corbusier, which offered a shifting viewpoint through the major spaces of the architecture.

Here, in both Gowan and Stirling's concerns, the building's dynamic visual experiences are disembodied, being unrelated to the architecture's main purpose, the interior of its body. Can such an architecture even have an interior?

The solid object

Stirling, interestingly, used Paul Rudolph's Art and Architecture Building at Yale University as the obvious contrast. It is Leicester's exact contemporary[60] and was already known to Stirling as visiting tutor. At Yale, Stirling strongly disapproved of the same material surfaces being used throughout, outside and in. Yet Leicester is ambiguous in its acceptance of any inside. There is no interior design, Stirling said, as all the elements are their own, quite separate, independent places. Did he simply mean there is no unifying palette of finishes? Workshops have harsh, crudely finished linings, with exposed services and structure unobscured, as might seem to befit an industrial interior. Lecture theatres are acoustic lined, reasonable, unmemorable commercial interiors. The intention throughout seems to be conventional. Perhaps it recalls how their conventional house interiors at Preston had learned the lesson of the over-defined insides of the Ham Common flats.

Circulation spaces, Stirling points out, provide 'the only consistent aesthetic element' of the building. Yet these spaces, exactly as with Rudolph at Yale, are treated as continuous with the outdoors, the finishes run through the glass, over and round all the surfaces – shiny, noisy, self-cleansing. Like the outside, they are handled with absolute precision – not a single cut tile. Stirling's contrast is now understandable, for this *is* outside; its 'hard, brittle reflective surfaces', as he said, 'appropriate to the outdoor climate'. It seems instinctively recognised that this building lodges in the memory as a collection of complexly wrapped, completely impenetrable forms.[61]

84

86

85

84–88 Circulation is the building's transparent, dynamic core; and it provides, in Stirling's words, 'its only consistent aesthetic element'. Photographs taken shortly after the building's completion show how from hall, entered at two levels, stairs (in fairfaced concrete) rise to platforms of varying shape and diminishing size (totally veneered in uncut red tile behind the waterfall of patent glazing). Fully glazed reading room under the office tower (87), and gallery at sixth floor (88).

87

88

89 Angles collide, massive section handrails float on pins and, with studied casualness, just stop short; escape stair and lavatory vent collage new significance.

90, 91 Tiny glazing units portray a vast skyscraper, while flimsy stilts hold the office tower as an awesome entrance porch. (The cladding has been changed in recent years and therefore these photographs, as with 92–95, date from the early 1960s.)

92–95 The glazed waterfall (93, photographed from within by James Stirling); and looking up to where the circulation hits the sky (94, 95).

89

90

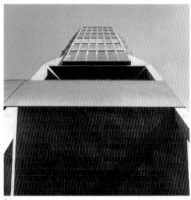

91

92

So impenetrable it could be solid; hewn, facetted on a grinding stone. The surfaces are skins; the podium, solid above its splayed base, is a brick curtain. Even when broken by double doors (under the ramp), they are covered by brick almost as if wallpaper. This seems a pointed detail, hinting towards the sensibility of the *Herausgefallen Steine* on the podium (car-park) wall at Stuttgart (though, interestingly, it seems to have come from Gowan).[62]

That Stirling is not interested in transparency as such, and that he sees this shift in Corbusier himself, was clear in his article on the Maisons Jaoul in the *Architectural Review*: the windows are no longer to be looked through but at, he argued; 'the wall is considered as a surface and not as a pattern'. This sensibility links Stirling with Paolozzi whose sculpture at this time had become an art of surface and not of mass. The glass skins at Leicester are opaque or translucent as much as transparent; a milky, silvery, facetted surface. The brick is sometimes paper-thin, the tiles are always laid vertically and unbonded to state their being a veneer. Right back to his 1952 Poole competition entry, Stirling's concern for material to articulate surface rather than represent structure has been clear. In his Poole report he spoke of 'brick, neither expressed as "infilling" to a frame nor expressed as structural wall, but rather as a "skin", clothing a facade …'.

By night, however, the building is quite different, becoming an essay in transparencies. In the circulation areas, the sparkle of the warm, tungsten spot lamps dotted around playing directly onto the red tiled surfaces contrasts, as one looks out, with the distant, cool and bluish light from the fluorescence in the ridges of the north-lights below. While from the outside of the building, the circulation shows as red splashes spilling from behind the black pencil of the stair, between the hard gleam of the offices and the solid, prismatic, light bands of the research block, and standing above a sea of cool, low intensity luminosity from the workshops; a gentle ghostly light.

The engineering image

Stirling & Gowan's image of engineering seems essentially object-centred; they imagine heavy industrial workshops; an architect's experience of engineering is of solid structures, to be made and tested under physical loads, concrete cubes to be compressed to destruction. A model is a three-dimensional object made in a workshop; modelling is a process of formal, sculptural composition.

Within this image, what was the place in the late 1950s at Leicester for an engineering which is less tactile, what of electrical and the growing electronic engineering, engineering which is clean, which also needs clean spaces to work in? Was Stirling & Gowan's image of engineering itself, as much as its architecture, grounded in the nineteenth-century Works?

When Heidegger said that technology is an end and not just a means, it was in his belief that, in the act of making, humanity discovers more about its own existence.[63] Is this the humanist or phenomenological sense in which Stirling & Gowan saw engineering? Architecture ought to deal with technology in a mediating role, enlightening and engaging with the users. Collaging pipes, industrial glazing and finishes to its formal ends, Leicester University Engineering Building does not talk about its own making.

Yet extruded aluminium sections are cut and carpented to fit on site, 'trimmed and fiddled', to quote Banham, 'until they answered to the outlines drawn on the surrounding tile-work and gave form to the original, and rather approximate, sketch that was supplied to the contractors'. Even the workshop roof-lights are handcrafted; every single diamond end was a different shape, because of deflection on the trusses, each one was slightly out of true and therefore individually formed. Is it, then, paradoxical that the 'engineering' building is far from 'engineering' built? It is essentially a craft building in its own production; but also perhaps in the image of its inhabitation.

The only escape, as Stirling argued in an important essay in 1957, from the inability to build with technical sophistication – and of course to escape the skin-deep prettiness of the Empiricists – is to develop a sensibility towards the industrial vernacular. 'The exploitation of local materials and methods is perhaps the only alternative to the conventional or the "contemporary" left open to the European architect faced with a minimum budget.' If the 'rational approach' could not be afforded in England, then 'creative thinking is now mainly directed towards the utilisation of existing building methods and labour forces'.

All this is spoken, just as was functionalism where we began, as if it were the spring of their architecture. It is just as much the justification of their taste. Gowan and Stirling were fascinated by such a tradition; Stirling had been collecting photographs of anonymous nineteenth-century Liverpool since student days in his home city. As he says, he was inspired by 'anything of any period which is in fact unself-

93

94

95

96

97

98

96, 97, 100–102 External geometry wraps the workshops.
98, 99 Rhetorical details expressing service are as carefully considered as Ledoux's. Chimney head and lifting tackle, as with the lavatory vent and rainwater spout seen earlier, are the vocabulary of *une architecture parlante* for the 1960s.

99

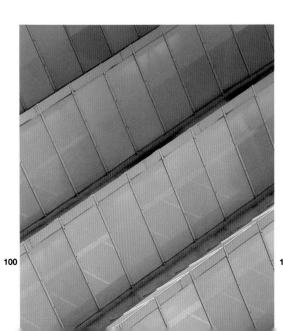

100

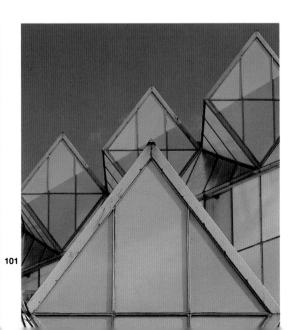

101

102

103, 104 The articulated corner. The brick-clad, framed research laboratory block is separated from the tile-clad, in-situ octagonal lift and service tower by a thin glazing strip which continues down past the landing slab. As is clearer on plan, the projecting laboratory windows only just don't touch the lift shaft. Services from the laboratories fly out into this foyer, bend through 90 degrees and fly on through the neat cover plate into the vertical service shaft seen in fig 104.

105–108 Contrast circulation space: inside lecture hall (105 and 107); an office (106); and inside circulation space (108).

103

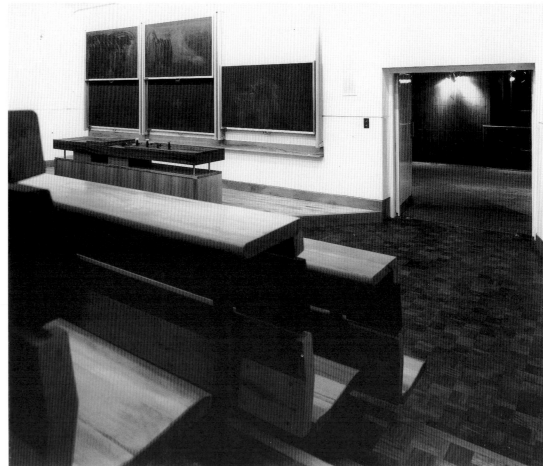

104

105

106

108

107

109

110

111

conscious and virtually anonymous… their outside appearance an efficient expression of their specific function'.

'Today Stonehenge is more significant than Christopher Wren'. That most powerful phrase from the same 1957 Stirling essay, implies this same sensibility. Yet it is nothing to do with exploiting an impoverished context. Nevertheless, much more than the style-spotters' handbook – of Melnikov, Sant'Elia, Wright, Kahn and so on – here is where Leicester germinated. When I persist with Frampton's calling Leicester the first European building clearly derived from Wright, Gowan simply shrugs: 'our models were English, not Wright'.

One way forward, Stirling suggested, was in 'contorting and exploiting ways and means.' This is seen in the use of components: both Gowan and Stirling were fascinated by creative specifying, by components as ready-mades to be exploited, by individual products used, ad-hoc, in eloquently new ways. And it is seen in the use of material: reversing normal conceptions, we find paper-thin brick skins, forms of wrap-round tiles, solid glass. 'I never select materials emotionally,' said Stirling in answer to a question; ' they are chosen entirely at a practical level, but then, of course, they must be transformed to cohere at a level of significance. It's not what you build of, but why and how you make it that determines the quality of our physical existence'.

Oh God, the details

Perhaps this is what the independent High Victorian, G E Street – who so fascinated Stirling – meant when he famously said that God was in the details. At Leicester, as Banham nicely put it, 'the architects achieved less a kind of anti-detailing than some form of un-detailing that would border on plain dereliction of duty were it not so patently right in this context'; or, rather, so patently wrenched out of context.

There is fastidiousness in the extreme: most careful detailing of the livid, hard red Accrington bricks, or of the closely matched Dutch tiles which dictate an intimate, chunky geometry. Look at how the tiles on the octagonal stair towers meet at the corner: showing the gap, as if they had been gently scored with a knife and bent slightly. Alongside this, the patent glazing is unaffectedly crude (quite different from Paxton and Turner), while the real interiors, as we saw, are left to fend for themselves as seems fit. This wonderful mixture, then, of fastidiousness and roughness, means the tile module can never become neurotic obsession. 'Both difficult and great', as Rowe said of the structural chamfer to

rectangle junction; 'tough-rough and delicately gentle, alert and intelligent'.

The formal, architectural detailing (more than its material surfaces) is never pursued with less than a quite unusual intellectual energy. Take just one example: the articulation of the forms where the research laboratory block meets the lift and service tower. The brick clad, framed tower is only inches from the tile clad, in-situ poured octagonal shaft. Connecting platforms stop short of a perimeter formed with a thin strip of sheer patent glazing. Projecting prismatic windows of the labs, with their horizontal louvres, only *just* don't touch the tiled lift shaft. Piped services fly into the circulation space from the labs, bend through 90 degrees and fly on, through a neat cover plate, into the vertical shaft. Both overwrought and under-designed, it is all astonishingly appropriate.

The art critic again

'It has been said that axonometric drawing has influenced the design of this building'. Stirling, typically, puts a distance. Certainly axonometric projection, like this building, relies essentially on the geometry of axes at 45 degrees to each other. Certainly, Wilford's sketches to explain the form of the cascading glass to the sub-contractor are unimaginable other than in axonometric. And Stirling was very proud of the cutaway axo he did of Leicester: clear, sharp, unshaded, unsentimental and purporting to reality (though it omitted the very glazing which Wilford's sketches explain).[64]

Certainly, it defines solids rather well (and thus is used by mechanical engineers); it encourages buildings to appear machine-like, objective, functionally transparent. Certainly, if architecture seeks to emulate the look of machinery – in its use of elements, scale, complexity of shape, chamfered corners, or whatever – axonometric almost generates its own forms. We can see Leicester here.

Inevitably, the axonometric encourages the toy-like; it tends towards a sculptural maquette of play forms; it even encourages a design process which casts functionally determined spaces in solid envelopes like play bricks. At the least, axonometric encourages the notion of modelling not as space but as solid; as a process of formal, sculptural composition, one at which Stirling was a master. This makes it imageable, memorable. We can see Leicester here too – even as on the 7½p postage stamp.

And so it fits: we have a building which plays games with scale. There is the pure pleasure of its strong, satisfying shapes. It is very small, but with tricks of scale plays at being

112

113

112 Glazing detail of
workshop interior.
113–115 Inside the ground
floor workshops.

114

115

116 Icon on a British stamp when not yet a decade old.

117 Between 'a mechanical hobgoblin … One could almost hear it clank' (Craig Hodgetts, 1976) and 'a pile of oxidising junk' (Martin Pawley, 1984) were the years of reassessment. Now an ambivalent icon, the tone for the 1980s was caught in a collage by Nils Ole-Lund, head of the Aarhus School of Architecture, Denmark.

118 From the start, students saw themselves aboard the *S S Stirling*. This expressive yet inarticulate sketch is a menu cover for the first annual dinner of the Engineering Society.

119 Sturdy frame of the tall construction testing workshop.

120 Above this, fits the clean and dry electrical workshop.

121 (overleaf) The rear of the workshop.

116

117

118

very large – the great tiny skyscraper. This sensibility of the sublime permeates: the vast entrance portal, and terrifyingly heavy lecture theatre overhead; the vertigiousness on the landing (where the clients had to insist firmly on handrails the architects would rather omit); and in the lantern-like office tower, with no walls at all, the glass sheet dropping sheer past the upstand lips of these shelves in the sky.

Kant's definition of the sublime is apposite here as to few other buildings: that aesthetic satisfaction which includes as one of its moments a negative experience, a shock, a blockage, an intimation of mortality.

The circulation area's glazing is compressed, a terribly narrow waterfall between solid red rocks. If Leicester tingles to the sublime in detail, it is just as satisfyingly picturesque as we move away. Both in its composition, which resolves with great poise the almost impossible problems of the tight site, and also, further back yet, as it balances the long low horizontality of Martin's proposed 'neo-Platonic' masterplan with a final flourish at the left hand end.[65]

There was even sublime sound – from the large bore pipes which descend alongside the stair, not hidden in a duct. With the water dropping 100 feet, and somewhere in the system a constriction or bend, an organ-pipe effect was triggered. Banham describes hearing what happened: 'As the hydraulics lab came up to full flow, a note of pure and unearthly beauty would be heard in the stair tower, building up through a perfect scale, but – unfortunately – getting louder as well, so that when it hit the octave it was more than the human ear could bear … I was with Jim Stirling the first time he heard it and his face was a study in baffled delight.'

Linking these qualities – ambiguities of scale, sculptural articulation and so on – we get a sense of compression, a compaction of elements. Matisse's aim was once defined as 'the art of condensed sensation.' This exactly fits Stirling & Gowan at Leicester.[66]

Returning finally to the axonometric, it presents a miniature of the real object; it seems to be held at arm's length, in the hand. In this way it has those same intrinsic qualities which Lévi-Strauss, in *The Savage Mind*, attributed to the 'miniature'. Conceptual understanding is promoted by the reversal of the usual process of cognition, by allowing knowledge to proceed from the whole to the parts; with the 'miniatures' functioning as (in Lévi-Strauss' term) 'objects of knowledge'.[67] The magnetism of the axonometric, so

poignant at Leicester, closely links with this notion of the miniature, the talisman, the gift. 'Well, my dear Jim, what a charming little toy!' was Colin Rowe's remark on finally arriving, with Stirling in Stevens' car, at the Engineering Building.

The end start

Leicester shows 'the maturity of original talents that may never need to worry about the problem of style again,' mused Banham at the time; 'confident now that this was something that will resolve itself in the process of satisfying the needs for which the building was created.' It had been, in Gowan's phrase, 'the style for the job'.

Clearly, Leicester couldn't be followed. It was the end of Brutalism – the last illustration in *The New Brutalism*, but used rather as H-R Hitchcock's last illustration, the Alexander Thomson church, in his *Early Victorian Architecture* as a forerunner. Pretending to play the game, fitting all our functionalist and programmatic presumptions, and then privately blowing them apart, it ended the easy flow of British postwar architecture. 'The Leicester building represented a finality for me', says Gowan. We therefore end here. Pausing for a fleeting glance forwards, we just make out Gowan suggesting he withdraw from the partnership – 'after completion, technical problems had to be resolved. I was critical of the outcome, Stirling delighted'. And we half glimpse Stirling, critical of Gowan's developing designs for a house in Hampstead, equally drawing apart. They seem both to be giving up teaching. A few months later, Wilford, who had been laid off as Leicester was nearing completion, is rung by Stirling, told of the divorce, and asked if he would assist him. Stirling's career vanishes into a blazingly public future; Gowan's, who thereafter practices alone, is increasingly private. While the equally remarkable and utterly different engineering building for Leicester's second university, by Short Ford, remains 30 years in the future.

Recently, describing Stirling at Leicester, Francesco Dal Co ended powerfully: 'to conclude an era is a privilege that only a real destructive mind can claim'. As Arthur Korn used to say, teaching back then in the 1950s at the AA – in a phrase he says he got from Breuer: 'a building should be conclusive'. 'After all', as was also said at the AA, though by John Ruskin exactly a century earlier, 'when a new style is invented, what can you do after that? Can you do more than build in it?'[68] Leicester is conclusive; a first.

119

120

Site plan

1 Leicester University
  Engineering Building
2 staff car park
3 rear block engineering
  annexe
4 Wyggeston School
5 university library
6 Victoria Park

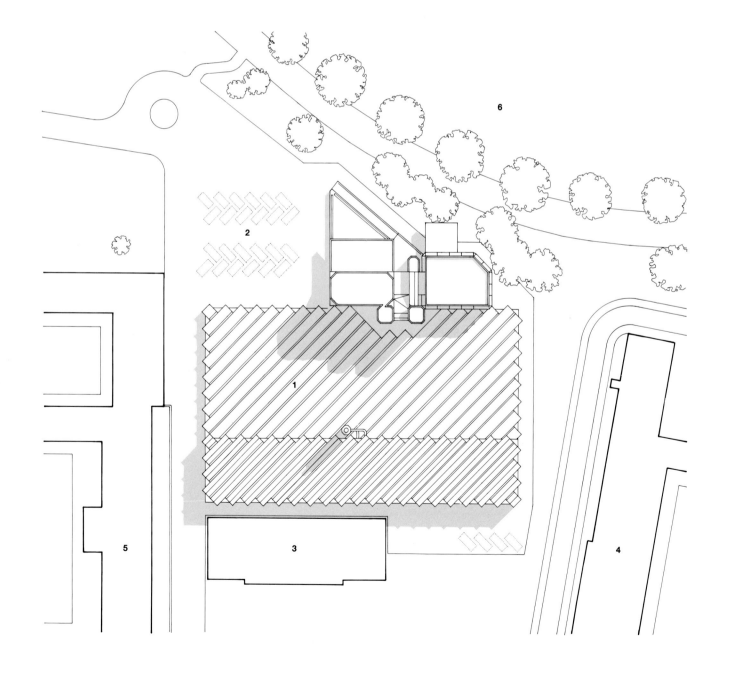

0   10m

0   30ft

Floor plans

Ground floor

1 entrance hall
2 cloakroom
3 student lavs (m)
4 staff lavs
5 student lavs (f)
6 ventilation plant
7 store
8 porter
9 workshops
10 hydraulics lab
11 heat lab
12 structures lab
13 electrical plant
14 boilers

First floor

15 small lecture theatre
16 terrace
17 lobby
18 upper part of entrance hall
19 upper part of workshops/labs
20 paint shop/stores
21 upper part of boiler room
22 instruction boiler

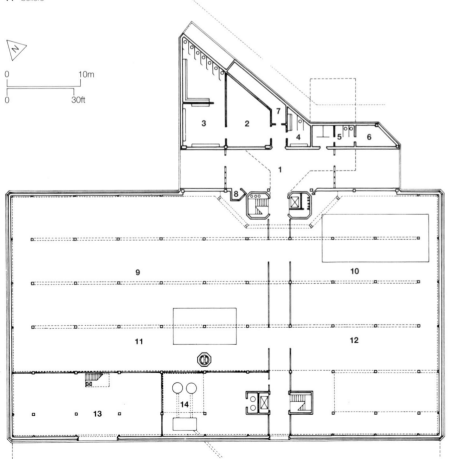

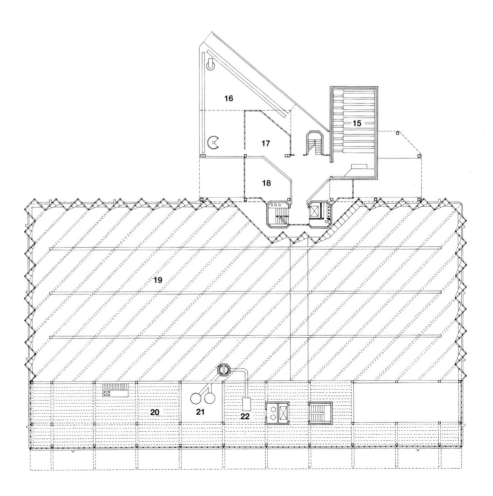

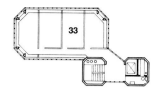

Eighth floor

33 staff offices

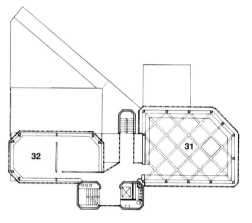

Sixth floor

31 metallurgy lab
32 head of department

Second floor

23 upper part of lecture theatre
24 large lecture theatre
25 upper part of boiler room
26 upper part of structures lab

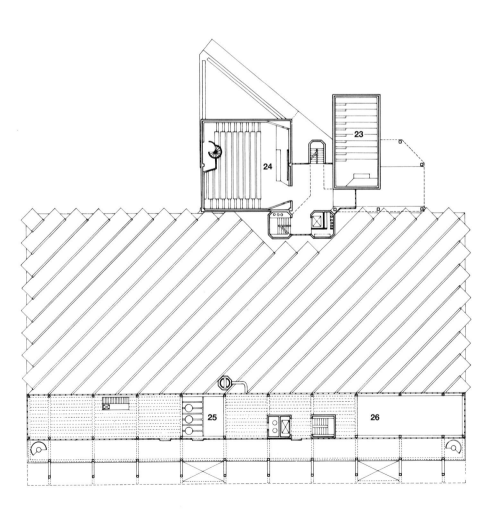

Fourth floor

27 library
28 machines lab
29 upper part of electrical labs
30 upper part of aerodynamics lab

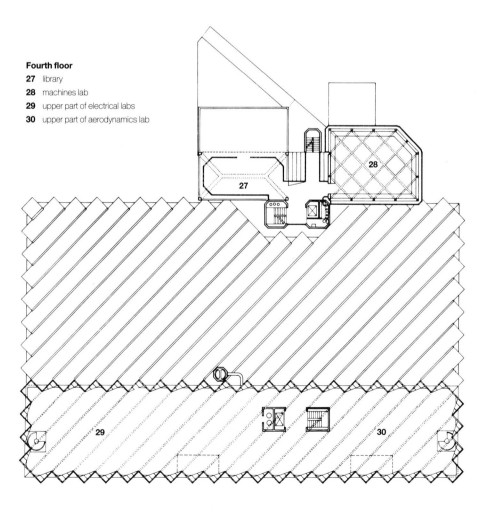

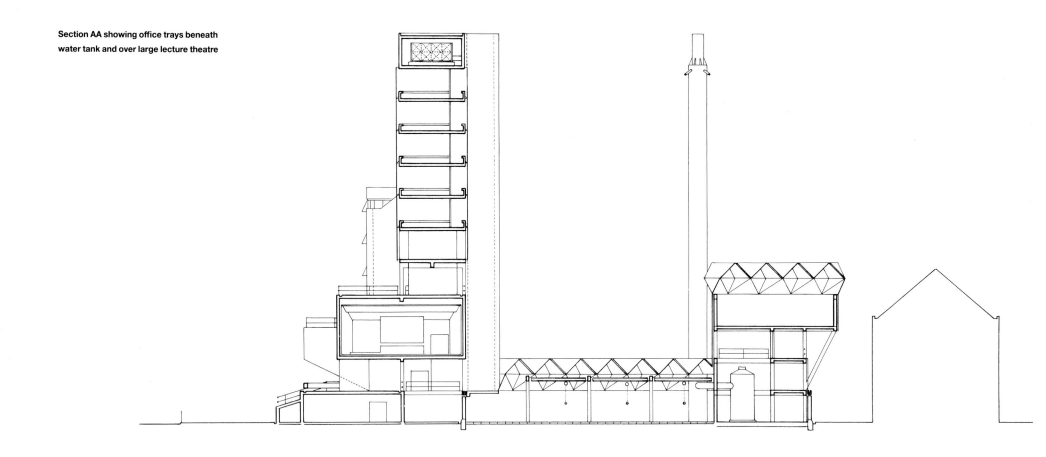

Section AA showing office trays beneath water tank and over large lecture theatre

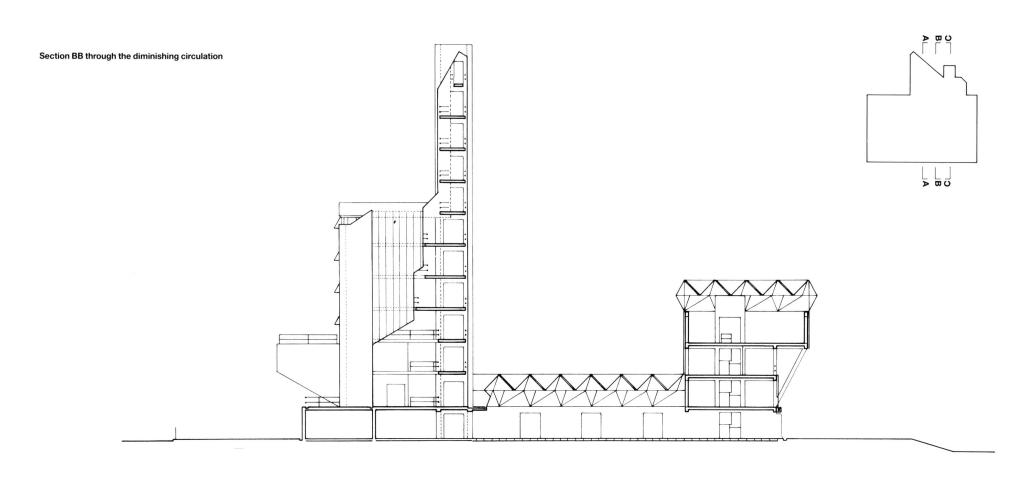

Section BB through the diminishing circulation

0 _____ 5m
0 _____ 15ft

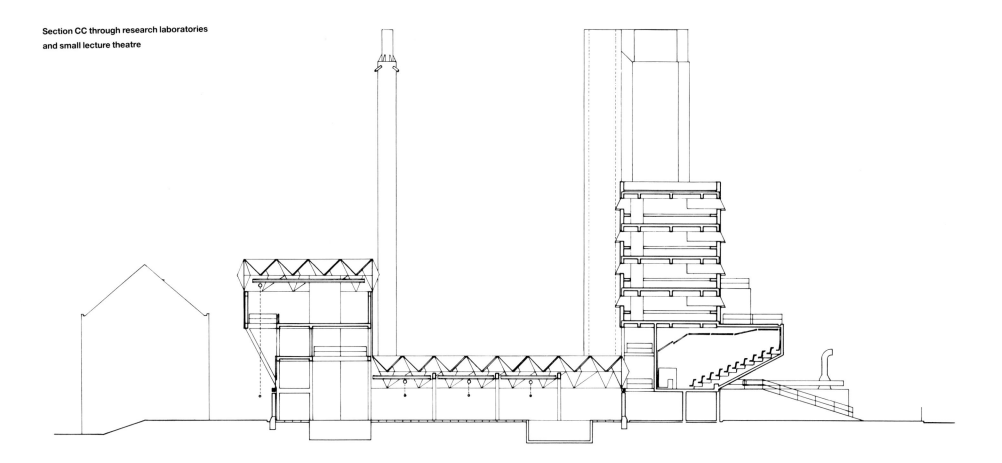

**Section CC through research laboratories
and small lecture theatre**

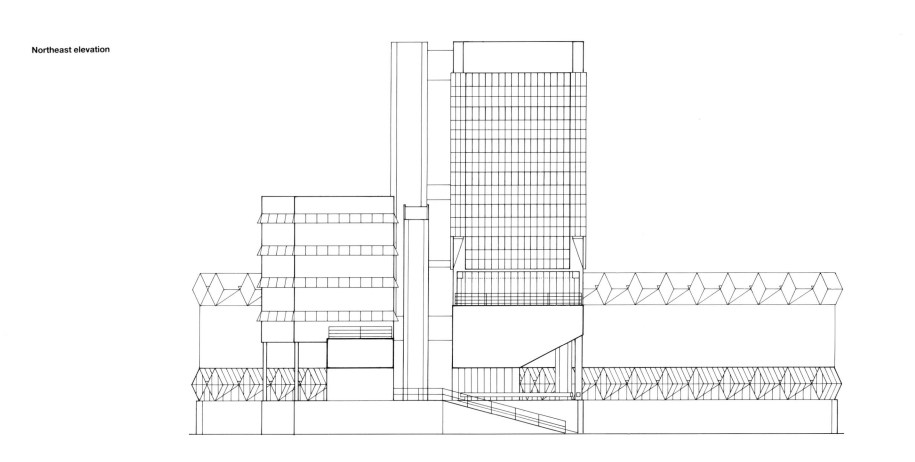

Northeast elevation

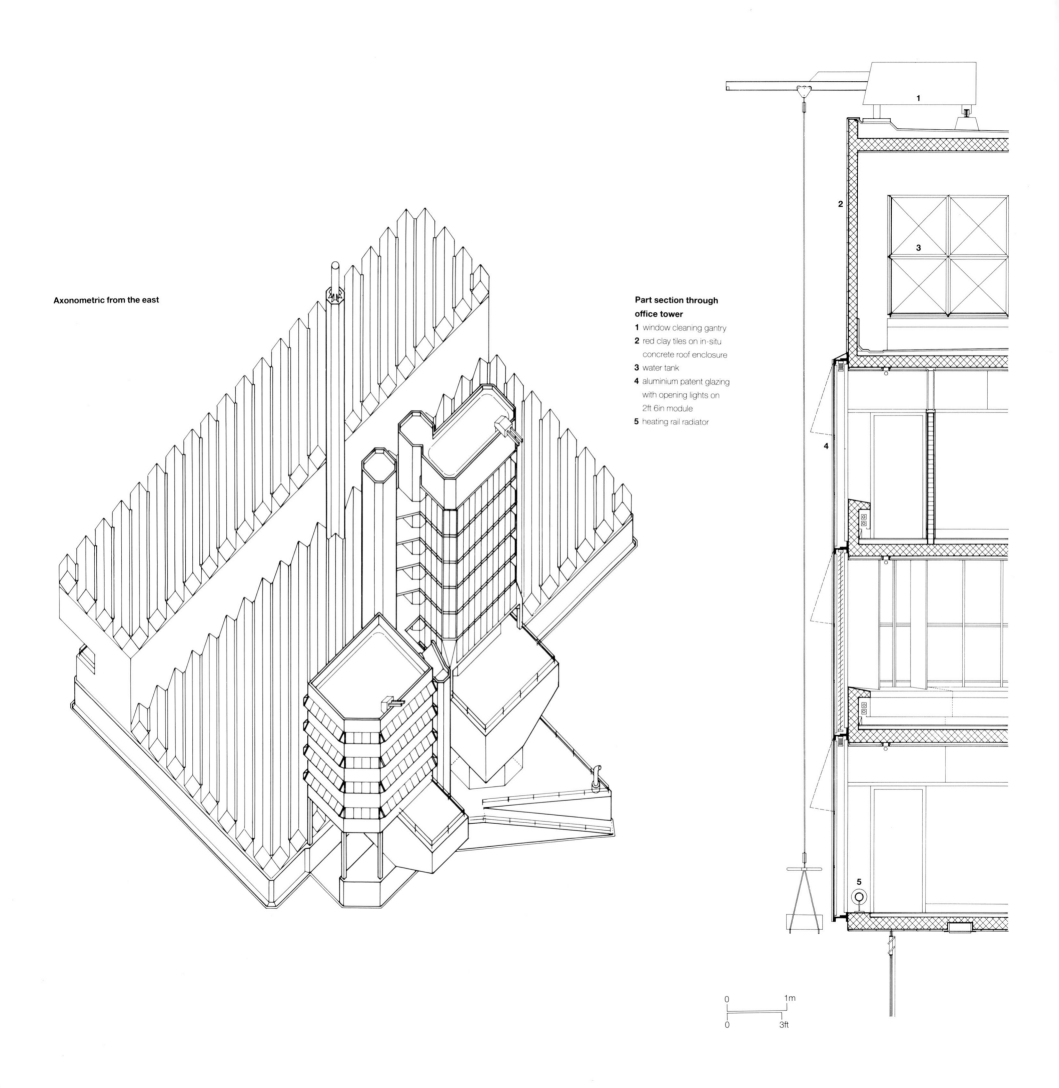

Axonometric from the east

**Part section through
office tower**

1 window cleaning gantry
2 red clay tiles on in-situ
  concrete roof enclosure
3 water tank
4 aluminium patent glazing
  with opening lights on
  2ft 6in module
5 heating rail radiator

1
2
3
4
5

0   1m

0   3ft

**Part section through
laboratory tower**

1 window cleaning gantry

2 force flow convector
   heating

3 ¾in heating flow and
   return in service bulkhead

4 hopper windows with
   ventilation louvres on
   underside, plyglass
   glazing unit-clear glass

5 13in cavity semi-
   engineering brickwork

6 in-situ concrete floor
   with diagonal diagrid
   floor beams

7 removable floor for
   hoisting equipment into
   laboratories

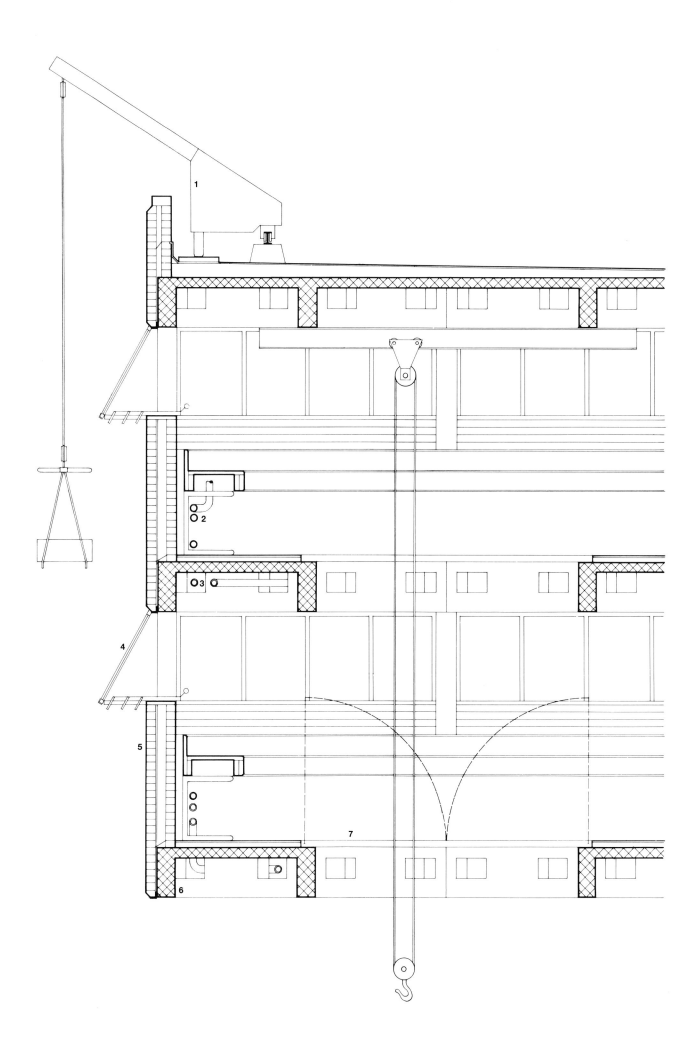

Axonometric looking south without end
wall of rear block, or cladding of circulation

**Sectional projection
through entrance
podium**

1 red clay tile
2 red clay tile drainage
   channel
3 RSJ encased in concrete
4 tubular steel structural
   support
5 13in cavity semi-
   engineering brickwork
6 in-situ concrete slab
7 red clay tile drainage
   channel
8 engineering brick edging
9 tarmac

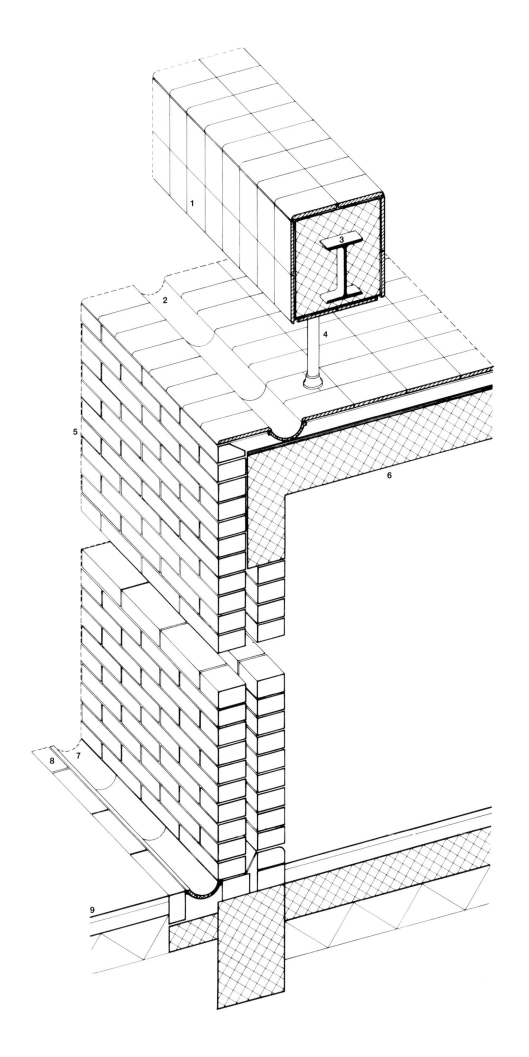

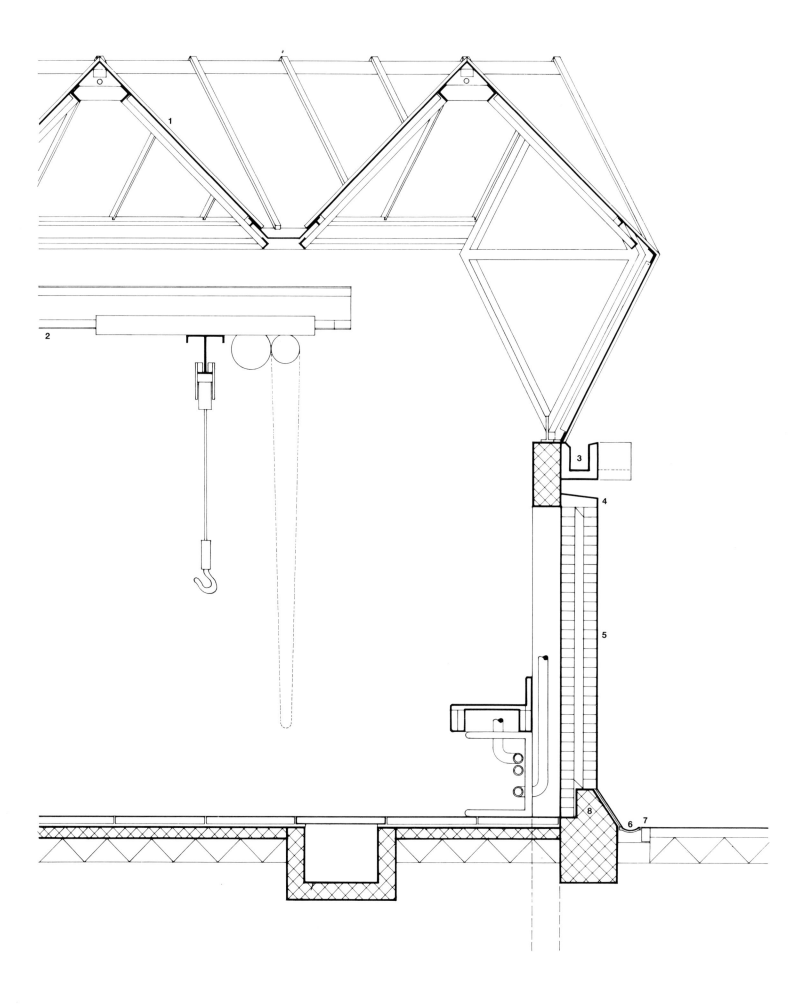

Part section through workshops

1 patent glazing with ply-glass units, on south side interlayer of foil, on north side interlayer of semi-opaque glass fibre
2 lifting beam for laboratory equipment
3 precast concrete gutter units with precast concrete overflows
4 brick coping
5 13in cavity semi-engineering brickwork
6 red clay tile drainage channel
7 engineering brick edging to drainage channel
8 concrete ground beam faced with brick slips laid vertically

0   1m

0   3ft

Flue terminal

1 chimney terminal
2 overflow
3 spun concrete pipe
4 firebrick lining
5 concrete outer face

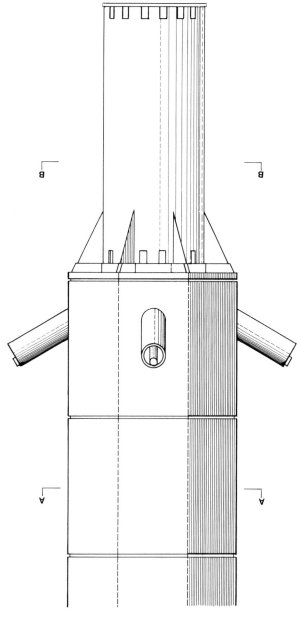

Elevation

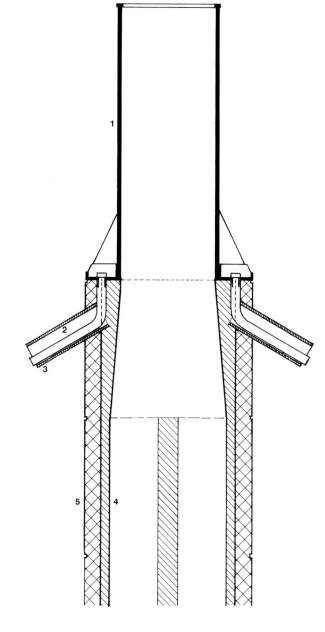

Section CC

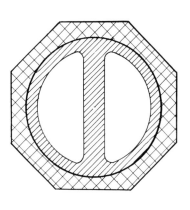

Plan AA

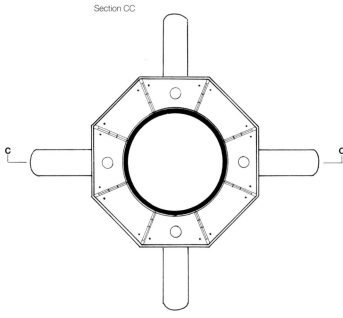

Plan BB

0   1m

0   3ft

Author's acknowledgement

I am grateful for the allocation of HEFCE research funding which allowed me to be released by The School of Architecture and Interior Design of the University of Brighton to work on this text, produced in early 1994. Thanks to all those who assisted me, especially James Gowan, Frank Newby and Michael Wilford. I am grateful to Irénée Scalbert for generously making available his recent essay on Leicester University Engineering Building which remains unpublished in Britain (see Bibliography). Finally, I gratefully acknowledge assistance from Jean Middleton and her Learning Resources colleagues at the University of Brighton.

But centrally I thank Stirling and Gowan for a building whose impact on a rudderless student in the sticks in the early 1960s still stirs the heart.

A note on units: When Leicester University Engineering Building was built, Britain's unit of linear measurement was the foot (subdivided into 12 inches). This text retains that measurement system, for reasons of historical accuracy but also for comprehension of meaning. For example, the building is based on a three-dimensional grid, built up of 10 foot cubes; a significance that would be lost in metric conversion. (A foot is 0.3048 metres.)

Notes

General note: Footnotes are limited to those which might be interesting; references to aid further inquiry only. Unreferenced quotations can be found in the Bibliography (often in *The Architectural Review,* December 1992), or they are from conversations with the author in early 1994.

1 Banham in interview with the author (taped) April 1976.

2 This book also featured works by Alison & Peter Smithson, Leslie Martin & Colin St John Wilson, Douglas Stephen & Partners, Colquhoun & Miller.

3 See K Morgan, *Labour in Power 1945–51*, Oxford University Press, 1984.

4 In 1957, Stirling wrote: 'The Hertfordshire schools might be considered our best post-war effort, but they do not set a standard either in conception or in style. They were, at least initially, motivated by a will to modernity. But one only has to compare the Crystal Palace to the Festival of Britain to appreciate the desperate state of our technical inventiveness today.' Stirling (1957).

5 See John McKean, 'The Royal Festival Hall', special issue of *The Architects' Journal*, 9 October 1991, where the cultural context 1945–51 is discussed, pp 24–36.

6 'Careless grace' is his definition of Sharawaggi, an eighteenth-century (pseudo-Chinese) landscape concept he expounded in *AR*. Later, Robert Maxwell similarly used Stendhal's phrase about the English: 'the carefully careless' in *Architectural Design*, April 1971.

7 Gowan in conversation, February 1994. Richards' text actually said, rather differently: 'the bane of the nineteenth century was the celebrity architect', *Circle*, edited by J Leslie Martin, Ben Nicholson and N Gabo, London, 1937, p184.

8 *An Introduction to* in much smaller type precedes *Modern Architecture* on the front but not on the spine of early editions; meanwhile, Pevsner's later editions become *Pioneers of Modern Architecture*.

9 *The Castles on the Ground* (illustrated John Piper), London, 1946.

10 Analogies were made to the English – as opposed to Scottish – tradition of faith in common-law precedent rather than statute law.

11 Replying to Peter Blundell Jones on the Staatsgalerie, Stuttgart, *The Architects' Journal,* February 1985

12 Four issues were published in 1938–9, edited by AA student Anthony Cox and published by Percy Lund Humphreys whose offices were, like the AA, in Bedford Square.

13 Banham (1968).

14 Stevens in interview with the author (taped) June 1976.

15 Banham in interview with the author (taped) April 1976.

16 Charles Jencks, *Modern Movements in Architecture*, Harmondsworth, 1973. (Note: Thomas Stevens is always known as Sam; just as Colin St John Wilson is always Sandy.)

17 *Architectural Principles in the Age of Humanism*, in *The Journal of the Courtauld and Warburg Institutes*. But the shortened title – apposite to young architects in a moment when they felt architecture was drifting rudderless – was encouraged by the publishers Tiranti who, when it appeared as a book in 1952, added *In The Age of Humanism* in much smaller type.

18 Summerson (1959).

19 Everyone else, recounts Wilson self-deprecatingly, had fallen asleep apart from Peter Carter who was operating the slides.

20 In conversation with the author, February 1994.

21 Alison and Peter Smithson had unique authority among their peers by having begun building: their uncompromising, 1949 winning design for a school on the north Norfolk coast (when they were aged 21 and 26 respectively) was built in the early 1950s.

22 In Auden's review in *Encounter*, June 1959, of Hannah Arendt's *Human Condition* (a book which would profoundly influence certain of this generation I discuss, notably Kenneth Frampton).

23 Perhaps it is in a misunderstanding of this comment by Stirling (1980), that certain US commentators on Stirling have talked as if Butterfield et al were actually called 'the Brutalists' in their day, and hence, in the 1950s, 'the New Brutalists' appear.

24 The Smithsons coined the phrase at the time and years later published a classic issue of *Architectural Design*, 'The Heroic Period', December 1965.

25 Gowan (1965).

26 All except Banham, of course, having trained as architects – though Rykwert had the distinction as a student of being thrown out of both the AA and the Courtauld.

27 Stirling (1980). The book was published by Oxford University Press in 1948, having grown from a wartime exhibition at the Warburg Institute. It was a unique publication in art history; the nearest equivalent for today's readers might be Joseph Campbell's large volumes on mythic imagery.

28 This story is repeated by various critics – Rowe, Eisenman – as told them by Stirling; Gowan recalls: 'Stirling told me he landed airborne in France, under attack, lay flat on the ground and was knocked out by the landshock of a nearby shell.' The flavour of a relationship can be sensed from the stories we tell about ourselves.

29 This is a later drawing by Leon Krier. Stirling came to the 'up view' through Krier's influence around 1970.

30 (sic) Others have discussed why he didn't say 'twenties', but we need not open it here.

31 'Lyons Israel & Ellis warned me about him,' Gowan adds; 'He was clearly a dodgy character; 'Stay with us! Be a partner!' they said …'

32 Perhaps best seen in the Greenwich housing schemes.

33 Fred Scott in *James Gowan: Architectural Monographs* 3, (1978).

34 In a similar way, the work each did in the years immediately after the partnership could also illuminate in retrospect. It would however be indulging in hindsight-history to introduce them here.

35 In *Contemporary Architects*, Muriel Emanuel (ed), Macmillan, London, 1979.

36 The publishers refocused the book as a connoisseur's collection of historic drawings as artworks, rearranged chronologically with almost all the modern drawings, including Stirling's and Gowan's, removed. Although much of the text and almost all the illustration selection is mine, I am nowhere mentioned in the final version, *Masterpieces of Architectural Drawing*, H Powell and D Leatherbarrow (eds), Orbis, London, 1982.

37 Scott as Note 33.

38 Cook, with various future Archigram colleagues, arrived at the AA in 1958.

39 Quinlan Terry, *The Architectural Review*, February 1993. (This was in a solicited appreciation of Stirling which the *AR* refused to publish with the others in December 1992, but did so when it was resubmitted as a letter.) Terry's architectural understanding is revealed in his next comment: 'it seemed obvious that the problem [detailing the diagonal roof-light structures] could be solved easily by making them parallel to the plan'.

40 General professional consciousness of such debates about linking buildings within master-planning 'skeletons' and 'structures' is clear from the questions asked after Stirling's talk at the RIBA in 1965. Fully aware that his own ideas – routes, formal patterns of growth, etc – were quite different, Leslie Martin expected Stirling & Gowan to bring to their isolated site an architecture of formal assertion.

41 I am most grateful for Irénée Scalbert's study, as yet unpublished in English (Scalbert 1993), for this information. Gowan adds that he attended both the briefing by Professor Parkes and a visit with him to the Cambridge Engineering labs without Stirling.

42 It is intriguing that both Stirling and Gowan had seen fit to publish this project; in Stirling's case, for arcane reasons of their own, he and Leon Krier carefully confused it with the final, built version.

43 ' I loved that spiral glass escape stair,' says Gowan, in conversation, February 1994. 'Whenever anyone said it's a ridiculous fire stair, I'd see the image of Eiffel standing on his one at the tower.'

44 Recognisably different from that built only in that it has two chimneys (see fig 57).

45 'The aerodynamic "venturi effect"? Shortly after the building opened, the professor took me up to his lab, opened the windows and every paper on his desk blew everywhere …' Gowan says today.

46 Pevsner's 1966 mistake, where this essay began, might be forgiven as a lapse; but when the latest revised edition of his *Buildings of England* (1984) talks of the 'narrow metal bridges spanning free, set back as the circulation space decreases upwards', well…

47 'Hi-tech or Mys-tech', talk at RIBA, 3 April 1984; published in *Proceedings of the RIBA.*

48 In conversation with the author, March 1994.

49 While others have credited Newby with this form, he recalls that it predated his involvement.

50 *The Architectural Review,* December 1992.

51 Listening to Newby, there is an overall sense that on this building the architects simply took form to the engineer and accepted the forms the engineers brought back. In his next two or three projects Stirling became much more structurally confident himself, being intimately involved with the raking structure at Cambridge (against which the glass roof leaned), and then at Oxford coming to Newby with the complete raking structural form already in place.

52 Gowan recalls them as steel; the '9 September' drawings state precast r.c..

53 Wilford recalls a meeting in 1960 at which the client firmly would not spend the additional cost recommended on anodising the aluminium.

54 Frank Newby in conversation with the author, March 1994. With the vertical ridges and horizontal concrete grooves, the assumption was that the tiles would be fixed solid, that the mortar would fill all grooves. But clearly this didn't happen and – on the cladding at the top, round the water tank – water which penetrated the tile joints could find vertical channels and run down to the flashing over the patent glazing. This flashing had not been sealed back into the concrete, and thus there was water penetration at this point.

55 Three responses offer reflected glimpses of professional images, roles and competences: first, when in the 1960s the Leicester professor of engineering wanted a holiday house, he called in Gowan. Secondly, when 25 years later the University had to deal with renovation and recladding, Samuely's were called in but other architects commissioned; neither the practices of Stirling & Wilford nor James Gowan were approached. Thirdly, when the building was listed as of historic interest in the 1990s and the faculty wanted to make changes, Michael Wilford was brought in; James Gowan was not approached, James Stirling was dead.

56 *Précis des Leçons*, 1802.

57 'Tot een be eldende architectuur', *De Stijl*, VI, 1924.

58 Scalbert (1993).

59 Kahn's building, Pennsylvania University Medical Laboratories, was quickly said to work poorly; Leicester engineering labs to work well. Both buildings were said by the style-spotters to derive from Wright's building for Johnson Wax at Racine. Kahn, when it was pointed out to him, went 'aha!'.

60 Appraised by Scully in *The Architectural Review* in the following issue.

61 This is so whether one is looking at ideas or at its sensuous imagery. In neither the 49 illustrations to Peter Eisenman's essay in *Oppositions* nor in *Global Architecture*'s pictorial portfolio is there a single interior photograph or comment.

62 I have never seen this detail either discussed or even illustrated. (In early photographs, such as Einzig's in *Architectural Design,* February 1964 they are simply unfaced, metal doors.) It came from an idea Gowan had recommended to an AA student of his around 1957, to hide the service entrance in his very naked, Miesian student project.

63 Paul Valéry in *Eupalinos*, quoted as the frontispiece to my book on Walter Segal (Birkhauser, Zurich, 1989), puts it more poetically.

64 'Reality' was a particular critical term used by The Ecclesiologists, those for whom Butterfield built. In 1851 they praised the Crystal Palace for being 'real.' In exactly the same sense they would have praised Leicester.

65 This effect was never realised, with Lasdun's and then Arup's towers following.

66 Eisenman's essay on the building (1974) talks of its 'extraordinary condensed iconic impact' as 'necessary to the very idea of monument'.

67 This is argued by Stuart Cohen, 'History as Drawing', *The Journal of Architectural Education*, Vol XXXII, No 1, September 1978.

68 John Ruskin, at an 'Architectural Association Conversazione', January 1857.

Architects and Consultants

Architects   James Stirling and James Gowan

Staff   Kit Evans, Michael Wilford, Quinlan Terry, Malcolm Higgs (Stirling names only Wilford and Higgs as assistants)

Structural engineer Frank Newby, of Felix J Samuely & Partners

Services engineer   Tom Smith, of Steensen, Varming & Mulcahy

Quantity surveyor Monk & Dunstone

Acoustic consultant Hope Bagenal

General contractor Wilson Lovatt & Sons Ltd

Subcontractors Glaziers: Faulkner Greene & Co; Mechanical services: Matthew Hall & Co; Lifts: Marryat & Scott Ltd; Plyglass: Plyglass Ltd; Structural steelworks: Hoveringham Engineering Ltd; Gutters: Harvey Ironworks Ltd; Monorails: British Monorail Ltd; Spiral staircase: Venduct Ltd; Doors: Metalcraft Ltd; Ductwork: Setonair Ltd; Runways: Cradle Runways Ltd; Acoustic treatment: Horace W Cullum & Co; Suspended ceiling: Universal Metal Furring & Lathing Co; Venetian blinds: Deans (Venetian blind division) Ltd; Ventilators: Colt Ventilation Ltd; Chalkboards: Westland Engineers Ltd; Flooring: G C Flooring Co

Chronology

1956 James Stirling and James Gowan leave Lyons Israel & Ellis and set up partnership.

1959 Begin Leicester University Engineering Building; Stirling & Gowan appointed mid 1959. Quinlan Terry, assistant three days a week 1959–61. July–December: two abortive plans and three models (all lost).

1960 July: Malcolm Higgs is appointed assistant to start in December. August: Michael Wilford joins. Building already has planning permission; less than a year to tender. December: Higgs starts in the office in week before Christmas.

1962 Bitterly cold winter 1962–63; site closed for three months.

1963 Partnership dissolved. Autumn: Leicester University Engineering Building occupied; interiors still incomplete when reviewed and photographed for magazines in Spring 1964.

Bibliography

A Contemporary context for the building (1954–66) (alphabetically)

Banham Reyner, (1957) 'Futurism and Modern Architecture', *RIBA Journal*, February 1957
Banham Reyner, (1966) 'The New Brutalism: Ethic or Aesthetic?', *The Architectural Press*, London, 1966
Banham Reyner, (1968) 'The Revenge of the Picturesque', in **Summerson** John (ed), *Concerning Architecture: Essays presented to Nikolaus Pevsner* (London: Allan Lane, The Penguin Press, 1968)
Gowan James, 'Curriculum', *The Architectural Review*, December 1959, Vol 126, pp 315–323
Gowan James, 'Notes on American Architecture', *Perspecta* 7, 1961, pp 77–82
Gowan James, (1965) 'Le Corbusier – his Impact on Four Generations', *RIBA Journal*, October 1965, Vol 72, pp 497–500
Korn Arthur, 'The Work of Stirling and Gowan', *Architect and Building News*, 7 January 1959, Vol 215, pp 8–23
Richards J M, 'Criticism: House near Cowes, Isle of Wight', *The Architects' Journal*, 24 July 1959, Vol 128, pp 119–22
Rowe Colin, (1959) 'The Blenheim of the Welfare State' (review of Stirling & Gowan's Churchill entry), *The Cambridge Review*, 31 October 1959
Rykwert Joseph, (1957) 'Meaning and Building' *Zodiac* 6, Milan, 1957
Stirling James, (1955) 'From Garches to Jaoul', *The Architectural Review*, September 1955
Stirling James, (1956) 'Ronchamp: Le Corbusier's Chapel and the Crisis of Rationalism', *The Architectural Review*, March 1956
Stirling James, 'Statement', 'This is Tomorrow' exhibition catalogue, Whitechapel Gallery, London 1956
Stirling James, (1957) 'Regionalism and Modern Architecture', in Trevor Dannatt (ed), *Architects' Year Book* 8, 1957, p 62
Stirling James, 'Young architects: A Personal View of the Present Situation', *Architectural Design*, June 1958
Stirling James, 'Packaged Deal and Prefabrication', *Design*, March 1959
Stirling James, 'The Functional Tradition and Expressionism', *Perspecta* 6, Yale, 1960, p 89
Summerson John, (1959) (Introduction to Trevor Dannatt, *Modern Architecture in Britain* (London: Batsford, 1959))

B Contemporary commentary on the building (1962–66) (chronologically)

'Work in Progress', *Architectural Design*, October 1962
Rowntree Diana, article in *The Guardian*, September 1963
Maxwell Robert, 'Frontiers of Inner Space', *Sunday Times* (Colour Supplement), 27 September 1963
Architectural Association Journal, December 1963
The Architects' Journal, 15 January 1964
Banham Reyner, (1964 A) 'Style for the Job', *New Statesman*, 14 February 1964 p 261
Frampton Kenneth, article in *Architectural Design*, February 1964
Jacobus John, article in *The Architectural Review*, April 1964
Hillman Judy, article in *Evening Standard*, 10 June 1964
Rykwert Joseph, 'Un Episoda Inglese', *Domus*, June 1964
Arquitectura 67, July 1964
Architectural Forum, August 1964
Glass, August 1964
Banham Reyner, (1964 B) 'The Word in Britain: Character', *Architectural Forum* August–September 1964
'Ten Buildings that Point to the Future', *Fortune Magazine*, October 1964
Architektur Heute, October 1964
Deutsche Bauzeitung, October, 1964
Bauwelt 43, October 1964
Hara Hiroshi and Futagawa, Yukio, 'Two works by James Stirling, A Portrait' (in addition to critique of the building), *Kokusai Kentiku*, Tokyo, January 1965
Frampton Kenneth, article in *Architecture and Urbanism* (*A+U*), February 1965
Stirling James, (1965) 'An architect's approach to architecture', paper given at the RIBA, 23 February 1965; article based on it in *RIBA Journal,* May 1965, p 231
Bouw, April 1965
Pevsner N, *Buildings of England: Leicestershire* (Harmondsworth: Penguin, April 1965)
L'Architecture d'Aujourd'hui, July 1965
British Aluminium 'Two Architects: James Stirling and James Gowan' (film), 1965
Stephens Douglas, Frampton, Kenneth & Carapetian, Michael, *British Buildings 1960–1964*, (London: Adam & Charles Black, 1965)
Bryant, G M, *Arkitekten* 18, Finland, 1966
The Brick Bulletin, January 1966
Stirling James, (1966) 'Anti-structure', a slide talk given at Bologna University to mark the retirement of Michelucci, November 1966. First published in *Zodiac* 18, Milan, 1968 (illustrated only with 12 photographs of glazing at Leicester)
Pevsner N, (1966) 'The Anti-pioneers' radio talk, BBC, end of 1966. Subsequently published in *The Listener*, 29 December 1966 and 5 January 1967

C The architects' accounts (since 1967) (alphabetically)

Monographs
James Gowan: Architectural Monographs 3, ed David Dunster (London: Academy Editions, 1978)
James Stirling, *RIBA Drawings Collection*, catalogue, April 1974
Stirling (1975) *James Stirling, Buildings and Projects 1950–1974*, Leo Krier and James Stirling (eds) (London: Thames & Hudson, 1975)
Stirling (1980) 'James Stirling: special profile to mark the award of the 1980 Royal Gold Medal' *Architectural Design* 7/8, 1980 (includes: Stirling, 'Speech of Acceptance of RIBA Gold Medal')
'James Stirling : A Profile' *Architectural Design*, 1982
Stirling (1984) *James Stirling Buildings and Projects*, Arnell & Bickford (eds) (London/New York: The Architectural Press/Rizzoli, 1984)
'James Stirling: Profile' *Architectural Design* 7/8, 1990 (includes: Stirling, James, 'Design Philosophy and Recent Work')
'James Stirling Memorial Issue', *The Architectural Review*, December 1992, Vol CXCI, No 1150
James Stirling 1926–1992; memorial issue of *ANY* (*Architecture New York*); No 2, September/October 1993 (includes: Wilford, Michael, speech at the Tribute to James Stirling, Solomon R Guggenheim Museum NY, 19 November 1992 and Wilford, Michael, 'A Conversation in London', with Cynthia Davidson)

D Commentary on the building (since 1967) (alphabetically)

Architecture Canada, April 1968
Banham Reyner, Introduction to James Stirling, *RIBA Drawings Collection*, catalogue, April 1974
BBC/Arts Council, 'James Stirling's Architecture' (film), London, 1973
BBC, Leicester Engineering Building, 'Building Sights' series, 1990 (10-minute film shown on BBC2)
Boyarsky Alvin, 'Stirling "Dimonstrationi"', *Architectural Design*, October 1968, pp 454–5
Brown I, *Architectural Forum*, April 1972
Colquhoun Alan, 'Architecture as a Continuous Text', *ANY* (*Architecture New York*) No 2, September/October 1993
De la Ciudad 1, February 1975
Eisenman Peter, 'Real and English: The Destruction of the Box 1', *Oppositions* 4, October 1974, pp 5–34
Frampton Kenneth, 'Stirling's Building', *Architectural Forum*, November 1968
Girouard Mark, 'Stirling's Gold', *Architectural Design* 7/8, 1980
Global Architecture 9, 'Leicester University Engineering Building and Cambridge University History Faculty Library', (text – Japanese only – Kiyonori Kikutake; photos Yukio Futagawa) ADA Edita, Japan, 1971
Hodges Craig, *Design Quarterly* 100, April 1976
Jacobus John, Introductory essay to *James Stirling, Buildings and Projects 1950–1974*, Leo Krier and James Stirling (eds) (London: Thames & Hudson, 1975)
Jencks Charles, 'Pop non-Pop', *Architectural Association Journal*, Winter 1968
Jencks Charles, 'Architecture 2000', *Studio Vista*, 1971
Kentiku Architecture, 'James Stirling Buildings and Projects (1950–1967)', January 1968
Maxwell Robert, 'James Stirling: Special Profile', *Architectural Design*, 1982
Maxwell Robert, 'Modern Architecture After Modernism', in *ANY* (*Architecture New York*) No 2, September/October 1993
McKean John, Extended profile of James Stirling, published in two parts: 'Inside Stirling', *Building Design*, 7 September 1979; and 'Stirling Quality' *Building Design*, 14 September 1979
Pawley Martin, 'Leicester Engineering: Building Revisits', *The Architects' Journal*, 6 June 1984, pp 43–48
Peters P, 'Glaeserne Grossform', *Baumeister*, December 1968
Rowe Colin, (1984) 'James Stirling: A Highly Personal and Very Disjointed Memoir', Introduction to *James Stirling Buildings and Projects*, Arnell & Bickford (eds) (London/New York, The Architectural Press/Rizzoli, 1984)
Rowe Colin, 'J F S, 1924–1992', an expanded version of his speech at the Tribute to James Stirling, Solomon R Guggenheim Museum NY, 19 November 1992, published in *ANY* (*Architecture New York*) No 2, September/October 1993
Scalbert Irénée, (1993) 'Le Leicester Building', essay in *Le Moniteur architecture AMC,* No 46, November 1993, pp 32–5 (with photos, plans, sections, models) (English text: 'The Design of the Leicester University Engineering Building')
Scott Fred, (1978) 'The Architecture of James Gowan', in *James Gowan, Architectural Monographs* 3, David Dunster (ed), (London: Academy Editions, 1978)
Stephens Thomas (Sam), 'Observations on New British Architecture', *Bauen & Wohnen*, Zurich, December 1967
Summerson John, 'Vitruvius Ludens', *The Architectural Review*, March 1983
Tafuri Manfredo, 'L'Architecture dans le Boudoir', *Oppositions* 3, May 1974
Walmsley Dominique, 'Leicester Engineering Building: its Post-Modern Role' *Journal of Architectural Education*, Vol 42, No 1, Fall 1988, pp 10–17

Foster Associates
Willis Faber & Dumas Building
Ipswich 1975

Gabriele Bramante

Photography
John Donat and Ken Kirkwood;
cover detail by Ken Kirkwood
Drawings
John Hewitt

1

1 Willis Faber Dumas' prismatic façade fractures and reflects an enigmatic version of the city.
2 In daylight the glass wall reveals nothing of the building within.
3 Buckminster Fuller's glass-domed USA pavilion at Expo 67, Montreal.
4 At ground level, the glass appears to slide into the pavement.

2

In daylight, the mysterious façade of the Willis Faber & Dumas insurance building recedes, reflecting and fracturing the architecture of the surrounding historic buildings, 1. Seen from the street, its unadorned tinted glass walls reflect everything and reveal nothing of the building within, 2.

Designed in 1970, at the time of the first Japanese pocket calculators, hot pants and the end of modern architecture as an unquestioned universal creed, Willis Faber Dumas was seen by its architects, its engineers and their exceptionally enlightened client as 'an extraordinary challenge'. At the age of thirty-five it was Norman Foster's first large-scale commission and was set to break every conceivable rule. The building's complex response to the historic urban fabric of Ipswich, its pioneering social programme and its many technological innovations are particularly relevant today now that the discussion of architecture has largely been reduced to style, and they are the subject of this book.

When completed in June 1975, Willis Faber Dumas set higher standards for office design throughout the western world. Even today, almost a quarter of a century later, the building still looks like something from the future and its impact remains profound.

The pioneering, totally suspended curved, glazed façade gave an entirely new meaning to the concept of glass architecture. Ever since Paxton had shown in 1851 that glass could be used on a vast scale to envelope a building like the Crystal Palace, glass as a building material has had its poetic protagonists. Even John Ruskin, inspired by Paxton, had been exhorting members of the Architectural Association to contemplate, of all things, the idea of a continuous glass dome over the city of London. He proclaimed: 'You shall put all London under one enchanted blazing glass dome that shall light the clouds with its flashing as far as the sea...'.

3

Norman Foster, inspired more recently by his good friend Buckminster Fuller, 3, had initially also envisaged an all-glass dome. As he later remarked in an interview: 'In 1970 Willis Faber Dumas was as close as you could get to an all-glass skin'.

And that skin is considerable. The passer-by is struck by the sheer size of the building; its perimeter wall stretches for nearly a quarter of a mile, and one is unsettled by the unfamiliarity of the almost indescribable shape. As the façade slides into the pavement like the face of a cliff, 4, there is no merging with nature except for the reflections that echo the trees.

4

But, beneath the skin, the building was generated by a complex response to context. Foster recalls; 'The response to the location was to produce a building that would swell right out to the edge of the site. It seemed appropriate to a market town where the key spaces are really the streets. The challenge was to reinforce that street pattern and not violate it by constructing a building with a different kind of geometry'.

7

5 The entrance hall floor is finished in 'Foster green' studded rubber, a material that in other hands might have utilitarian overtones.
6, 7 Continuously moving escalators provide a mechanized '*promenade architecturale*'.

Spatial transparency

When the building was first completed and the entrance lobby formed one continuous spatial sequence, the eye could travel freely across and beyond the pool, preparing the visitor for the spatial transparency of the subsequent upper levels. Today, the lobby has lost some of its spatial force due to the later intervention of a continuous partition which bisects the foyer to enclose additional computer rooms. Therefore, sadly, one can now no longer feel the sequence of the ground-floor space, nor see immediately its spectacular swimming pool.

The atmosphere in the entrance lobby at Willis Faber Dumas is highly unusual. There is no display of corporate wealth. The architects deliberately underplayed the treatment of the immediate entrance area in order to heighten the drama of the architectural promenade through the building. The ground-floor decor is purposely spartan to provide, instead, the best possible finishes for the workers on the office floors. There are no lush carpets or polished marble; the floor is of studded lime-green rubber, which more usually has tough, utilitarian, overtones, **5**.

This modest passage through the understated foyer, however, greatly heightens the effect of the subsequent skyward explosion of space. Passing through security, one is suddenly liberated by the breathtaking freedom of the cascading central escalators, creating a celebration of movement through which the building declares itself. In the spirit of Le Corbusier's '*promenade architecturale*' the magic of the moving belt is the key to the building's success, **6**.

There is a rush of adrenalin as one is swept up by the spectacular energy of the escalators soaring towards the sky. There are many friendly chance encounters and office workers greet and recognize each other as they sail past subsequent floors on their escalator sorties up and down, **7**.

Willis Faber Dumas has an exceptionally low staff turn-over and a tremendous community spirit. It serves as a splendid example of how spatial forms can influence human interactions. Employees may feel ambivalent about the building's façade but they are united in their love for its interior. Indeed, the passage of time has consolidated the success of Willis Faber Dumas and how well it enhances the lives and supports the activities of its 1300 workers. 'It is a rare achievement for a large modern office building to be so clearly liked' was the citation when in 1990 the RIBA acclaimed Willis Faber Dumas 'the finest work by a British designer anywhere in the world between 1965 and 1983'.

Kenneth Knight, who set up the client body that supervised the project and acted as co-ordinator between Willis Faber & Dumas and the design team, attributes part of the building's success to the dialogue that Foster established with his client. Foster's approach to architecture remains characterized by a deep desire to improve the working conditions for the people who may spend up to a third of their lives in the same building. 'I always start by analysing people's working patterns to create a place that helps employees

5

6

9

8 Polished aluminium ceilings reflect the light and increase the apparent scale of the office floors.

9 Escalators ascend towards the light of the roof-level restaurant.

10 The restaurant is a simple Miesian enclosure.

11 Office workers enjoying the amenity of the building's roof-level garden.

12 At night the building throws off its daytime character and becomes brilliantly transparent, revealing itself to the city.

8

work more efficiently and which, above all, fulfils their social and spiritual needs. The architect's aspirations for artistic self-expression must take second place.'

Willis Faber Dumas consists of four floors which are fused around one spectacular open space by the diagonal cut of the central circulation zone. Only the two middle floors are offices. They are open plan and designed to be truly flexible, with large spans between structural columns, 30km of continuous in-floor bus-bars, free-standing desks and movable, low-height partitions that allow the floors to absorb major organizational changes freely. With identical chairs, desks and partitions it can be difficult to work out who is in charge. Such lack of internal office hierarchy dictates a very democratic form of management. Even in the complete absence of enclosed offices, confidentiality has never posed a problem; however, new managers accustomed to personal executive suites invariably take time to make the transition.

The secret of the building's well-controlled climate essentially lies in its unusually deep plan, its special solar glass, its fully integrated services and the perimeter buffer zone where air is blown directly onto the glass. Where Mies van der Rohe had failed, and on his own admission had 'never come to grips with the problem of how to heat or cool a glass building', Foster's team managed to tackle the unfinished business of indoor climatic control.

In the absence of solid walls, light floods rather than filters into the building. The incoming light is coloured by the luxurious green carpets and reflected by the polished aluminium ceilings, creating the most dazzling and delirious effect with people's movements multiplied in the burnished overhead plane, **8**. Casting one's gaze across the vast open-plan space the eye comes to rest on distant vanishing points; it is difficult to know what is within or without. There are no limits imposed and no intervening elements to break the breathtaking views. With only windows as walls the building simply spills out into the city. Moving up the escalators towards the light, an environment for complete relaxation slowly reveals itself, **9**. The roof-top restaurant, like the lower office floors, enjoys the simple quality of spatial freedom. An open deck with freely spaced tables and chairs, the restaurant could hardly be simpler in its formal orchestration, **10**.

On warm summer days, employees spill out onto the lawn to picnic or stroll in their private roof-top garden, **11**. Here, in the spirit of Mies van der Rohe, 'nature, architecture and man are brought together in a higher unity'.

Glass in the city

At night all the rules are reversed. The building's dark façade slowly dissolves. Only now can the glass walls reveal their secrets to outsiders, as the black leviathan metamorphosizes into a crystalline cage, inhabited only by the beauty of light, **12**.

The whole building shines like a lantern creating the splendid illusion that the night is more glorious than the day. The office floors are now free-floating

10

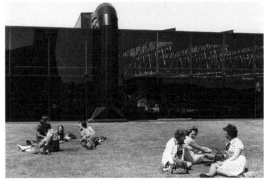

11

12

14

13

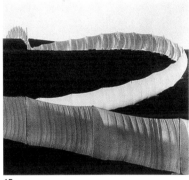

15

decks defying all forces of gravity. The structural columns on the rectilinear grid dematerialize in the darkness and cease to punctuate the space.

Ever since Paxton's Crystal Palace, the idea of a lantern-like building had captivated entire generations of architects; Mies van der Rohe's visionary model of a glass sky scraper of 1920, **13**, L. Nikolski's Swimming Bath Project of 1927, the Osram Publicity Tower of 1929, **14**, and the Phillips Light Company Column of the same year, are the most significant examples of many such visionary schemes.

But, perhaps the most unexpected was Frank Lloyd Wright's personal vision of 'glass architecture' when he wrote in 1928: 'Imagine a city luminous at night; buildings woven of glass. Such a city would clean itself in the rain and would need no fire alarms. Glass, the curse of the classic, is a tempting material now about to be explored…'.

Paul Scheerbart, for his part, was totally obsessed with the possibilities of glass as a building material. A poet, rather than an architect, and Bruno Taut's great inspiration, he summarized his utopian dreams in 1920 in the now classic title *Glass Architecture*, where he writes with great vision: 'We live for the most part in closed rooms. If we want our culture to rise to a higher level, we must change our architecture. We can only do that by introducing glass architecture which lets in the sun, the stars and the moon, not merely through a few windows, but through every possible wall, which will be made entirely of glass. The new environment we thus create, will bring us a new culture'. Scheerbart went on to say: 'Aeronauts will show their indignation at unlit glass buildings. And on Venus and Mars they will stare in wonder and no longer recognise the surface of the earth'.

The glass wall at Willis Faber Dumas was not a new vision but it represented a great technological breakthrough. It was from Eames, Prouvé and principally Buckminster Fuller that Foster had learned to break with convention and to accept the challenge of pushing technology beyond its present boundaries. Like Heidegger, the philosopher, Foster firmly believes that discovery is architecture's morality. And a building that does not discover a hitherto unknown element of existence is simply immoral, since it is only the sequence of discoveries that constitutes the history of architecture.

Foster firmly rejects the popular view that stylistic considerations are the basis for good architecture. He believes passionately that technology is more than a method; it is a world in itself and where it reaches its real fulfilment it transcends into architecture.

The more we study this building, the greater becomes our admiration for its true originality, its clarity of articulation, its independence of thought and above all its social aspiration to raise standards for the people who work in it. For Norman Foster, material and spiritual needs, technology and architecture have grown together into a singular unity with one expressing the other.

16 Cut-away isometric drawing showing the building's strikingly clear vertical zoning. The first and second floors provide open-plan office space. Above, is a staff restaurant and roof garden; below, at ground level, are reception, swimming pool, plant rooms and computer banks.

17 Foster's response to the location was to produce a low-rise building that would swell right out to the edge of the site. From top to bottom: the existing buildings are low and extend to the edges of their sites to form narrow winding streets. A fast programme meant that the design and site acquisition had to proceed in tandem. The exact site area and the possibility of street closures meant that the proposal had to be open-ended until late in the design stage. The proposal had two principal structural components, an internal 14m square column grid and a perimeter 'necklace' of columns. The large span inner structure was capable of spanning roads should closures not prove possible.

Road closures allowed the final scheme to develop a clear, cohesive form. The perimeter necklace of columns followed the new site boundary while the inner grid was aligned to accommodate an atrium and swimming pool in their optimum positions. The building is served by four discrete minor cores which responded to both servicing and escape stair requirements. They also allowed the potential sub-division of office floors to allow for possible future sub-tenancies.

The commission and the brief

Willis Faber & Dumas, now known as Willis Corroon, is one of the world's largest insurance brokers and an old established City of London firm. They are acting underwriting agents for Lloyds and operate large maritime syndicates. In 1912 the company had to settle the loss of the ill-fated Titanic at a cost of £1 million and continues to cover risks for Cunard. Even NASA's moon buggy was once on the books.

In August 1970, Willis Faber & Dumas decided to rationalize its operations and decentralize all its administrative departments, from its satellite offices in Southend and its head office in London, to a less expensive location in Ipswich. Ipswich is a charming, medium-sized, medieval market town with narrow streets and much black and white Tudor architecture. Only 75 minutes from London, it seemed particularly attractive due to its busy port and growing economic base.

In the search for a suitable architect to design the new building, the company contacted the RIBA who recommended twelve practices. Of these the client's project committee selected six possible firms: Ahrends Burton & Koralek, Arup Associates, Foster Associates, H.T. Cadbury Brown, Powell & Moya and Sheppard Robson. Eventually a second shortlist emerged with only ABK, Arup and Foster Associates in the running. According to the project committee's report, Foster Associates were appointed because Norman Foster seemed a singularly able man and had been involved in large open-plan projects with IBM and Fred Olsen at the time. But, of greatest importance to the client was Foster's undertaking to be personally involved throughout the project.

The Ipswich headquarters needed to be more than just a 'paper factory' to handle the company's increased administrative work-load and provide essential clerical back-up for the 300 or so brokers retained at Head Office in London. Specifically, the brief asked for a distinguished building that would be 'neither over-ambitious nor pedestrian'. It had to provide at least 21,000m² of office space to accommodate a large work-force of 1350 people with no less than 1200 workstations. Foster's response involved office floors that would be extremely flexible, able to absorb future organizational changes and to improve working efficiency.

To alleviate the mundane nature of the administrative work, Willis Faber & Dumas, with great foresight, asked for 'an office environment sympathetic to human values'. Norman Foster later recalled that 'all they had was a lot of boring old office space... The challenge was to produce something better than the Dickensian squalor in which they seemed to exist'. Initially, Foster's team spent much time at Willis Faber & Dumas' Southend office to compile lengthy questionnaires and carefully observe existing work patterns. The results of this rigorous initial research, which remains characteristic of Foster's problem-solving approach, were analysed through colour-coded charts. These revealed that great advantages could be gained from a totally open-plan and dynamic office environment.

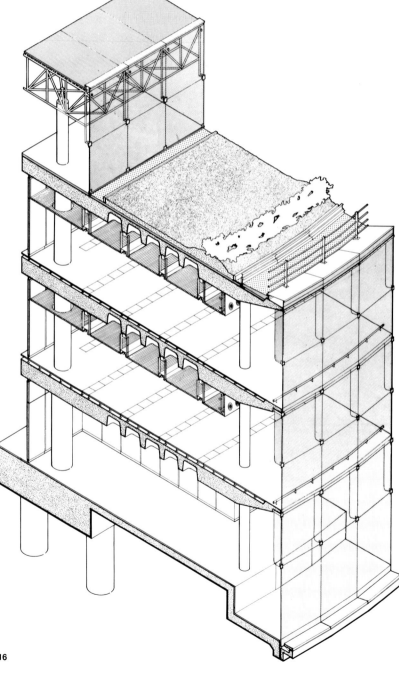

16

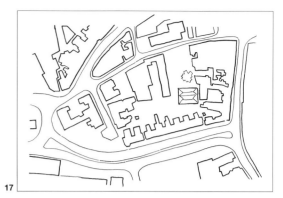

By stretching the plan to the periphery of the site only four floors were needed to meet the client's space requirement of 21,000m². A strikingly clear lay-out emerged, **16**. The first and second floors were developed as identical open-plan office space. These floors were backed-up by two service floors: above, were a staff restaurant and roof garden, with reception, swimming pool, plant, computer banks and loading docks located below.

Initially no provisions were made for car parking. However, Willis Faber & Dumas later bought the adjacent multi-storey car park to provide parking for employees. In 1980 part of the car park was converted into over-spill office space by Michael Hopkins and Partners.

Developing a structural logic

The building's structure had to be developed alongside the architectural concept. Anthony Hunt was engaged as the structural engineer. For both him and his team, Willis Faber Dumas was a natural progression of the work they had been developing with Foster Associates. Hunt's projects, ranging from Reliance Controls, IBM Northern Road and most recently Olsen at Millwall Dock, were becoming larger and increasingly complex.

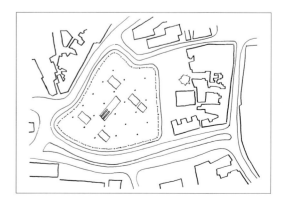

From the outset the architects and engineers were faced with an unusually difficult situation in which they had to design for an expandable and, as yet, undefined site, **17**. As Foster explained later, 'We had a client who didn't know whether he could buy one piece of land or another. The acquisition pattern was one of the most difficult things to come to grips with. They would come up with a site – we would be designing away for that site, while across the road they would be negotiating for another parcel of land. This scheme-on-scheme-off seesaw lasted for several months'.

The original concept for the building had to take account of a central site split by a road, into two parts, one much larger than the other. Early structural schemes considered a building on each site with a bridge over the road, linking the two. The bridge proved to be a complicated, large-span structure. Thankfully, at this point, the client negotiated for the road to be closed.

From then on, the structural concepts concentrated on a single building designed to straddle any site configuration. All the services in the road, in particular the mains drainage pipes and the international telephone cables to Europe, had to be re-routed.

When Willis Faber & Dumas finally completed its lengthy land negotiations, the company had acquired 7000m² of built-up property at the edge of the town between the historic northern part and the bleak southern zone. The existing buildings on the site were demolished and a new building line was drawn. The planning authorities imposed new height restrictions and a total ban on any high-rise development. This did not pose a problem to Foster whose design strategy had led naturally to the development of a low and deep-plan building which would optimize the site coverage and generate a low-rise building in keeping with the surrounding streets. Another factor,

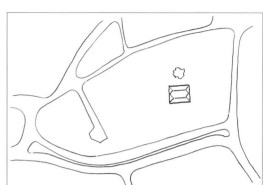

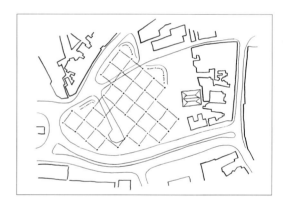

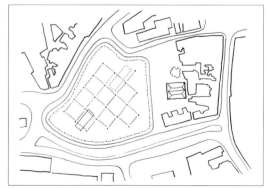

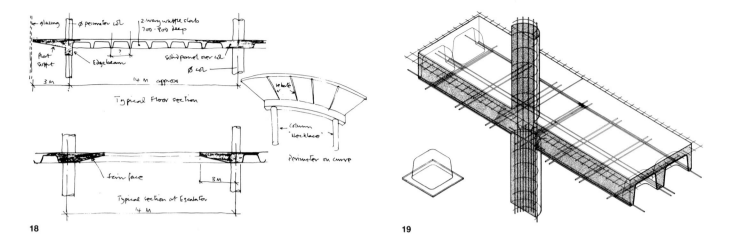

18

19

18 Extracts from structural engineer Tony Hunt's sketchbooks for the project showing the development of a typical floor section.
19 Cut-away isometric detail of the building's 700mm constant depth flat plate and waffle concrete floor structure and reinforced concrete columns; the depth of the slab was calculated to avoid the need for downstands.
20 A sequence of sixteen sketches by Foster taken

however, did impose serious constraints: no access was allowed from the ring road or within the radius of the Merlin roundabout. Therefore, the service access could only come off Princess Street. Maintaining the integrity of the glass wall meant that the loading bay had to be inside the building.

Furthermore, the architects and structural engineers were severely constrained by the existing basements and extensive underground services, a high water-table and variable ground conditions. The ballast and fill over the base layer of chalk were generally 8m thick, but on one corner of the site the chalk bed was 26m down. Swallow holes were also reported in the chalk and one was subsequently encountered. There was also a need to build swiftly and economically on a very tight urban site.

Structural design

For the superstructure, Foster's design options sought a balance between the widest possible and the most economic spans to achieve optimum space planning. In close collaboration with the engineer, Anthony Hunt, and the quantity surveyor, the Foster team first identified possible floor beam and column alternatives, and then systematically evaluated numerous grids and possible material combinations (for example steel, steel and concrete, pre-cast concrete or total *in-situ*). Hunt's sketches, **18**, give a fascinating insight into the underlining logic of an engineer's problem-solving approach.

After a detailed analysis of identified floor types, a constant depth flat plate and waffle concrete floor structure was designed in order to reduce the overall height and weight of the building, **19**. This solution depended on using *in-situ* reinforced concrete columns. Where earlier alternatives had examined hollow structural columns through which all services could pass, the final solution depended on a continuous service void above the suspended ceiling, with four non-structural service cores feeding all the vertical supplies. This had the great advantage that the superstructure could be a straightforward concrete frame totally free of servicing considerations. At the same time, the perimeter and escalator cantilevers were being developed, resulting finally in a solid slab tapering in thickness from the root to the glazed perimeter and central void respectively.

The final structural grid was based on columns set at 14m centres, with an edge necklace of more tightly spaced columns that could freely embrace the irregular shape of the site. The inspired combination of the rectilinear internal grid and the free-flowing perimeter columns at once determined the shape of the building and successfully dealt with the problem of left-over space. Since the meandering façade posed unusual load and deflection problems, a 7m spacing was used for the perimeter columns. They form a secondary structural system that is unrelated to the primary 14 × 14m grid.

This totally flexible system could straddle such fixed elements as loading docks, service cores, escalators, swimming pool, underground fire escape routes, and the limited basement.[1]

20

a

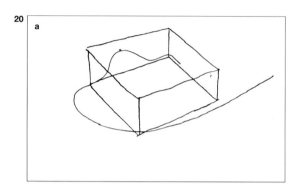

b

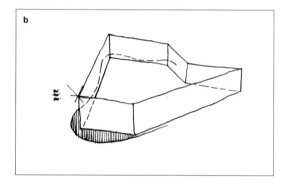

c

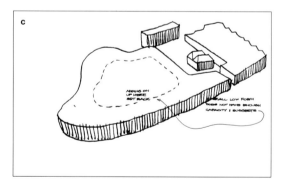

d

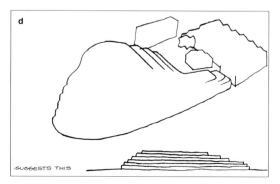

from a set of twenty-one he produced to explain and clarify his early ideas for the overall form of the building. The original numbering can be seen in the top right-hand corner of each sketch. Foster's notes on each sketch are as follows:

a simple geometry not acceptable for environmental reasons; **b** valuable site area unused – awkward corners negate simple runs – pin-wheel solutions and centre well; **c** overall podium block does not have enough capacity. Consider set backs; **d** suggests this – accommodates changes of height and light angles but structurally awkward with plan/section/space conflict; **e** OK but problems of separate access escape structure and why two not one building?; **f** difficult to divert services along preferred route – difficult to build over part of site – suggests one form; **g** combination of pool/ movement/café terraces in heart of building. Makes for social and technical conflicts – a building type not related to overlaps. Socially suggests usable space reduced significantly; **h** ideal pool construction but unless larger 60' span feasible, then problems; **j** preferred location for pool and other larger-span elements – socially (day and weekend) more interesting – compatible with strata studies; **k** obvious traditional structural answer but assumes core fixed quickly and forever – very questionable; **l** suggested as a preferred structural/servicing/ planning grid. 40' x 40' or 40' x 60'?; **m** reintroduction in new guise and more appropriate form of escalator route; **n** could develop so that roof is predominantly glazed. Shouts for overall glazed envelope.

o Great possibilities! But we lack time and immediate expertise at technical level; **p** technical problems realizable from 20th May. RBF visit – maybe we run parallel but time surely sends us back to TH-phased design, even though less desirable and all problems of a building on a building;

q could generate a unique roofscape/ trees/ gardens/ sun/ views out.

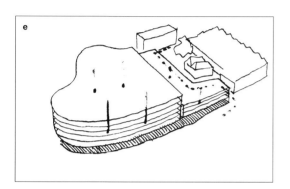

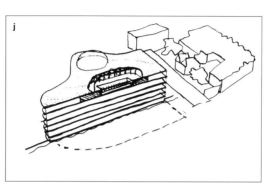

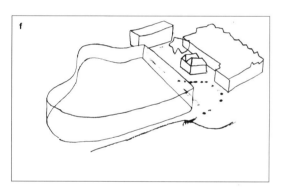

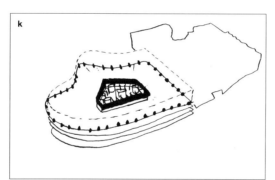

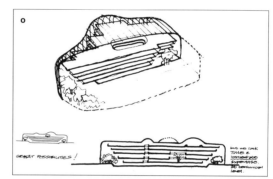

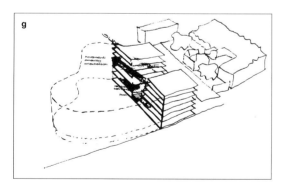

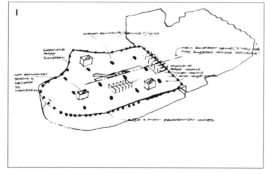

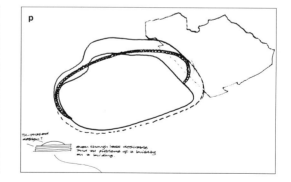

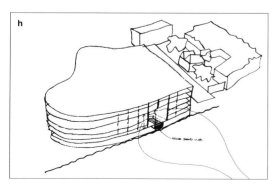

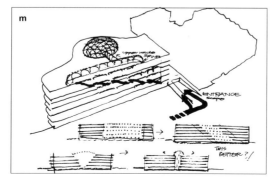

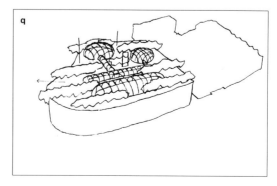

21 Willis Faber Dumas has one of the first 'level deck' pools where the water surface is contiguous with the floor plane.
22 The restaurant appears as an independent single storey building in the roof garden.
23 Detail of the restaurant's space-frame roof structure.
24 Construction begins on site in May 1972.

21

The large spans and high loading criteria (due to significant paper storage) dictated grouped pile foundations with the substructure elements, like the small basement, swimming pool and the fire escape tunnel tied into the pile caps to avoid floatation.

Because of the variable ground, exceptionally deep 30m piles had to be bored through the upper layers to reach the bedrock, using liners through the upper layers. All piles were large in diameter (1.07m and 1.22m) in order to avoid differential settlement. Each of the twenty-two main columns rests on at least four piles with *in-situ* pile caps. The forty-two perimeter columns stand on two piles each.

The 25m long pool hull is fully suspended between pile caps using its walls as beams. Incidentally, it was one of the first 'level deck' pools, like those designed by Luis Barragán, where the water over-flows into a perimeter trough to give the illusion of a single continuous plane, **21**.

Anthony Hunt's specially devised waffle slab for the floors, proved an ingenious solution. The waffles, 700mm deep with 250mm wide ribs, were developed on a 1m grid to suit the architectural planning grid. The slab's primary advantage was that it could easily accommodate the building's wide range of loading conditions. To counter the structure's high shear loads, additional strength could be gained, without increasing structural depth, by simply filling in waffles around a column head. Every 14m, where column meets slab, a 6m^2 solid reinforced concrete panel occurs in the slab to provide shear transfer.

The building's irregular shape and variable column grid dictated that the design should accommodate thermal stresses without the inclusion of the normally indispensable expansion joints. Therefore, to control structural movement, extra reinforcement to columns and slabs was used. The roof slab could be designed in the same way as the building's other floor slabs, without the need for an expansion joint, due to the high level of structural insulation afforded by the turfed roof.

The roof restaurant was treated very much as an independent single-storey steel-frame building, **22**. Its structure reflecting the 14m grid with reinforced concrete columns continued through from below to a white-painted tubular-steel space-frame supporting the glazed roof, **23**. Wall glazing is hung from the top edge of the space deck with the glass braced by special rocking arms.

Construction sequence

In May 1972 construction started on site, **24**. Bovis was chosen as the main contractor in a highly unconventional arrangement for the time; entering a management/fixed fee contract with the client, a contract that Bovis itself had pioneered. All elements of the building were put out to tender by the quantity surveyor who prepared the Bills of Quantities, and subcontracted by Bovis, who, as management contractor, assumed complete responsibility for all site operations and guaranteed quality control.

24

22

23

25, 26 Construction followed
a progressive sequence.
27 Hydraulically-levelled
table formwork was erected
bay by bay.
28 View of the glass curtain wall
during erection; the floor slabs
cantilever 3m and taper at the
perimeter to meet the glass.

25

26

27

The three-day week, a result of the miners' strike of 1973, complicated pre-planning and ordering during the construction stage. For example, serious steel shortages meant that the design of the roof pavilion had to be completely re-considered.

The programme demanded a progressive sequence of construction; the roof structure was completed in some areas whilst the building was still rising from the ground in other parts of the site, **25**, **26**. Fortunately, the selected structure of a flat, waffle slab permitted the use of hydraulically-levelled table formwork to be used bay by bay, **27**.

To further speed up construction, the contractors elected to deck-out the table forms prior to placing the GRP (glass reinforced plastic) waffle moulds. Concrete pours were pre-booked well in advance to avoid the problems of the three-day week and the building was successfully completed on time and within its original budget.

In its final form the concrete structure is simplicity itself: a square grid of internal columns, a waffle slab, further set of edge columns, and a 3m wide, tapered cantilever, **28**.

The building's frame was the only site-based wet trade and it went up in nine months. All other elements – fire walls, roof structure, external cladding and internal partitions – were of prefabricated, dry construction. Plaster work was eliminated and all partitions were constructed of galvanized metal sections. The advantages were better quality control, cost reduction, speed of erection and 'the delight of using materials of this age'. Foster's approach was that 'if a product was not available – and hardly anything was – then we designed one and collaborated with the manufacturers to make it'.

28

The glass wall

Willis Faber Dumas' glass wall was Foster's greatest design challenge and one which led to the most daring solution. Foster's team began by evaluating all available mullion support systems. Foster, however, did not want to use mullions at Willis Faber Dumas because, to him, the building's undulating line suggested a continuous skin – vertical mullions would have filleted the free-flowing form into a series of glazed segments. Ideally, the design team wanted to use a system similar to the one they had just prototyped for their new offices in Fitzroy Street, London. This system relied only on internal glass fins and silicon joints. It was the first application of silicon as a structural material and pioneered the glass technology without which the glass wall at Willis Faber Dumas would not have been possible.

To achieve the desired effect of a continuous sweeping wall, the glass had to be hung like a curtain. But this had never been done before. Foster recalls, 'Everyone thought we were crazy and that it was technically not feasible. The traditional engineering view was that you just can't do that'.

To meet the challenge of the glass wall, the design team was split down the middle to develop two separate assemblies; one supported by vertical

31

29 The final all-glass wall solution remained unresolved until late in the project, hence an alternative system was detailed which relied on suspended stainless steel tubular mullions to give the glass structural support.

30 The final solution adapted the standard patch fittings of Pilkington's planar system to cope with the angled junctions created by the building's curved perimeter. The geometry was calculated carefully to suit all requirements.

31 Early presentation drawings by Helmut Jacoby show the glass wall supported by a suspended steel mullion system.

32 A design sketch by Norman Foster suggesting that the clamping strip along the top edge of each glass facet be separated from the parapet capping.

33 Detail of a typical patch-plate fitting.

29

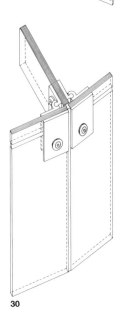

30

mullions, **29**, the other totally suspended, **30**. If the experimental suspended system failed, they would have had the mullion system to fall back on. Foster asked Martin Francis to co-ordinate the necessary research for the suspended system. Francis was a trained cabinet maker, who knew little about glass but was a creative thinker and had worked in industry. His first priority on joining the design team was to determine the parameters that would affect a totally suspended glass wall.

It was only at the eleventh hour that Foster's team demonstrated to everyone's satisfaction the technical feasibility of a fully suspended glass system. In fact, most of the office's presentation drawings still show the glass wall with internal tubular steel mullions, **31**.

The all-glass suspended solution was only possible because glass is strongest in tension. Foster recalls, 'We had to do all the calculations and working drawings to convince Pilkington, who at first rejected the idea, that it was not only feasible but very cost effective, since all we needed was glass and glue'. In fact, the final suspended solution was marginally cheaper than the standard mullion system.

With the help of the Technical Advisory Service, Fosters negotiated an unusual contract with Pilkington who were very helpful. It was a trade off: Foster Associates surrendered their design rights to Pilkington, who in return accepted full design responsibility. The deal has paid off handsomely for Pilkington, who still market the system internationally. For a while they ran double-page adverts with the headline: '900 pane installation, largest suspended glass façade in the world…' and a quote from Lance Wright's editorial in *The Architectural Review*: 'Perhaps once in a decade will an industrial company find itself involved in a project so ambitious, that the challenge becomes irresistible'.

Modern Art Glass was sub-contracted to install the glass wall whilst Pilkington and Foster's team entered into an intensive working programme to solve the particular problems of the building shape, movement, tolerances and overall size. Martin Francis remained the vital link between Pilkington and the design team throughout.

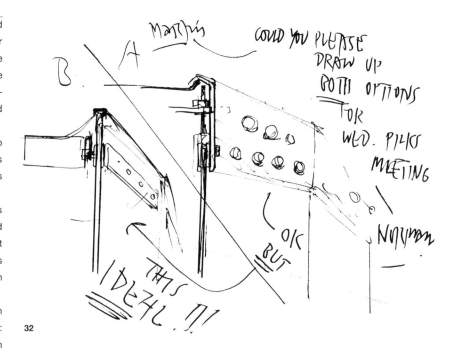

32

Glass in suspension

The entire glass wall is suspended from one continuous rail running around the roof perimeter. Amazingly, the dead weight of each 2m wide and three storey high glazing module is independently suspended from a single bolt located centrally at its top. The load is spread across the width of the glass at that point by means of a metal clamping strip and fibre gasket. There is no other means of support, **32**.

At each four-way junction (i.e. at floor and mid-floor levels) the individual glazing panels are connected by a small corner plate or so-called 'patch fittings'. Pilkington re-jigged their standard brass patch plates to cope with the angled junctions created by the curves of the building, **33**. The plate

33

geometry had to be carefully calculated to take up all changes of direction. The patch fittings secure one sheet of glass to the one immediately above or below it, never to sheets on either side; the gap around each plate is sealed with silicon.

Internal glass fins are independently attached to the cantilevered concrete floor slabs, **34**; and the glass fins are secured to the glass wall using specially developed sliding patch fittings. The internal glass fins do not hold the glass wall up, they simply restrain it against lateral wind loads whilst allowing vertical movement caused by thermal effects and building movement.

Since the glass wall forms no direct connection with the concrete frame the problems of structural creep in the cantilevers, which can continue for up to ten years after the building's completion, did not have to be considered.

Wind loads

The wind loads on the building are extremely high, in fact almost the same as the office floor loads. Calculation proved difficult. No existing wind codes could cope with the building's unique problem of an irregular shape, totally sealed but with the possibility of a large accidental opening and the different heights of surrounding buildings with complex spaces in between. Detailed data had to be prepared. This involved taking aerial photographs, charting heights and sizes of all adjacent buildings, allowing for future buildings in the area and analysing local weather conditions. All data was tabulated by the Building Research Establishment in London; it prepared a complete schedule of maximum wind forces on the building that verified the theoretical design assumptions made. This allowed the fixings for the glass wall and the size of the internal glass fins to be calculated. The glass fins are only a half-storey high. Earlier design proposals, using full-height glass fins from floor to soffit, were abandoned because of the anticipated differential movement in the perimeter cantilevers.

Glass wall assembly

Much doubt surrounded the on-site assembly of the glass wall. Previously, all glazing systems relied on taking site dimensions once the openings of the building existed; the glass would then be cut to fit. At Ipswich this was not possible.

Aesthetic, structural and manufacturing considerations had already determined the size of each glass panel as a 2m × 2.5m module. Therefore a new assembly method had to be developed that would match manufacturing tolerances with given site dimensions. This was only feasible because of very precise setting-out and careful initial surveying. Moreover, to absorb any minor discrepancies in the concrete frame, each glass panel had a built-in tolerance of 50mm in any direction provided by oversized fixing holes. The glass panels could now be factory finished whilst the concrete was still being poured on site. This method worked well.

34

36

35 Bolting a 'patch plate' fitting into place.
36 Removable metal plates in the pavement allow access to the drainage gully at the base of the glass wall.
37 Individual glass panels can be easily replaced; as was demonstrated by this panel failure shortly after the building's official opening.

38 A page taken from Norman Foster's project sketchbook; Foster's sketch defines the problem of how to treat the floor slab and its soffit where it approaches the all-glass wall.

35

First, the internal glass fins were installed to form a kind of window frame. Starting from the top, the glass plates were then lifted into position and the patch fittings bolted into place, **35**, with the large fixing holes allowing for any slight misalignment of the fins. The joints between glass panels were simply sealed with silicon.

In summary, this assembly method had many distinct advantages. All the glass panels could be pre-fabricated before the concrete frame was complete. All the glass could be the same size, with emphasis on variable joint width. And, since the fixed glass fins pre-determined the position of each glass panel, the on-site erection procedure was greatly simplified. The oversized bolt holes allowed the necessary tolerances. Even though the façade is curved, no curved glass sections had to be fabricated. The same 2m × 2.5m module could be used throughout. The building's many curves are, in fact, all straight edges meeting at angles carefully calculated by computer. This standardized approach greatly reduced costs and made it easy for future glass plates to be replaced.

Water drainage

There are no external drain pipes at Willis Faber Dumas. Rain water simply washes off the walls and is collected in a gully in the pavement along the perimeter line. The wall's lower-most glass panels, the only ones cut to allow for falling site levels, simply drop into this gap. The glass is not restrained along its bottom edge and hangs freely inside the gully to move up and down. Access to the gully is through removable metal plates in the pavement, **36**.

In the absence of leaking down pipes and dripping sills, the building's sleek and seamless façade is remarkably maintenance free: the rooftop trolleys are lowered only at three monthly intervals to clean the glass.

Safety considerations

Willis Faber Dumas' 12mm glass is thicker than a car windscreen but toughened in the same way. If damaged, the shattered granules tend to stay in place. Michael Hopkins, then a partner at Foster Associates, said on completion of the building: 'The glass wall is incredibly strong – like a wall of bricks'. However, only a week after the official opening one of the glass plates did shatter, **37**. Although six plates of glass are suspended in series from each clamping strip, the lower plates will not collapse if a breakage occurs higher up; this is due to the structural silicon joints pioneered on the glass façade at Fitzroy Street, which allow loads to be transferred sideways.

The building's natural tolerance was demonstrated in the 1987 hurricane, when the glass wall was deflected 100mm in some areas but only two plates actually failed. The support brackets simply slid horizontally across their locating holes; these brackets were just slackened off and re-located. Foster recalls an earlier test of the building's durability: 'The edge of the building is on a route to Ipswich football ground and there were a lot of reservations

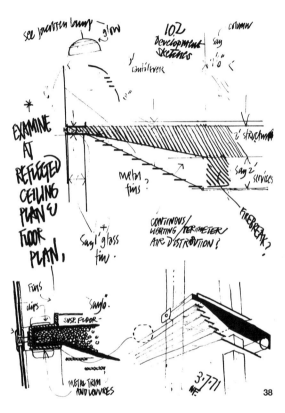

38

37

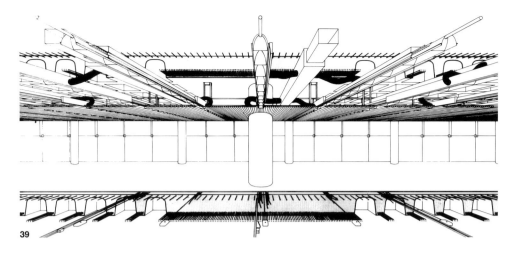

39

39 The building's ceiling system was pioneered by the Foster office; light fittings were specially designed to give efficient illumination without glare at spacings wider than the accepted norm. Wiring channels were incorporated within the chassis of each lighting strip and return air was deliberately drawn through the light fittings to absorb heat at source.

40 The ceiling system is able to accommodate the building's curved edge with ease.

41 A Norman Foster sketch exploring the detailing of the aluminium strip ceiling at its edge condition.

42 The purpose-designed lighting system incorporates highly polished deep, concave, reflectors which help to achieve the required brightness and distribution of light over large office floor areas.

about the ability of the glass wall to withstand the onslaught of the Ipswich football supporters en route. The question was posed, "What would happen if somebody threw a brick at it?" We tested this on a mock-up and what happened was that it bounced back'. Apart from occasional vandal damage, the most likely reasons for failure are the amount of torque applied to each patch fitting and excessive heating or cooling in a particular area.

An integrated servicing system

From day one, Foster's team set themselves the difficult task of developing a totally integrated, custom-made ceiling and floor system that considerably exceeded the standards of the time, **38**, **39**. Foster wanted an intelligent system where all components would interact with each other; for example, light fittings that could double as air extract vents. Such technical innovations did not come about easily but were the result of the office's long-term commitment to technology-transfer and the relentless improvement of available systems.

After every proprietary ceiling system had been examined, countless study models and mock-ups were made and eliminated. With functional and aesthetic considerations as the most significant factors, a specially made aluminium system finally emerged. It consisted of 30mm wide, highly polished aluminium channels with fully integrated luminaires and air supply ducts.

The primary aim was to maintain a clear ceiling line, free of protruding secondary fittings. This was achieved by suspending the ceiling from specially designed H-frames which allowed for three-dimensional adjustment. The H-frames held cross supports for the aluminium channels and neatly integrated all necessary services such as the air conditioning, smoke detectors, emergency lighting and sprinkler heads. No less than 40 miles of aluminium channel were required to make up the ceiling plane of just one floor.

The next problem was how to terminate the aluminium channels along the building's irregular perimeter line. The solution involved cutting each channel to a different length, creating a stepped-back edge profile that stops short of the glass wall against a vertical panel, **40**, **41**. The panel forms a downstand to the concrete cantilever which contains the directional air ducts that constantly blow air onto the glass wall to condition the perimeter zone and prevent condensation. The cantilever tapers out towards the glass wall to create the thinnest possible junction between floors.

Within the ceiling, the lighting tracks in each office level house over 2500 luminaires. The luminaires are precision engineered and fitted with parabolic reflectors. The reflectors are highly polished, deep, and concave to achieve the desired brightness and glare ratings and uniform lighting levels – difficult to attain over a vast floor area of 6500m², **42**.

As Foster later remarked: 'to create that kind of lighting system we had to tear up all existing lighting codes and take a completely different stand'. The grid's 2m spacing is significantly wider than the accepted standard for offices

40

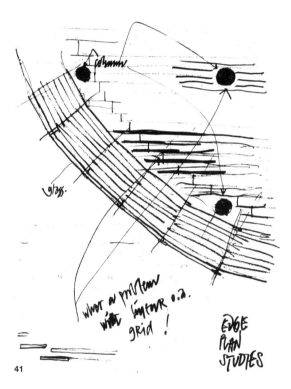

41

42

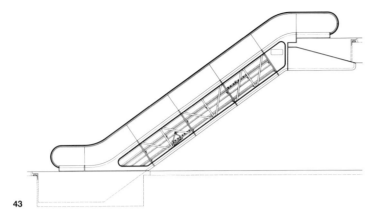

43 Following the principle that all main service installations would be open to view, the escalators incorporate glass-sided panels that reveal their inner workings.
44 Foster's sketches exploring the dynamic of three levels of escalators rising up through the building to the light of the roof-top restaurant.

43

and posed the potential problem of patchy lighting levels. However, any patchiness was eliminated by laying throughout a bright green carpet which reflects the predominant colour component of the fluorescent lights.

The polished ceiling, which sets up secondary reflections and brings natural light deep into the open plan, further compensated for the wider lighting grid. The ceiling dissolves and reflects everything, with the muted glare of its thousand mirrors creating an environment where it is difficult to tell whether the lights are in use or not.

All the air conditioning takes place through openings in the light fittings. Air is supplied at the rate of 40 litres per second and extracted at the rate of 25 litres per second (the difference of 15 litres per second goes towards toilet and kitchen extraction) via ventilation boots attached to and running alongside the luminaires, conveniently cooling them in the process. The integrated air conditioning system was a brilliant solution that enormously simplified all ducting, saving material, installation and maintenance costs.

At equal intervals along the lighting track aluminium plates, specially designed to match the reflectors, are fitted. These conceal sprinkler heads, smoke detectors and emergency lighting.

A flexible floor

In the early 1970s no one could have foreseen the explosive growth in computerization and information technology. When typewriters and telephones were the only visible office equipment it was a far-sighted decision to specify a floor services system that would allow the electrical services to absorb future growth and provide maximum flexibility. Subsequently, the company's extensive computerization, with terminals at each desk, has been accommodated effortlessly by the totally flexible initial design. In fact, no extra sub-stations or electrical cables were required to service the greatly increased loads. In a 1989 company report, Willis Faber Dumas quantified the advantages: 'In real terms the building is now able to handle a staggering two and a half times the business with the same number of staff'.

Insurance brokers need a dynamic working environment since the nature of their work requires frequent office re-organization. The convention at the time was to bury the service trunking in the floor screed with all the outlets fixed, and invariably in the wrong place. In 1970 totally raised floors were still unusual in England. Where they had been used, they would constitute a tangled web of disparate elements brought together in an on-site shot-gun marriage.

Since no existing flooring system offered a sufficiently flexible solution, Foster's team, together with the respective manufacturers and engineers, set about developing their own prototype, using the architects' model shop to experiment with full scale mock ups.

The most radical innovation in the raised floors are the integrated service trenches that provide a floor zone free of projecting access traps. On each

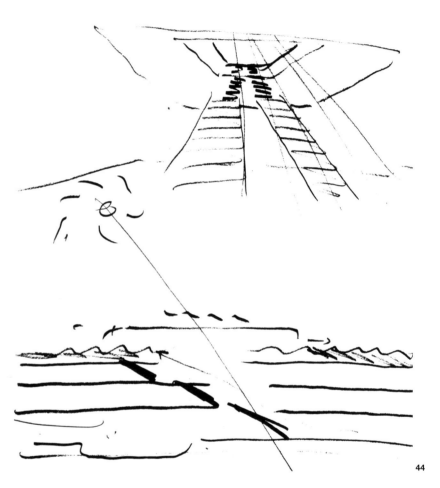

44

office floor the trenches run directly below the overhead lighting track, following the same 2m wide grid. Each trench contains a continuous run of plug-in power ducts or so called 'bus-bars'. Thousands of custom-made 13 amp sockets were developed for the system. The sockets can be plugged into the bus-bar at any point along its length. This makes office re-organization very easy. To reconnect a work station simply involves lifting any one of the continuous access panels and plugging into the bus-bar. All wires are neatly threaded through carefully detailed holes in the plastic rim of the trench flaps.

As new syndicates are formed or dissolved, and departments expand or contract, people can be moved without major organizational changes. At present the bus-bars feed about 1400 work stations but this number could be increased easily. With great foresight, the bus-bars were specified to carry loads of up to 30 amps – not required at the time but now needed for desktop terminals. Every length of duct is protected by its own 50 amp circuit breaker in one of the riser cubicles. The service trenches also hold the IBM 3750 direct line telephone system linking Ipswich to Head Office in London. The original system is still in use.

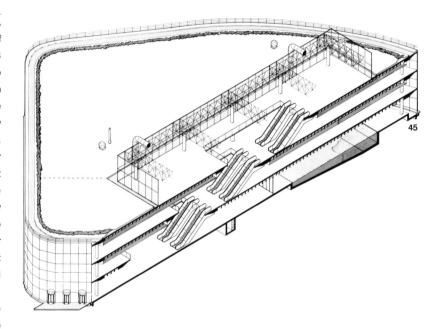

45

Since the two enormous office floors at Willis Faber Dumas had to function on a sub-lettable basis, each floor has four independent service cores to facilitate four major spatial sub-divisions. Therefore, the building's service lift and document lift are separate and not integrated into the service cores.

The four service cores are fed from two packaged sub-stations in the main plant room. Each sub-station has a power output of 2MW. The transformers for each sub-station are cast in resin. This is significant because it was the first commercial application of its kind. The advantages of cast resin transformers over oil-filled types are that they have a high temporary overload capacity, are only half the size and require reduced fire precautions.

Taking advantage of the roof

This is one of the few well documented cases where a roof garden has been included at no extra capital cost. Considered in isolation, a grass roof is more expensive than a conventional flat roof. At Willis Faber Dumas, however, other factors outweighed the greater initial construction costs. For instance, the greatly increased insulation afforded by the soil layer meant significant reductions in heating and cooling costs. Early calculations showed that insulation would be so good as to eliminate totally the need for an expansion joint across the building, removing at a stroke an entire line of columns and associated foundations.

Another, more potent, argument for the roof garden was its amenity value. The architects took a creative view and argued that the garden would reduce staff turn-over and thus prove cost effective in the long run. To convince the client, a visit to the Derry & Toms Building in London, famous for its roof-top garden, **47**, was arranged. The client was impressed but nervous about the

46 Foster's decision to 'recreate the site' at roof level by covering it with grass broke new ground in office building design. The declared aim was to provide an additional amenity for office staff but secondary practical advantages quickly became apparent; the soil layer proved to be highly insulative and eliminated the need for any expansion joints within the structure.

47 Derry and Toms' roof garden, an early source of inspiration.

48 A perimeter hedge conceals the roof parapet.

49 View into the ground-floor main-frame computer and data processing suite.

46

idea of maintaining a full scale garden. When the architects suggested a straightforward expanse of grass, **46**, agreement was reached.

Early drawings show the roof garden doubling as a heliport, affording a quick touch down for stressed executives. This proposal was never seriously considered, however, because of the problems of over-flying built-up areas and the impossibly low approach angle.

Like the floors, the roof is constructed of reinforced concrete waffle slabs. The screed falls at 1:50 towards the drainage points which are at 20m intervals. Lorry loads of ceramic tiles, seconds from a local pottery, were used as protection on top of the asphalt. The turf covering was then built up in four distinctive layers. Generally the covering is 225mm thick increasing to 550mm where the lawn gently banks up towards the perimeter. The soil consists of 35% peat, 35% sterilized loam and 30% sharp sand.

Planting in the one acre garden remains limited to grass and the *Euonymus Japonica* perimeter hedge which conceals the roof parapet, **48**, thus creating the splendid illusion of a ground level garden. A continuous walkway or jogging track runs between the planted hedge and the roof edge. The small terrace area outside the restaurant and the track are the only hard surfaces and were originally finished with studded rubber flooring which had to be removed when the underlying screed started to break up. Now, a pitch epoxy resin coating with a non-slip grit coating has been applied. The path slopes gently towards the lawn allowing rain water to run into the drainage layer under the grass via holes in the kerb.

The pop-up sprinklers that irrigate the lawn are fed from the main water supply in two of the four service cores. The whole system is controlled by an electronic timer. By supplying the sprinklers from only two cores and then further reducing the demand by sub-dividing the roof into ten irrigation zones, it was possible to avoid a sudden drop in water pressure throughout the rest of the building. In addition, the water pressure in the mains is boosted by one horse power electric pumps to create sufficient pressure for the sprinklers.

Originally, sealed floodlights with spike fittings were installed throughout the garden but since they posed a continuous hazard to lawn mowers they had to be removed. Now, a string of lights along the kerb and several recessed into the lawn illuminate the garden at night.

47

48

Fire control

From the outset, the building's open escalator well posed a potentially serious problem. Smoke, the greatest hazard in any fire, could quickly penetrate every floor. The open well is not a risk in itself. The difficulty was that if the office floors had been compartmented to meet the fire regulations set down for unprotected perimeter areas – a regulation that applies only in urban areas – then the escalator well would have had to be fire separated. The solution was the introduction of sprinklers as a way of getting a waiver on the compartmentalization regulations. The client, as insurance brokers, also supported the idea of sprinklers in office buildings, a solution that in the end was no more expensive than installing fire partitions.

In addition, several preventative measures were built into the design: the narrow junction where the concrete cantilever tapers out to meet the glass wall had to act as a smoke barrier. To find a malleable material with the necessary resistance was a tricky problem. After much testing, a flexible neoprene fin was used to fill the gap. This constitutes the only smoke trap between floors. In addition, extra smoke detectors, alarm bells, fire extinguishers and hose reels had to be fitted and continue to be tested at regular intervals.

The unmanned computers, **49**, which work the building's telephone exchange are further protected by CO_2 outlets to minimize the risk of water damage. All computer areas operated by people are cooled and protected by underfloor water pipes running at a depth of 300mm. To protect against accidental water damage, special sensors were installed under the floor to detect any possible leaks.

The kitchen is fitted with its own dry powder release system. Elsewhere, sprinklers were installed in the ceiling and ceiling cavities where electrical services run. Furthermore, great care was taken to use fire resistant materials throughout the building for example: metal ceilings, galvanized partitions and glass walls. The fully metal-encased staircases in each of the four service cores are the building's fire escape routes.

49

Energy considerations

The continuous glass wall at Willis Faber Dumas suggests an extremely high-energy building. Surprisingly, however, the building is enormously energy friendly. Its electricity consumption is 35% less than that of a conventional office building with the same floor area. This astonishing fact is due to a series of innovative and extremely subtle energy conscious design features.

The building's projected energy consumption before completion was: gas – 250,000 therms per annum; electricity – 8,000,000kWh per annum. These estimates assumed five day operating periods for the office spaces with constant usage of the main frame computer and swimming pool.

For 1976, the first full year of operation the figures were: gas – 170,000 therms; electricity – 5,829,000kWh. The owner's skill in managing the building's energy system over the years is reflected in the excellent figures for 1983: gas – 77,674 therms; electricity – 5,142,390kWh. Energy consumption has actually fallen despite greatly increased demand; particularly for local data processing equipment, a ten-fold increase in remote VDU stations and a large number of additional computer systems installed throughout the office space.

The building's very substantial fall in gas consumption was acknowledged by the Gas Council's regional award for energy conservation in 1984. These unexpected results delighted client, architect and engineers alike, especially

50, 51 Willis Faber Dumas'
plant is located at ground level,
clearly visible to passers-by
and those using the building.
With everything on view, great
attention was paid to the design
of the plantroom layout, pipe
routes and internal lighting.
52 At dusk, as the reflective
surface of the glass wall
dissolves, the internal workings
of the plantroom are revealed,
like the engines of some
great liner.

since the building has three extra high energy facilities not found in conventional office buildings of similar size: the powerful mainframe computer (used by the company even in the 1970s), the competition length swimming pool, and a kitchen providing 700 meals daily.

Whilst a balanced view was taken between social benefits and running costs, the most significant factors of the building's surprisingly low energy consumption are: its compact shape and the unusually deep plan – in places up to 108m across which dramatically reduces the floor to window ratio to half that of a conventional office building.

To service the building's given floor area a bank of twelve lifts would have been required. Instead, the two central escalators are infinitely cheaper to run and maintain.

In addition, it was found that in winter, the heavily body-tinted glass absorbs more solar energy than expected. In summer, the glass guards against extensive heat gain, whilst still admitting high levels of natural light. Thus air conditioning and artificial lighting are kept to a minimum. Although there is no serious overheating due to solar gain, the staff still lobbied to have vertical blinds installed to control glare. These are now hardly used but have a reassuring psychological effect.

Artificial lighting is the greatest energy waster in most office buildings, partly because traditional light fittings diffuse a great deal of their light onto the ceiling. The specially prototyped parabolic reflectors at Willis Faber Dumas, however, maximize downlighting to such an extent that single 85W fluorescent tubes could be used where a pair would normally have been necessary. With a floor to ceiling height of 2.66m an illuminance of 750 lux is achieved. Even though the 2m centre lighting grid is wider than accepted by standard lighting codes, no additional task lighting is needed.

This significant saving in electrical energy consumption is primarily due to the reflector's highly polished concave scoops that focus the light directly onto the working surface where it matters most. Of the 5000 lumen produced by each fitting, 3000 lumen are directed downwards. This 60% lighting efficiency compares extremely well with the 30–40% efficiency of standard light fittings.

On the office floors, the fully integrated air conditioning consumes only 65% of the energy of a conventional system. Its efficiency lies primarily in the ingenious positioning of the air intake and air outlet vents within each recessed light fitting. The system recycles the heat from the light fittings, office machines and staff. Efficiency is further improved by extracting air through the light fittings thus prolonging the life of the fluorescent tubes (no over heating) and the constant air current keeps the fittings clean which means low maintenance, high reflective quality and greater light output.

This form of creative heat recovery, coupled with the air exhausts over the fluorescent tubes makes the building's lighting and temperature control extremely energy efficient.

50

51

The air handling system in the restaurant is similar to that for the offices, except that distribution is by long throw diffusers, since there is no suspended ceiling. The swimming pool enclosure is serviced by a fixed 100% fresh air supply and extract system. The pool itself has water filtration, treatment and heating facilities. The main computer space has complete air conditioning systems independent of the rest of the building.

All services are kept simple. Only the most straightforward systems were installed: natural gas fired boilers for heating, hermetic centrifugal refrigeration plant for cooling, packaged sub-stations, and a back-up diesel generator in case of power failure. These were the most economical systems in terms of capital costs, but perhaps not the most sophisticated in terms of technology; however, they remain extremely effective in terms of running costs.

The costly complexity that often results when undue emphasis is placed on achieving the lowest possible fuel consumption was avoided. Instead, the architects' primary consideration was to create a good and stimulating working environment that would improve productivity and thus be energy efficient in the widest sense.

Placing the plantroom on the ground floor was less expensive than putting it at roof level or below ground. Consequently, the visual impact of the street-level plantroom became an important design consideration, 50, 51. What do you put into the shop window of an insurance company? At Willis Faber Dumas, the architects elevated the plantroom to a piece of mechanical sculpture. Clearly visible from all sides through continuous glass partitions, the strong image of the meticulously detailed plant, with its dramatic nocturnal lighting effects, was intended to be symbolic of how the rest of the building works, 52.

To further increase energy efficiency, in 1980 Willis Faber Dumas installed a computerized monitoring system and introduced a series of cost-saving measures. For example, a heating circuit bypass was installed.

Whilst the building's boiler plant has to run 24 hours a day to service the swimming pool, the building's heating system is shut down at night. During maintenance work, engineers noticed that, at night, hot water from the boilers continued to circulate through the coils of the office floors' air handling units. Without the fans running, heated air was freely escaping from the building through the air handling units as well as the fresh air intakes. The simple expedient of installing two position by-pass valves at the boiler plant, to cut off the water-flow to the coils in the air handling units, produced a surprisingly large annual energy saving.

Operating experience also showed that in winter a lower air volume could be supplied to all areas of the building. This was achieved by throttling manual dampers on the inlets of the air handling unit. Electrical power consumption was thereby cut. As a further measure, the swimming pool air handling unit, running at all times, was fitted with a heat recovery system. This consisted of

52

53 A radical concern for the well-being of those using the building led to the incorporation of the competition standard swimming pool which has provided a social focus for office staff and their families since it opened.

54 Frank Dickens, who draws the Bristow cartoon strip, was engaged by the design team to use his skills to communicate the spirit of the building and how it would be different to the traditional office. Norman Foster recalls, 'he got completely carried away with the idea and produced a sequence of about 40 of these images'.

'runaround' coils in the intake and extract ducts. Ways are now being investigated to incorporate the pool into the general services system by using its thermal storage capacity as a heat tank.[2]

Ahead of its time

53

It is remarkable that Willis Faber Dumas, designed three years before the energy crisis of 1973, was already conceived as an energy-conscious building. Today, most of its energy saving features, as well as its many ingenious technological innovations, are taken for granted. The most real and lasting significance of the building lies in its underlying ideology: to reinstate the fundamental values of architecture – to design with the utmost human consideration.

At Willis Faber Dumas, the life of the building emanates from its people and how they determine to use it. For instance, the end of a working day finds children waiting in the foyer to go swimming with their parents, **53**. At first, some staff had to adjust to seeing families at their place of work, but the building's forces unite everyone in a friendly and personal atmosphere.

In terms of its human values, Willis Faber Dumas remains today, more than fifteen years after its completion, ahead of its time. In April 1991, when the staff swimming pool suddenly came under threat the Department of the Environment intervened quickly to spotlight the building and stop plans to pour concrete into the pool to create 2136m[2] of additional office space. It is a rare honour for a contemporary building to be protected by law, but Willis Faber Dumas is exceptional, for it is a commercial building that has become a great social success. Willis Faber Dumas now enjoys the singular status of being the youngest listed building in the United Kingdom and only the third post-war building to be given Grade 1 status; Coventry Cathedral and the Royal Festival Hall being the other two.[3]

In 1975, when the Rt Hon. Harold MacMillan spoke on the occasion of the building's opening ceremony, he immediately singled out its unusual recreational facilities. 'Looking at the swimming pool, the roof garden, the restaurant, the gymnasium and the rest', he said, 'I am reminded of a story many years ago, when ICI built what was then thought to be one of the most modern offices in London, on the Thames Embankment. The founder of the great enterprise, Sir Alfred Mond, was taking a visitor round the wonderful structure. His guest said "How many people work here?" "Oh", said Sir Alfred, "ten per cent, not more." 'I hope', said MacMillan, 'and this is a rather cynical observation, that in spite of all these amenities, or perhaps because of them, you will be able to advance to a higher figure.' Willis Faber Dumas should be remembered best for its pioneering social and spiritual aspirations, conceived at a time when nobody thought of the recreational needs of the office floor, and few recognized that a stimulating and spiritually uplifting office environment invariably leads to higher productivity.

Notes

1 By law, commercial buildings need to store enough water to maintain a 24 hour supply. To avoid additional structural reinforcement, the water tank at Willis Faber Dumas is not on the roof but placed below ground. The so-called Borsari tank is a reinforced concrete drum lined with special ceramic tiles; it has a diameter of 10m and a depth of 3.4m.

2 For further details see *Energy Conservation and Use in the Willis Faber and Dumas Building, Ipswich* by Loren Butt, Hutchinson, 1985.

3 Other notable post-war buildings that have been listed are: Royal Festival Hall in London (1951), Coventry Cathedral (1962) and the Economist Building in London (1964).

Chronology

1970–1972

Design
January 1971–December 1972

Date of tender
January 1973

Contract period
March 1973–July 1974

Official Opening
2 June 1975 by Rt Hon. Harold MacMillan, who was father-in-law to company chairman Julien Faber

Dimensions

Site
7,000m² irregular shape

Gross floor area
21,255m²

Building height
Four storeys/21.5m

Clear span of structural frame
14m

Length of glass wall
320m

Functional unit
1200 people (17.71 m²)

Structure

Internal columns
1m diameter from ground floor to first floor; 800mm diameter from first to third floor; centred at 14m.

Perimeter columns
600mm diameter from ground to third floor; centred at 7m; set back 3m from the glass wall. The 1m drop in site level is taken up by a change of level within the building.

Upper floors and roof
700mm deep reinforced concrete waffle slab with ribs at 1m centres. Cantilevers are solid and tapered.

Ground floor slab and pool
reinforced concrete fully suspended between pile caps.

Roof
steel tubular lattice girders.

Foundations
in situ bored piles with *in situ* pile caps.

Additional data

Carpet
Heavy duty contract Wilton broadloom, 80% wool, 20% Bri-nylon, accentuated tuft anchorage, through-to-back-weave, non-fray finish, colour green, width 3.66m. 14,500m² specially woven at CMC's Wessex Wilton plant.

Glass wall
12mm Armourplate Antisun Solar Control Glass, bronze tinted, pre-stressed, by Pilkington Bros Ltd, 14m high, 320m long continuous glass wall. Total glazed area 4,500m² consisting of 930 plates measuring 2m x 2.5m, total weight over 50 tons.

Silicon
ICI Silicone Building Sealant, Abrosil 1081, one part sealant. Supplied by Adshead Ratcliffe & Co. Ltd.

Swimming pool
Open daily 7 am–10 pm. Average use 70 people per day. Used regularly by employees' families after school and at weekends.

Cost

Overall cost per m²
£232.06 (building alone)
£234.40 (building and external works)

Final account cost
£4,982,062

Basis of tender
Management fee contract

Management Contractor
Bovis Construction Ltd

Project Director
David Wolf

Project Manager
M.E. Stafford

Awards

1976 Business & Industry Panel for the Environment Award of the Royal Society of Arts

1976 R.S. Reynolds Memorial Award

1977 RIBA Award

1984 Gas Council Regional Award for energy conservation

1990 RIBA Trustees Medal

Willis Faber Dumas' suspended glass wall extends over 320 metres enclosing 21,000 square metres of office space. By stretching the building out to the site boundaries and covering the entire site area the office space specified in the brief could be provided on just three floors. In fact, the building's entire administrative function is located on only two of these floors, both almost entirely open plan and each housing up to 600 people. Some support functions, such as the restaurant and kitchens are located at roof level; others such as computer rooms and plant are placed on public view at ground level.

Willis Faber Dumas' plantrooms are placed prominently on public view at ground level. The all-glass sheath that envelops the building meant that there was no place to 'hide' the mechanical plant; instead, the Foster team made a virtue of necessity, turning the concept of showing the building's inner workings into a carefully detailed and colourful display. Placing the plant at ground level also follows structural logic, allowing the heavy machinery the best support and minimizing the risk of vibration.

'In daylight, the one acre of mirror glass exterior wall uniformly reflects and augments the historic neighbouring structures. At night, with its customized, mirror-finished aluminium ceiling reflecting an evenly illuminated interior, the building becomes an enclosed urban plaza. The darkened and quiet neighbour-hood which inscribes it after night-fall is then provided with an exciting vista into the active world within.'
RS Reynolds Memorial Award Citation, April 1976

Three banks of escalators, left, speed the flow of people through Willis Faber Dumas' open heart. As well as being very efficient movers of office staff, the escalators also offer opportunities for chance encounters and brief conversations; they have become one of the building's social focuses.

Two views of the office floors, above left and right, taken in the 1970s and 1990s respectively show how effortlessly the advent of the computer and changing workplace requirements have been accommodated. Perimeter areas, right, are kept free, as originally intended, for use as circulation routes and *ad hoc* meeting spaces.

The escalators, opposite page, can be seen as a microcosm of the building itself; they were specially detailed to incorporate glass side panels which reveal their inner workings to general view.

Elsewhere, the themes of lightness and transparency predominate. The minimal use of fixing plates allows the glass wall, even when viewed from an acute angle or through overlapping glass fins, to dissolve, revealing uninterrupted views of the city beyond.

Polished aluminium ceilings, above, assist the even spread of light throughout the deep-plan office floors.

Escalators rise up through four floors, culminating at the staff restaurant where the green carpet leads out onto the turf of the roof garden.

The restaurant, left, is bathed in light from all sides. Glazing of the roof-top pavilion is similar in most respects to the main façade; the glass is supported by special rocking arms from the top edge of the tubular steel roof structure. Detail, right, of the junction between concrete column and tubular steel roof trusses.

Two views into Willis Faber
Dumas' main-frame computer
suite as originally completed in
the 1970s.

Willis Faber Dumas' swimming pool has been one of its principal sources of inspiration: Ben Johnson's painting, above, commissioned in 1984, captures its spirit perfectly. Before its recent closure, such moments of tranquillity were rare, however; on average more than 70 people used the pool per day. It became an ideal meeting point for office staff and their families after hours and at weekends.

Site plan

The site was originally split by two existing roads into three distinct parcels of land; the entire area became available several months into the project allowing the building to take a clear and cohesive form.

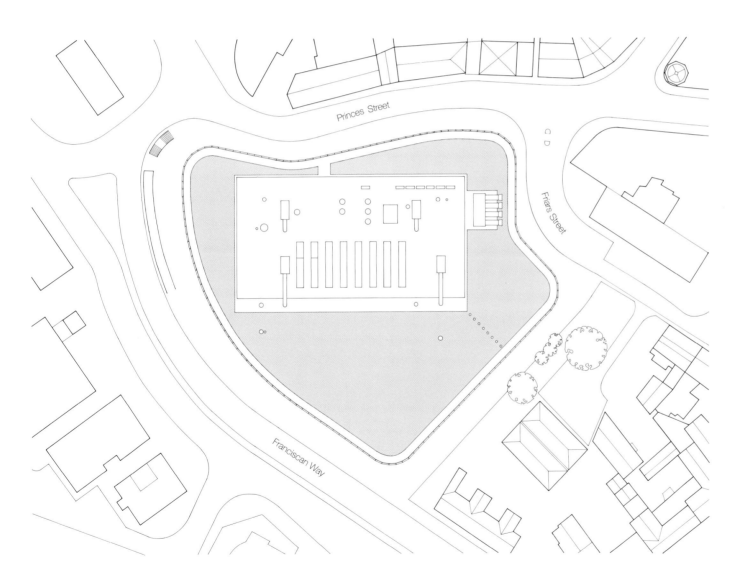

Princes Street

Friars Street

Franciscan Way

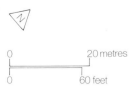

N

0 — 20 metres

0 — 60 feet

Ground floor plan

1 entrance
2 reception
3 escalators
4 coffee bar
5 swimming pool
6 changing rooms
7 gymnasium
8 crèche
9 wcs
10 data processing
11 document lift
12 engineers
13 tape store
14 computers
15 telex room
16 reprographics
17 chillers
18 generators
19 loading bay
20 plant
21 switch room

First floor plan

1 escalator atrium
2 service lift
3 document lift
4 office space
5 plant
6 store rooms
7 wcs

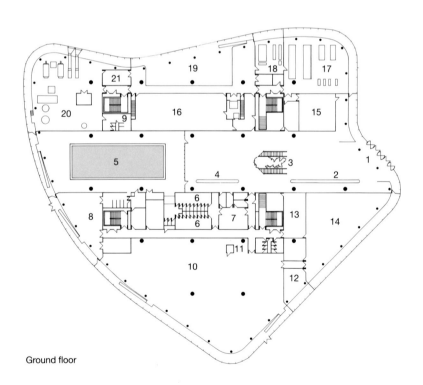

Ground floor

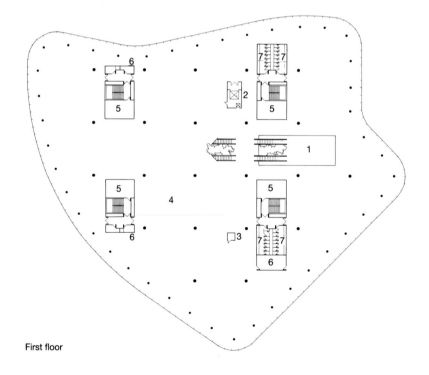

First floor

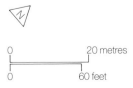

0   20 metres

0   60 feet

Second floor plan

1 escalator atrium
2 service lift
3 document lift
4 office space
5 plant
6 store rooms
7 wcs

Roof level plan

1 escalator atrium
2 service lift
3 wcs
4 cold storage
5 plant
6 kitchen
7 servery

8 cafeteria
9 restaurant
10 dishwashing
11 roof garden
12 perimeter walkway
13 cooling tower

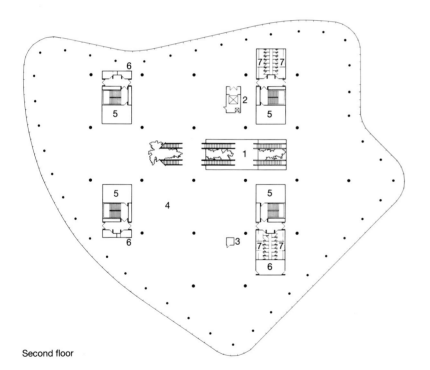

Second floor

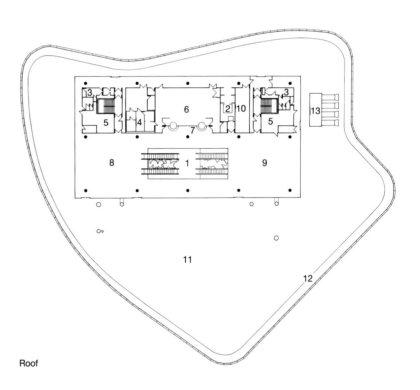

Roof

Longitudinal and lateral sections
through escalator atrium

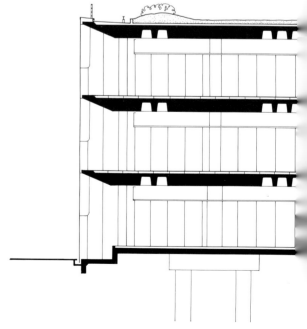

Longitudinal section

Lateral section

0   5 metres

0   15 feet

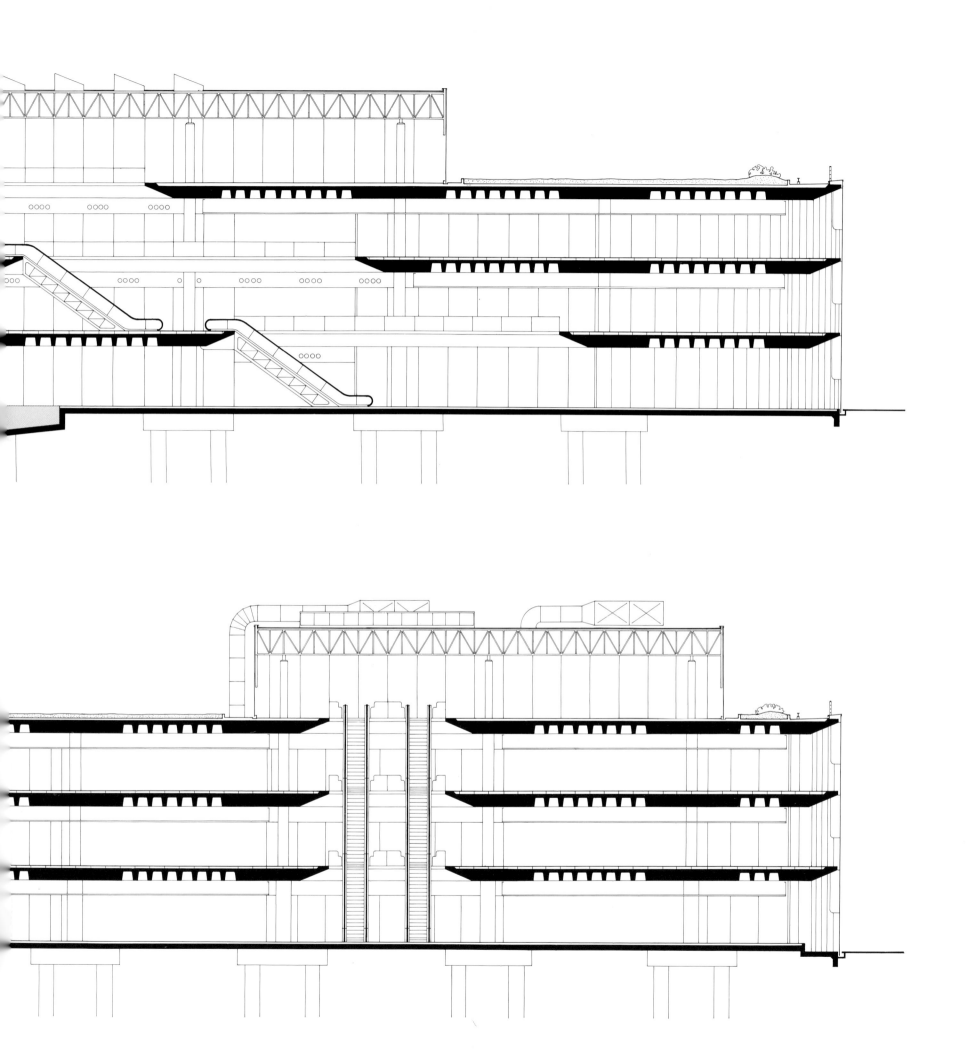

Detail sections through office suspended ceiling system

1 700mm deep reinforced concrete waffle-slab
2 aluminium channel extrusion polished finish
3 20mm glass fibre acoustic absorption mat
4 hanger support
5 sprinkler supply pipe
6 air boot diffuser with flexible connection to supply air duct
7 light fitting
8 primary lighting electrical distribution
9 air extract
10 local lighting electrical distribution

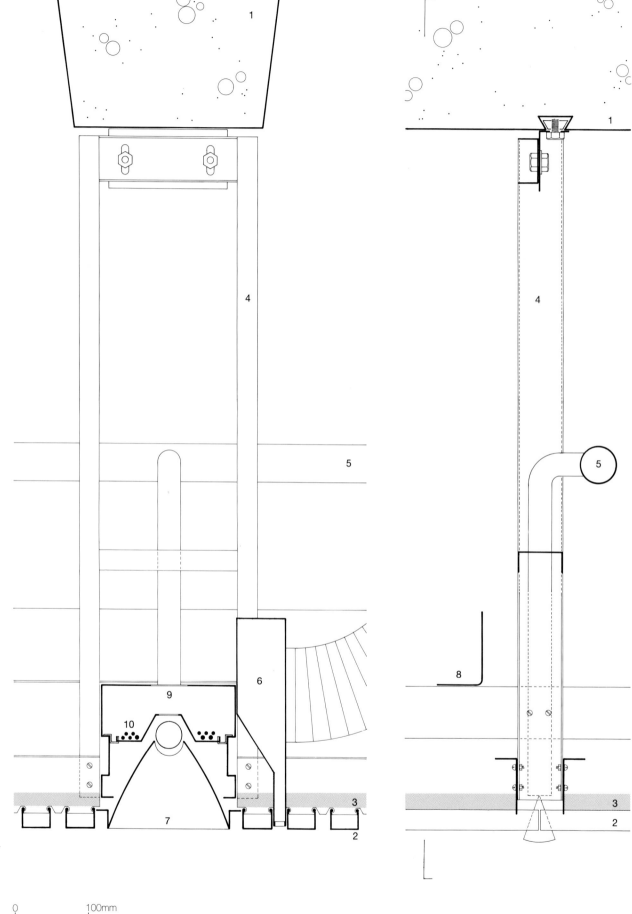

0   100mm

0   4 inches

Patch plate details; modified fitting, top and standard fitting

The Foster team adapted the standard Pilkington bronze patch-plate system to cope with the angled junctions caused by the building's shifting geometry. The usual rectangular slot of the flat glass wall system was modified to an 'open hinge' arrangement whose geometry could change to meet all situations.

Exploded isometric of the glass wall assembly

This drawing prepared by the Foster design team explains the key elements in the glass wall assembly. The full three-storey height of each two-metre wide glass facet is suspended independently from a single bolt located centrally at the head of each module. Loads are spread across the width of the glass at that point by means of clamping strips. Patch fittings at floor and mid-floor level connect each glass plate to its neighbour below. Lateral restraint against wind loads is provided by half-storey height glass fins which are attached independently to the soffit of each concrete floor structure. These are linked to the main façade by means of a sliding patch fitting which restrains horizontal movement but allows for thermal and building movement in the vertical plane. Joints between panels are sealed with clear silicon.

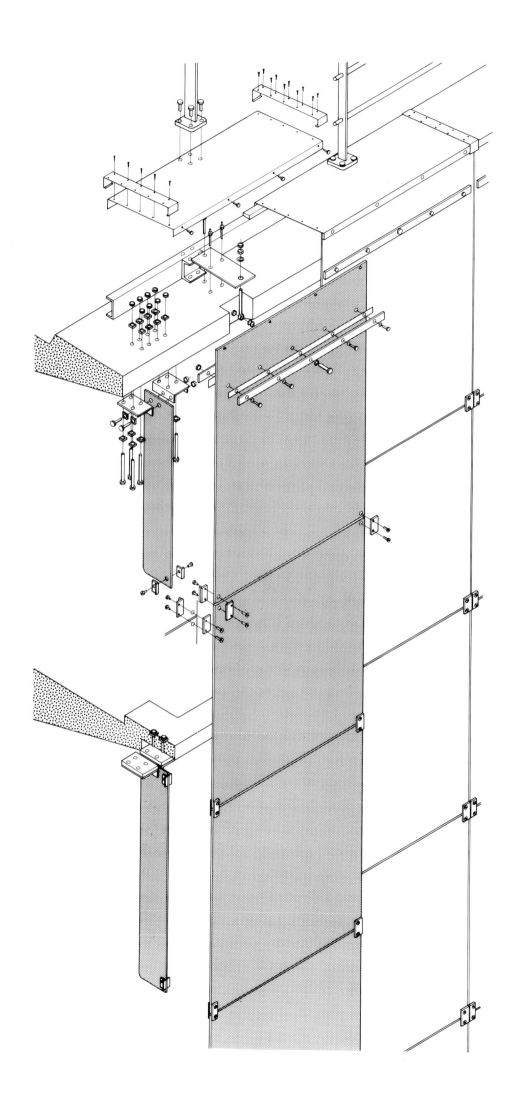

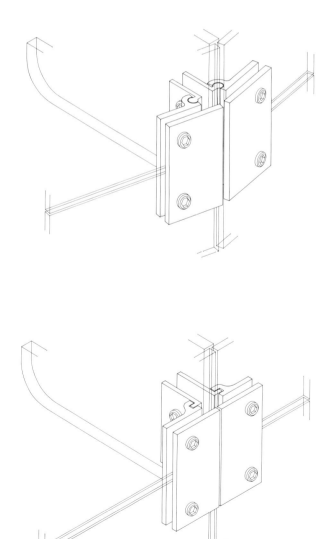

Detail section through glass wall at ground level

1 12mm armourplate antisun bronze glass

2 studded rubber floor and nosing

3 45mm screed with 35 x 35mm aluminium angle stop riveted to aluminium flat

4 neoprene gasket

5 Pilkington patch fitting fixed back to unistrut insert cast into concrete

6 concrete floor slab and edge beam

7 precast concrete

8 steel access section supported on nib and retained by 5mm thick brass straps. Note precast concrete profile beyond

9 leaf grating

10 rainwater drainage trap

11 precast concrete pavement slab

12 40mm diameter tube rail between 12mm steel plate uprights bolted to slab

gutter with nib

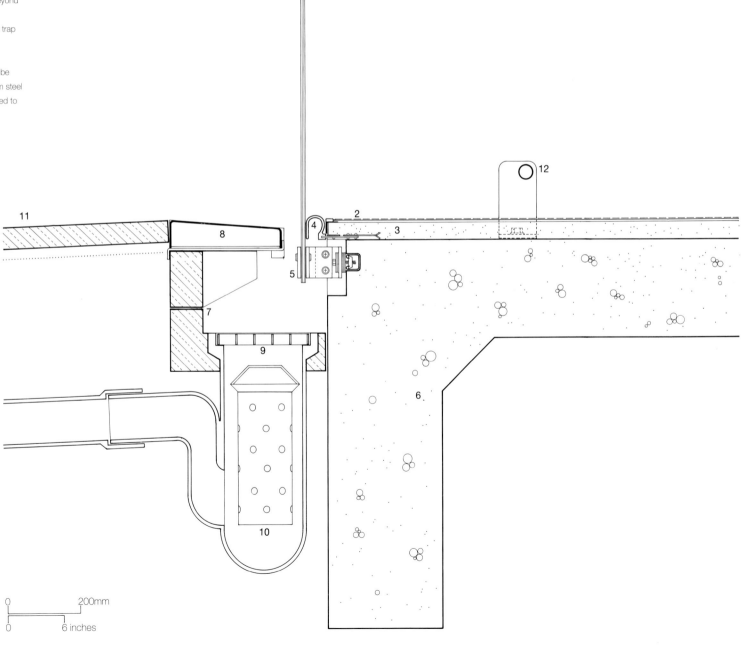

0 ____ 200mm

0 ____ 6 inches

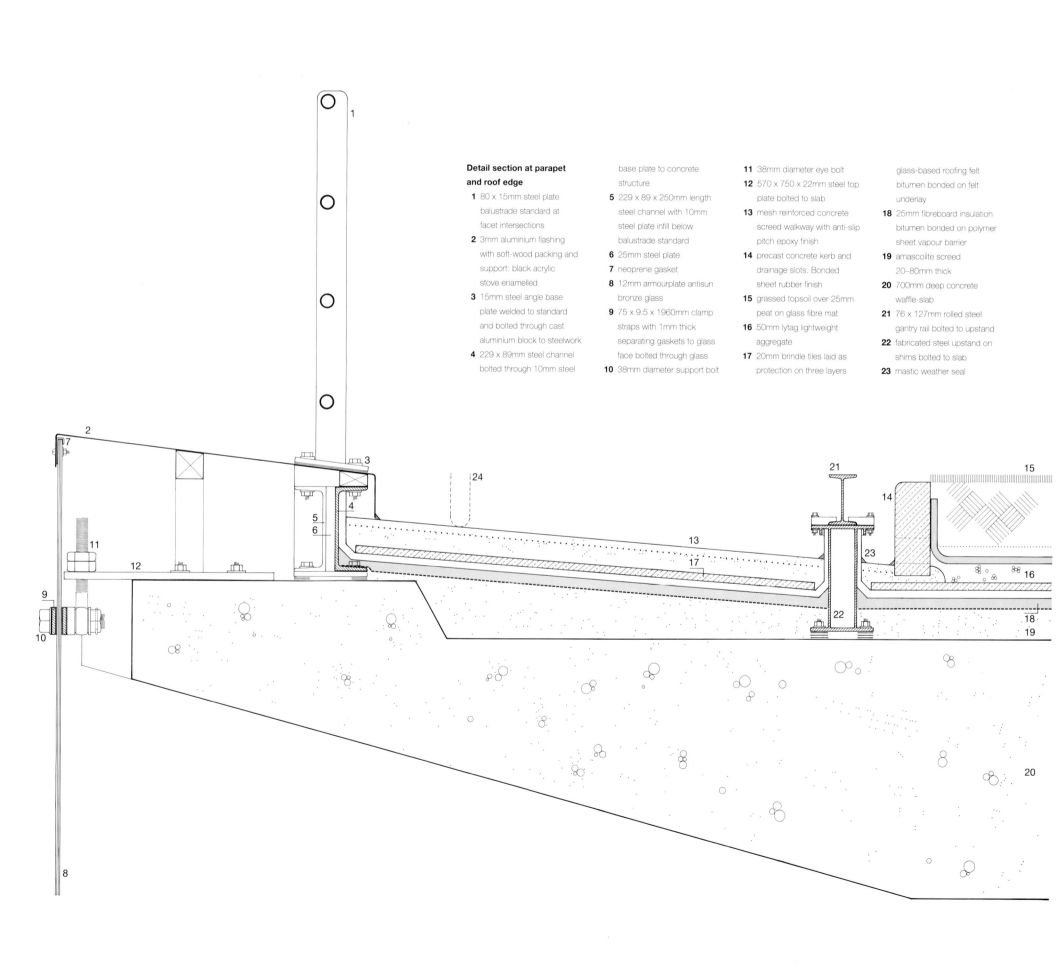

**Detail section at parapet
and roof edge**

1 80 x 15mm steel plate
balustrade standard at
facet intersections

2 3mm aluminium flashing
with soft-wood packing and
support: black acrylic
stove enamelled

3 15mm steel angle base
plate welded to standard
and bolted through cast
aluminium block to steelwork

4 229 x 89mm steel channel
bolted through 10mm steel

base plate to concrete
structure

5 229 x 89 x 250mm length
steel channel with 10mm
steel plate infill below
balustrade standard

6 25mm steel plate

7 neoprene gasket

8 12mm armourplate antisun
bronze glass

9 75 x 9.5 x 1960mm clamp
straps with 1mm thick
separating gaskets to glass
face bolted through glass

10 38mm diameter support bolt

11 38mm diameter eye bolt

12 570 x 750 x 22mm steel top
plate bolted to slab

13 mesh reinforced concrete
screed walkway with anti-slip
pitch epoxy finish

14 precast concrete kerb and
drainage slots. Bonded
sheet rubber finish

15 grassed topsoil over 25mm
peat on glass fibre mat

16 50mm lytag lightweight
aggregate

17 20mm brindle tiles laid as
protection on three layers

glass-based roofing felt
bitumen bonded on felt
underlay

18 25mm fibreboard insulation
bitumen bonded on polymer
sheet vapour barrier

19 amascolite screed
20–80mm thick

20 700mm deep concrete
waffle-slab

21 76 x 127mm rolled steel
gantry rail bolted to upstand

22 fabricated steel upstand on
shims bolted to slab

23 mastic weather seal

Detail section through restaurant glass wall and cill fixing

1 12mm armourplate antisun bronze glass

2 patch fitting fixed back to angle

3 100 x 100 x 6mm continuous aluminium angle bolted through 80 x 25mm hardwood block to steel channel

4 neoprene weathering gasket fixed to angle

5 carpet on screed

6 mesh reinforced concrete screed with anti-slip pitch epoxy finish

7 rainwater outlet beyond

8 precast concrete kerb with bonded sheet rubber finish

9 grassed topsoil over 25mm peat on glass fibre mat

10 50mm lytag lightweight aggregate

11 20mm brindle tiles laid as protection on three layers glass-based roofing felt bitumen bonded on felt underlay

12 25mm fibreboard insulation bitumen bonded on polymer sheet vapour barrier

13 amascolite screed 20–80mm thick

14 700mm deep concrete waffle-slab

15 cast iron gulley with leaf grating

16 cast iron rainwater outlet and grating

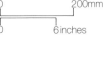

0   200mm

0   6 inches

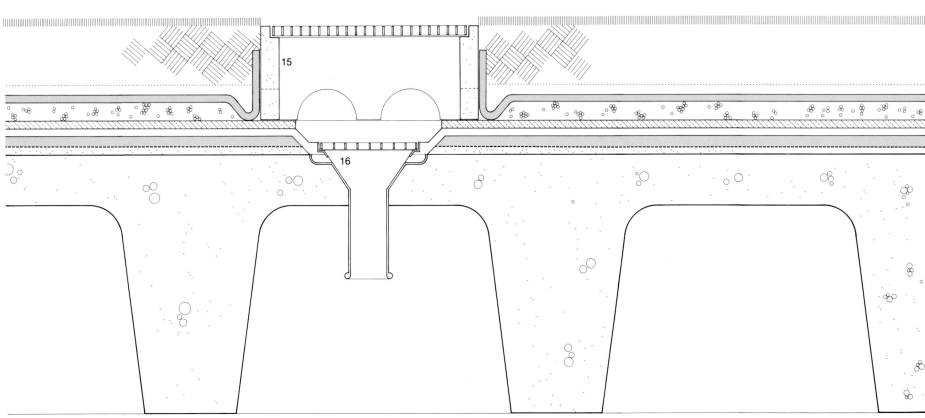

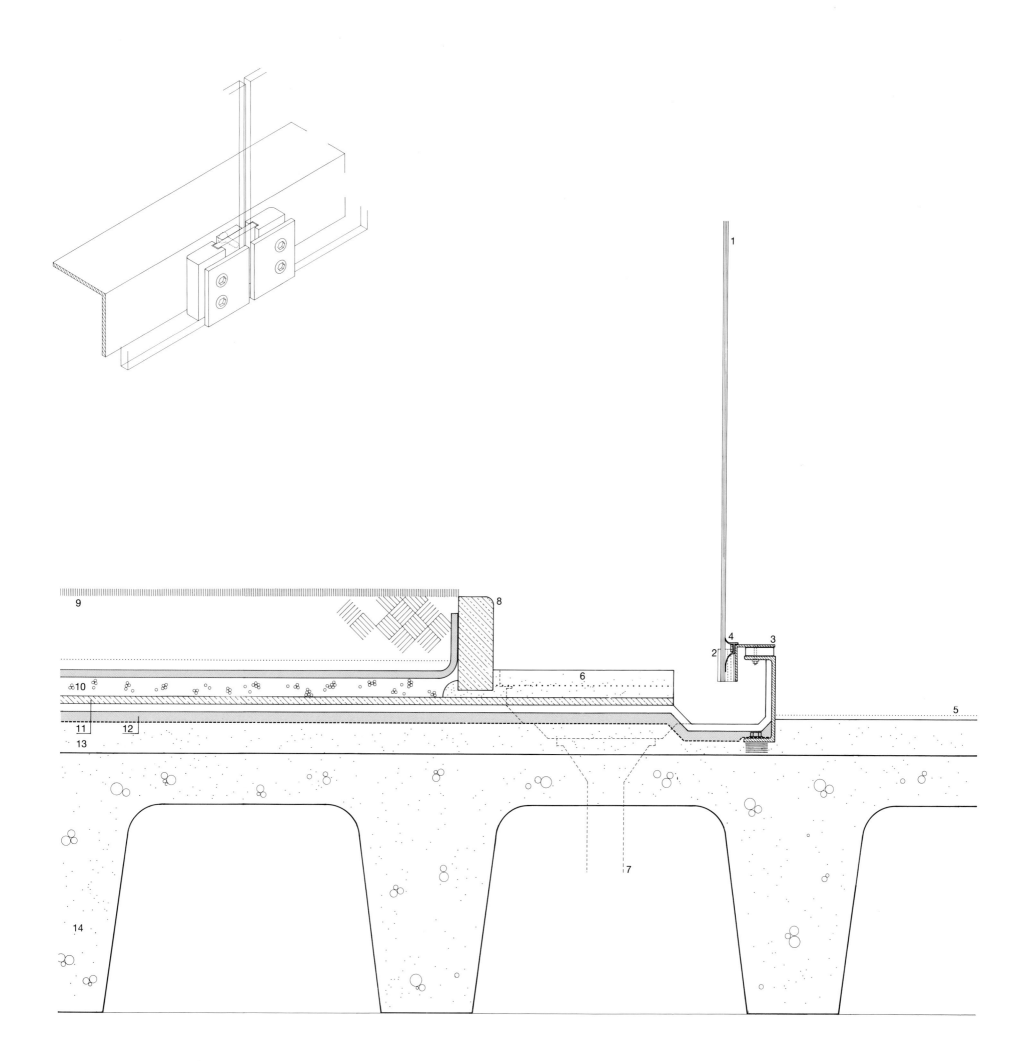

Specifications

Location 16 Friars Street, Ipswich, Suffolk. The mainline railway station is close by and is reached from London Liverpool Street in 75 minutes.

Client Willis Faber & Dumas Ltd, now Willis Corroon plc.

Client project committee Organized by Kenneth Knight, then company secretary of the Willis Faber Dumas Group. It comprised the immediate past-chairman of the group John Roscoe, the company secretary John Waite, the director in charge of buildings Steve Harding and the director in charge of staff. It was later joined by another senior executive director and the deputy chairman, who assumed overall responsibility for the project.

Company profile The company which owns the 'Willis Faber Dumas' building in Ipswich is now called Willis Corroon plc, of which Willis Faber Dumas and Willis Faber & Dumas are subsidiaries. Willis Corroon was formed in October 1990 by the merger of Willis Faber Dumas plc and the Corroon & Black Corporation of the United States. Willis Corroon is one of the world's largest insurance brokers. The Willis Faber Dumas side of the group goes back to the early 19th century with the formation of Henry Willis & Company in the City of London.

The Faber and Dumas names were the result of mergers, in 1897 and 1928, with other City companies. The Corroon & Black side originated in 1905 with the formation of R.F. Corroon & Company in the United States. Most of Willis Corroon's business comes from overseas. As a result of the 1990 merger it now has a very strong presence in the United States. However, the company has done business for many years in virtually every country in the world, and has particularly strong links with Japan, India, the Soviet Union and the principal European economies. The company currently handles annual gross premiums of about £5 billion with profits in excess of £100 million. World-wide the group employs over 11,000 people. Willis Faber & Dumas regards itself as the broker to the world's insurance industry; its administrative and accounting services, supporting the brokers at the London headquarters, are housed in the Ipswich building.

Architects and Consultants

Architects Sir Norman Foster & Partners, formerly Foster Associates, Riverside Three, 22 Hester Road, London SW11 4AN.

Project team David Bailey, Reg Bradley, Arthur Branthwaite, Loren Butt, Chubby Chhabra, Ian Dowsett, Roy Fleetwood, Norman Foster, Wendy Foster, Birkin Haward, Neil Holt, Michael Hopkins, David Johns, Jan Kaplicky, Rainer Koch, Truls Ovrum, Louis Pillar, Tony Pritchard, Ian Ritchie, Ken Shuttleworth, Mark Sutcliffe, Judith Warren, John Wharton, John Yates

Perspectives Helmut Jacoby, Jo van Heyningen

Models John Wharton

Project architects Mark Sutcliffe, Birkin Haward

Management Contractor Bovis Construction Ltd

Mechanical and Electrical Engineers Foster Associates; Loren Butt, Chubby Chhabra

Structural Engineers Anthony Hunt Associates; Anthony Hunt, David Hemmings

Civil Engineer John Taylor & Sons

Quantity Surveyors Davis Langdon & Everest

Partner in charge Clyde Malby

Project Surveyor Alec Waller

Acoustics Sound Research Laboratories

External wall consultants Martin Francis

Drainage Adrian Wilder

Landscape consultant John Allen

Contractors and Suppliers

Air-tube system Dialled Dispatches

Adhesives epoxy Shell Composites Ltd

Air-handling units Luwa (UK) Ltd; F.H.Biddle Ltd

Attenuators, grilles Trox Bros Ltd

Boilers Allan Ygnis Boilers Ltd

Carpet Carpet Manufacturing Co, Gilt Edge

Ceilings, suspended office area Brazier & Sons Ltd

Ceramic tiling and grilles to swimming pool Dennis M. Williams Ltd

Clocks Gent & Co.

CO_2 system Mather & Platt Ltd

Cold rooms R.E.A. Botts Ltd

Computer system, 1975 installation IBM 3750

Cooker, hob, dishwasher, refrigerator NEFF

Diesel generator Petbow Ltd

Diffusers, servery Waterloo Grille Co.

Doors, revolving T.B. Coleman & Sons Ltd

Doors, sliding Automatic Doors Ltd

Door closers Warshaw Building Supplies Ltd

Electrical contractor William Steward Ltd

Emergency lighting cubicles Chloride Industrial Batteries Ltd

Emergency lighting fittings Merchant Adventurers Ltd; NEM Co.

Entrance matting/external Avon Rubber Co.

Entrance matting/internal Jaymart Rubber & Plastics Ltd

Environmental services Drake & Scull Engineering

Escalators Marryat & Scott Ltd

Escalator well, balustrades Modern Art Glass

Fire shutter and controls Roller Shutters Ltd

Flexible ductwork Van den Bosch Ltd

Floor, raised H.H. Robertson (UK) Ltd

Floor, rubber Carl Freudenberg & Co. (UK) Ltd

Floor grilles Netaline Aire Distribution Products Ltd

Flue dilution fans Woods of Colchester Ltd

Foundations Cementation Piling & Foundations Ltd

Furniture, chairs and conference tables (Charles Eames) Herman Miller (UK) Ltd

Furniture, office Meredew Contract Furnishing

Furniture, PU workstations Programme Contract Interiors

Glass bends for doors G.T. & W. Ide Ltd

Glass wall Pilkington Bros Ltd; Modern Art Glass Ltd

Glass wall cleaning system Gascoigne Gush & Dent (Engineering) Ltd

Glazing for roof restaurant James Clark & Eaton Ltd

High-level air return panels D. Burkle & Sons Ltd

Lighting fittings Moorlite Electrical Ltd; Concord Lighting International Ltd; Merchant Adventurers Ltd; Thorn Lighting Ltd

Manual fire alarm installation Vesta Fire Alarms Ltd; Gent & Co.

Mechanical services Drake & Scull Ltd

Mobile filing racks Dexion Ltd

Partitions and high-level face panels Hauserman Ltd

Passenger and goods lift Marryat & Scott Ltd

Pneumatic valves and Controls Satchwell Control System Division

Public address system General Telephone System Ltd

Ramps Kensizer Engineering Co.

Reinforced Concrete Superstructure Diespeker Concrete Co. Ltd

Resin transformer Brentford Electric Ltd

Roof ceiling, stove-enamelled suppliers Burgess Architectural Products Ltd

Rooflights Pillar Patent Glazing Ltd

Roof waterproofing Briggs Amasco Ltd

Screeds C & P Plastering Ltd

Sprinkler system Matthew Hall (Mechanical Services) Ltd

Stainless steel Zealand Engineering Co.

Staircases Portia (Engineering) Ltd

Staircase balustrades Starkie Gardner Ltd

Steel Roof Structure Tubeworkers Ltd

Underfloor trunking, pvc pipework Key Terrain Ltd

Richard Rogers Partnership
Lloyd's Building
London 1978–86

Kenneth Powell

Photography
Richard Bryant, Martin Charles and others;
cover detail by Arcaid/Richard Bryant
Drawings
Richard Rogers Partnership, John Hewitt
Introduction
Patrick Heron

Blue Cranes in the Sky
Patrick Heron

'Only the really new can be truly traditional.'
T.S. Eliot

'A style is not a style until it has its beauty. But the beauty is born of the necessity; it is not an arbitrary choice; it is rather the exact solution of a problem.'
Herbert Read

Before the building was complete, walking along in the direction of Leadenhall Street (thinking of something else – although looking for Lloyd's), it surprised me: suddenly there it was, wrapped in flapping polythene, not unreminiscent of some of those fantasies illustrated in Claes Oldenburg's drawings or of a cliff wrapped by Christo, but far more interesting than either. A truly great building, like a great painting, always transmits its electricity the very instant it is first glimpsed. It is instantly recognized for what it is – however physically obscured it may be at first sighting. Similarly, a thin vertical slice of Picasso's *Guernica*, seen five rooms away in a museum, immediately makes such a vital communication that we are instantly certain of the magnitude of the statement that will be unfolded into total availability for us by merely moving closer, the obtruding walls or screens withdrawing themselves as we advance. Likewise, Salisbury Cathedral is already an electrifying architectural presence when still visually fragmented (half a spire, two fifths of a transept gable-end) by the near chimneys or roofs of houses in the approaches. And somehow, when one reaches the Cathedral Close, and the great façades are still visually only a third available to your eye because of the densely opaque foliage of strategically placed trees, your possession of an accurate awareness of the complete architectural reality of the building is not only not impaired by such visual fragmentation, but it is actually enhanced by it, as in a Cubist collage. In fact, there is even additional excitement and pleasure in the process itself of scanning from a visible section of, say, the nave, through (or past) nearby obstacles, to, say, a section of the tower just below the spire – and then joining these together mentally. And all this occurs, incidentally, despite the fact that Salisbury is placed, like a wedding cake in the middle of a table, well away from all encroachment. With most medieval cathedrals the crowding-in, around their walls, of other, unrelated buildings greatly increases this incidence of interruptions to the full viewing of the whole edifice. In fact, there is no 'full viewing' possible (and never was) of most cathedrals – even of York Minster.

Hemmed-in in the City
In the case of Pompidou, Piano and Rogers had done a Salisbury, in the sense that the great cake had had a table-top of horizontal space around it from the beginning. On three sides, at any rate, it is visible in its totality. But with Lloyd's the Richard Rogers Partnership (Rogers, John Young, Marco Goldschmied and Mike Davies) were faced with the hemmed-in cathedral situation to an extreme degree. Furthermore, they had to use a site of extreme and highly irregular complexity, a fragment of the ancient City of London's medieval street plan – and they have used it all, right out to the very kerbstone limits of Leadenhall Street, Lime Street and the less visible boundaries of Leadenhall Market's various properties. From this extremely irregular ground plan, whose complexity is almost too varied and subtle to have suggested any sort of 'geometry', Rogers has shot straight up skyward with a cluster of, as it were, conjoined towers, in themselves of the utmost geometric purity and sheerness. In plan these 'towers' occupy the awkward corners of the site rather as the cells of a honeycomb are extended into the most irregular of spaces. But it is in the very great contrast between the sensed medieval *plan* and the absolutely stark and stunningly geometric *elevations* of these towers that Lloyd's great fascination has one of its main sources.

All of which I suggest, not in order to point to some possible symbolism (all symbolism bores me) but in order to try to describe (if possible) one of the most astonishing artistic triumphs of our time. For that is what Lloyd's is: it is the greatest building to have arisen in the City of London since Sir Christopher Wren finally put the gold cross in the sky above the dome of St Paul's. What Richard Rogers' great building has graced the City skyline with are five steel cranes of exquisite blue: in time they will be seen to be just as beautiful as that orb and cross which constitute the final uppermost punctuation, over Wren's masterpiece.

Vertical crag
But to return to earth – or, rather, to Leadenhall Street, and to that first encounter with Lloyd's, which converted me instantly – there it was, a pale grey piece of hovering verticality, unidentifiable as material or structure, as yet: just a vertical crag reaching slenderly upwards, a mere wedge of battleship-grey, somehow notched with immensely regular teeth vertically, some rounded, others square-sharp, all the way up. The whole construction wedged, downwards, into and behind the 'normal' shapes of the street, out of which it seemed to grow with extreme naturalness…

That was a way of putting it – not very architectural. But my sole excuse for this article is that Lloyd's, from the first, has proved an overwhelming experience from a *purely aesthetic, purely visual standpoint*. And such an experience deserves to be communicated, if possible: demands it, in fact. But, of course, a building is architecture; it is not sculpture, for instance. Indeed, the quotation from Herbert Read I started with was one I made in a short speech in the Lecture Theatre of the RIBA, in Portland Place, the night the ICA was founded, in the autumn of 1949 – and Herbert was sitting in the front row (Ernesto Rogers and F.E. McWilliam were among the other five speakers). There I said: 'Naum Gabo's constructions are miniature and useless buildings: they are idealized, and again useless,

machines; that is to say, their use is aesthetic… [they make visible] the poetry of space, of organized air…'. Thirty odd years later we see the mature architecture of the Rogers office extending those very aesthetic criteria which a Constructivist sculptor, among others, pioneered – but arriving at his breathtakingly sheer and perfect forms in stainless steel, glass and concrete, by way of another route than that of the painter's or sculptor's purely aesthetic conscious concerns.

What is so brilliant and profound about the Lloyd's building is that at last it is patently impossible to separate out the two great elements whose fusion has always been indispensable in any great architecture of any time or place – its revolutionary and totally economic physical usefulness: and its total aesthetic satisfaction. Great beauty in a building only exists when these two apparently distinct areas of human need are seen to be *co-existing* in every single detail, however large or small; in every relationship of parts; and in every disposition of all major masses. This is most certainly the achievement at Lloyd's. Nothing at Lloyd's is there *only* for its aesthetic; nothing is there *only* for its use. What was so retrogressive, so decadent, about post-modernism was its actual, conscious *separation* of these qualities!

Of course, one notes that the architect and his team (for 'team' it has always been in Rogers' case, as he himself never tires of acknowledging) speak of their work as though the myriad solutions which the huge building *materializes*, were primarily practical. They barely break with the convention, in the realm of architectural exposition or discussion, which, almost unconsciously it seems, proscribes a direct discussion of the *aesthetic* itself. Yet the logic of the aesthetic is as absolute – and as scientific – as the logic of physical functions. The practical brilliance of the 'solution' of placing all the

services (lavatories, lifts, ventilating ducts, and so on) up the *outside* of the building is quite unanswerable; but if Rogers had not, as an artist, already *loved the appearance* of all the shining, geometric forms that this would expose to the whole of London outside – he would have adopted a different set of 'practical' solutions. Architecture all the time juggles function and pure aesthetic choice.

A hundred angles

My references to Gothic cathedrals, earlier on, were made not so much to imply that Lloyd's is of a complexity, and on a scale, that is the most ambitious imaginable (though it is) but rather to stress that (a) because of the city-density of its site the building will always be read as a presence glimpsed, in fragments, from a hundred angles, through and over (and under!) a hundred gaps and interstices in the surrounding architectural jungle; and (b) that its geometry will thus be something that will excite us although only seen from very acute angles, and never from 'straight in front'. The architect's elevations would be available, in reality, only to a helicopter pilot hovering at a point 90 degrees out from the *centre* of each 'façade', or elevation subject. No-one would sense, looking up at Lloyd's, that the great core, or body, of the complex was a neat rectangular box, inside which a gigantic rectangular slot of space over 200 feet deep, was sunk. The service towers, so dominantly visible, totally disguise that great central symmetry, which is the main body of the building. By the exquisite asymmetry of their positioning, at the corners of the irregular site, they assume an enormously varied set of visual relationships with one another *and* with the barely-sensed box of the core. The richness of this arrangement shows in the fact that, for instance, these towers all seem to be of different heights – when they are not.

Spaces and solids

As you walk about outside Lloyd's you are supplied with a huge vertical configuration of exceedingly definite forms whose definite and precise relationships *change* with every step you take. If one sees the 12 lavatory-pods which rise in a column above one another, or the 12 semi-circular stair-platforms, making another vertical column (the spaces *between* each box or half-circle being as precise in proportion as the boxes themselves, of course: spaces and solids, as in great painting, being of equal value) – if you see all this in an elevation drawing, you would merely note the exquisite proportion of each unit – each sharp rectilinear box being perfect in proportion, and each punctuated with an exquisitely placed circular window (a Nicholson relief could not be more beautiful in its relating of circle to rectangle) – and you would note the perfect *regularity* of the spacing, in the vertical arrangement of these boxes. But translated into a 300 foot stainless-steel building that regularity is overlaid, in your awareness, by the distortions of *perspective*: they soar away upwards, getting smaller and bluer. And, of course, any solid object, walked round, swells and contracts and changes its silhouette, as well as all its internal relationships, a million times. If our eyes could take instant snapshots of what we actually see, at every second, these would prove the point. A great building is one which supplies a moving tapestry of highly satisfactory and significant moving shapes (and colours) to all who approach it. And, of course, it continues to feed your eyes with endlessly satisfying formal relationships as you finally enter – for a building is a sculpture you can go inside. Once inside, it is your entire visual field, from eyelid to eyelid, which is occupied by the configurations controlled by the architect. Wherever you look, whatever you see composes into the equivalent of pictorial compositions. At every step you take, ele-

ments typical of the Rogers team's highly personal formal language arrange and rearrange themselves. And one is also extremely aware that all and every detail – handrails, window-frames, doorknobs – is a perfect microcosm of the building's largest features – or rather, a microcosmic variant.

The fact that this idiom has been given the label 'high-tech' is now a disadvantage. High-tech is fine in so far as it focuses attention on the nature of the component parts of a Rogers building; but it is intellectually obstructive as a description of his art as architecture. It is an inadequate term in our consideration of almost any *total* building by Rogers, because, although it is unquestionable that each and every component part of a building by his office looks mechanical in origin, and is often convincingly like the parts of a machine (and nearly all of them are made off-site), nevertheless all these spars, braces, brackets, plates, tubes, grids of every description, strips and rods of stainless-steel – all in being finally slotted together into a three-dimensional *design* thereby lose much of their individual identity. And it is design which involves real space, in all its dimensions, enclosing it, excluding it, threading it, making it 'visible' by *delineating* it. All these parts, mechanically produced, are 'delineators'.

But all art is primarily a matter of organizational configuration: it is how you relate one unit, one element to another, or one cluster or group of elements to another group, that gives rise to the art-work. It is almost irrelevant just *what* each component of such visual organization may be. A garden already exists, for instance, the moment three stones, a clump of grass, a handful of sand or pebbles and three weeds are first isolated and then related.

In the case of Lloyd's (getting on for 20,000 drawings were made in Rogers' office, one gathers) the parts are all very beautiful in their own right – as single objects scattered on the foundry floor, for instance. And in passing, one may reflect that the 'prefabricated' carved pieces of stone that must have littered the masons' yards of York, so long ago, would also have looked very 'geometric', very abstract, and unlike the tree or plant-like vaults and columns they were destined to sink *their* individual outlines into. In the so-to-speak mosaic-of-parts-in-relief of the external walls of Lloyd's, in Lime Street, one gets a good view, for instance, of those 'shapes' that look rather like the suction-head of a vacuum cleaner which you would use for cleaning carpets. It is repeated at mesmerizing intervals and its 'decorative' effect is stunning. It is as beautiful as a detail, as any capital of a pilaster on a stone façade might be. But the aesthetic excitement is multiplied by the knowledge of its precise physical function; the feeling resulting from knowing of its *double* necessity.

Unity in disparity

There is another feature of Lloyd's which I find most exciting. In painting, I've always been aware of that even consistency of touch, or design, right across the picture surface, which is the minor artist's short cut to unity. Instead, I've always looked for evidence of those startling changes of gear which only the great painters manage, and in which one finds that the unifying rhythms, so to speak, are all superficially at variance with one another, from area to area of the canvas. Tight, heavy, regular brush strokes in one part giving way, in an adjacent area, to wildly looping, barely-touching-the-surface gestures: geometrically weighty forms suddenly abutting on feathery, speckled or scribbled surfaces; and so on and all within the same painting; all settling down together into a stupendous sense of absolute formal unity – *despite* all these abrupt *changes of gear*. There is abundant evidence of this unity in disparity in Lloyd's.

For instance, the immaculate stainless-steel surfaces of the stairs and lavatories stacked in the six satellite towers have a feeling of great plastic (in Roger Fry's sense) weightiness; a feeling almost of being as heavy as a sculpture in turned steel. They have the immensely certain pulse, or beat, of the great Cubist paintings of Picasso or Braque: a very definite, very regular articulation. But the great vertical pipes, pillars and ducts (some in concrete: most in glittering steel) which go up alongside, have a much lighter feel.

Capitals on columns

And *all* these vertical stripes and stacks of the satellite towers are, of course, in very sharp, formal contrast with *all* the surfaces of the main building, where glass predominates, elegantly, delicately, in a pattern of rectangular subdivisions. But most pronounced of all these 'changes of gear' are the four, three-storey plant-rooms which sit right up on top of four of the satellite towers. These are really in the sky, and are therefore prominent all over the City. And their whole placement, up there, great, pale, lightweight, steel boxes *balancing*, one feels, on the narrower columns of the respective satellite towers, is a stroke of formal genius. Not only do they give that most original 'top-heavy' look to the building's sky-profile (they project out from their column-like tower supports – indeed, now one thinks of it, they're rather like wide capitals on thin columns) but they seem positively flimsy in construction, and in their cladding, which looks like corrugated pale-blue paper from a distance.

This exquisite feeling of comparative temporariness, this apparent slightness of construction, by comparison with the towers below, is a reflection of the architect's proclaimed aim in making their contents (the plant which may need renewing from time to time) more easily accessible for replacement, than it would be buried in the entrails of the building.

But still outside, one notices certain other significant idiom-shifts, or changes of tempo. There are the very slimly drawn spiral stairs which twist their way up alongside the blank stainless-steel panels of the walls of the four plant-rooms. The skinny, writhing, extremely linear corkscrew spirals are contrasted wonderfully with the blankness of those cubes in the sky. It is again *on top* of the 'paper-thin', sharply square boxes of the four plant-rooms, balanced up there against the sky, that the final touches of the four blue cranes have been *drawn in* in blue. Blue against blue – or grey or yellow, according to the London weather. They are rather like the wine glass Picasso merely indicates, merely draws in, on top of a box-like table he's painted in so powerfully and broadly. They are also a signature in the City's sky; *here*, below, is Lloyd's… in case it is almost invisible at the moment in question because the steel of the towers just happens to have gone pale lemon-yellow-grey, making a sort of hole in Leadenhall Street – and all because the afternoon sky behind you *is* lemon, just for a moment. Reflective steel takes on a hundred differing colours, tones – just whatever the day is supplying. The whole building can turn into a deep ultramarine blue, with bars of dark violet or pale cerulean blue across it…

Then the massive rectangle of the main body of Lloyd's is itself disguised further by the fact of the four terraces, stepping down from north-east to south-west, which define the upper limits of four sections of the great cube. These add enormously to the subtlety of the almost unanalysable image the whole building presents and ensure the complete and final disguising of the great central cube – rescuing it from any trace of the monolithic, for instance. But so does the insertion, along the exact centre of this truly cubist core, of the astonishing atrium. Again, it is the atrium's delicacy of definition which con-

trasts so satisfactorily with the cubist solidity of the main building, the very slender beams, spars and braces which define this great glass vault over 200 feet above the heads of the thousands of underwriters swarming below, or gliding up and across the well, under the atrium, on criss-crossed escalators whose undersides glow yellow-gold, from hidden lights. And the quality of the light which filters down in the immensely lofty atrium is magically soft yet clear – a blend of daylight and artificial light sprayed down, so to speak, from the undersides of the numerous floors which open onto it. Pale blue carpet everywhere contributes to this soft clarity of light, no doubt. And so also, one feels, do the phenomenally smooth surfaces of the great, jointed concrete pillars, over 200 feet high, which support the atrium, visible from top to bottom (echoes of the Purbeck marble 'drainpipes' which, standing free, and bracketed, accompany the stone piers in the nave at Salisbury). These great pillars (concrete cast on site against steel shuttering) have a luminous, matt grey surface of fascinating subtlety: almost impossible to focus on, so unfamiliar as a texture/colour/material. 'Are they really concrete? Not matt silk?'

Built against the odds

If Pompidou was to some extent a triumph for iconoclastic daring on the part of governments from which such boldness was not altogether unthinkable – and its 30,000 visitors daily is a verdict none can ignore – Lloyd's has, far more surprisingly, been commissioned, *and built*, in the very heart of the most aesthetically reactionary and cautious part of London.

Personally I think it is unquestionably Richard Rogers' masterpiece. Seeing it through to completion – in spite of a climate in which architectural criticism has plunged to new depths of sheer decadence – is certainly as great a tribute to the team's genius as designing it was in the first place. **P.H.**

Opposite The building cascades down towards Leadenhall Market revealing its great atrium.
Left Because of the city-density of its site the building will always be read as a presence glimpsed, in fragments, from a hundred angles.

1

2

3

4

1 The market had its beginnings in Lloyd's coffee house, where shipowners and merchants met.
2 From the 1770s to the 1920s Lloyd's operated from the prestigious confines of the Royal Exchange in the heart of the City.
3 The Royal Exchange was an imposing location which Lloyd's eventually outgrew.
4 Edwin Cooper gave Lloyd's a triumphal gateway from Leadenhall Street – a feature which the Rogers scheme preserved.

A Modern Marketplace

No other modern building in London has achieved the iconic status of Lloyd's. Completed in 1986, it has become a symbol of the capital, and of the City of London in particular, as well as an emblem of the renaissance of British architecture in the 1980s. Built as the headquarters of an organization which is one of the foundations of British capitalism, it is a radical, even a revolutionary, structure which embodies the Richard Rogers Partnership's vision of a new urbanism. Created for an historic and, in some respects, conservative corporation, it was designed to accommodate change. No new City building of the post-war era has so fearlessly rejected the compromise of historical pastiche – of 'keeping in keeping' – and yet none has made such a positive contribution to the historic locality in which it stands. At once forward-looking and, at the same time, evocative of some of the most captivating visions of the heroic age of modern architecture, Lloyd's is a building which is full of tensions and contradictions. A machine for making money? A place for people? An abstractly beautiful piece of sculpture? Lloyd's is all these and more. It appears, in retrospect, as the product of a heroic moment in British architecture. Yet Lloyd's was not the product of chance circumstances but of a unique process of partnership and collaboration. It is the outcome of that rare virtue in the modern building world: inspired and intelligent patronage.

Lloyd's of London is a marketplace. Like other markets, it is a meeting place for buyers and sellers. The stall-holders in this market, the underwriters, sell an invisible commodity: insurance. The buyers – the brokers – in this, the world's biggest insurance market, act, directly or indirectly, for millions of individuals around the world, who want to insure anything from a family car to a space laboratory, from a house to a chain of hotels, from a motor launch to an oil-rig. (Marine insurance remains the mainstay of Lloyd's.) This is a place which trades in risks. The risks can be huge and are spread between a large number of individuals, many of whom rarely, if ever, enter the Lloyd's building. Sometimes the worst happens. A major disaster means that the syndicates of 'names' who underwrite policies have to pay up. Fortunes have been made – and lost – at Lloyd's. In the end, someone has to pay. The essence of Lloyd's is taking risks – it is neither static nor staid. Nor is it a monolithic corporate body, like the big banks and insurance companies which are its City neighbours. Lloyd's is a club, where the members elect the Committee and pay the administrative staff. It is a place for individualists, a fact which Richard Rogers and his team could never forget when they were designing its new headquarters.

When the Rogers practice first got to know Lloyd's, in 1977, the famous City institution had moved the centre of its operations twice in half a century. Lloyd's takes its name from Edward Lloyd, a Welshman who opened a coffee house in Tower Street, close to the Tower of London, in 1688. It became a meeting place for seafarers, shipowners, merchants and for the first underwriters, who insured ships and their cargoes. By the 1770s Lloyd's had left the coffee house era and found accommodation in the Royal Exchange – a token of its growing importance and respectability. It was to stay there until the

8

5

6

7

5 Cooper's great Roman arch
led to a handsome corridor,
linking the street with the heart
of the institution.
6 The 1928 Cooper building
housed a 'Room' of great dignity
– but it soon became inadequate
and, after 1958, was subdivided
as offices.
7 In 1958 the new Lloyd's
building was opened, linked by a
bridge to the 1928 block. It was
designed to 'see Lloyd's into the
21st century'.
8 The 1958 Room was seen
as the final answer to Lloyd's
space problems but soon
proved too small.

1920s when the sheer scale of its operations made a move inevitable. A site was acquired in Leadenhall Street and Sir Edwin Cooper, an architect who was a favourite with prestigious City institutions, was commissioned to design the new building. The site was, in fact, quite awkward, since most of the frontage on to the main thoroughfare of Leadenhall Street had been taken up by another Cooper-designed block, Royal Mail House. Cooper, however, gave Lloyd's a powerful presence by contriving its main entrance through an imposing triumphal arch. A majestic corridor led from the main door to the 'Room', a grandiose 16,000 square foot space where underwriting business was conducted. Completed in 1928, Cooper's building was soon inadequate in size. Luckily, Royal Mail House came on to the market and was acquired by Lloyd's in 1936. The two buildings were rather untidily joined together, producing a lot of circuitous corridors and inconvenient spaces.

Lloyd's survived the Second World War and the Cooper building was untouched by the German bombs which flattened the adjacent site just across Lime Street. Foreseeing the need for expansion, Lloyd's sensibly bought this land in 1950. In 1952 work started on a 'new' Lloyd's. Though the existing buildings were to remain, it was planned to move the 'Room', the Chairman's suite, the members' restaurant (traditionally known as the 'Captains' Room') and the other principal facilities into the new building. The architect of the new building was Terence Heysham, a former assistant of Edwin Cooper who had assumed the latter's mantle as 'architect to Lloyd's'. Rejecting the modernism which had captured the public's imagination in the recent Festival of Britain, Heysham produced a suave but rather bland exercise in stripped Classicism, a comfortable rather than a challenging building. It was linked to the 1928 building by a bridge, 38 feet above Lime Street.

After Heysham's Lloyd's opened in 1958, the 1928 building (with Royal Mail House incorporated) was extensively altered internally to provide offices and space for the administrative staff – Cooper's Room was ruthlessly partitioned. The accommodation was, an old Lloyd's hand remembered, "appallingly tatty – but the staff didn't count for much in those days". The 1958 building inspired a mixed response. Well-built of traditional materials and faced in the City's favoured Portland stone, it lacked the rich character of Cooper's Lloyd's – one wit described its rather anaemic style as "late French lavatorial". Marine underwriters, who were accommodated on the ground floor, tended to like Heysham's Room. Others, banished to a gallery, were less content. The matter of 'who sits where' was to come to the fore again when Rogers' building was being planned. The location of the 'boxes' from which the underwriters operate has always been seen as significant in terms of attracting business.

It was the continued growth of Lloyd's during the 1960s and 1970s which made Heysham's building, designed to 'see Lloyd's into the 21st century', redundant. The Room, with a capacity of 1,500, was simply too small. More underwriting space was needed – and quickly if Lloyd's was not to suffer. Some little-used spaces within the 1958 building were requisitioned and there was talk of building a link across Lime Street so that the old and new Rooms could be joined together. (The City Corporation made it clear that this would

9

not be countenanced – the street was public property.) The answer seemed
to lie in the 1928 building, which could be refurbished or even totally rebuilt
within the existing walls. Alternatively, the best solution might be to demolish
it and commission a new building. But there were problems with this
approach. The Cooper building was listed (grade II) by the government in
1977 and there was no guarantee that consent would be given to pull it down.

At this stage, it looked likely that the job of rebuilding would go to Arup
Associates, a practice which had recently completed new administrative
offices for Lloyd's at Chatham in Kent. The difficult process of decanting had
been masterminded by Lloyd's head of administration, Courtenay Blackmore.
Appointed to Lloyd's in 1971, Blackmore (1922–92) had no training in architectural matters (after a distinguished war service he had worked as a person-
nel manager for ICI in the north-east of England) but was to become a significant figure in British architecture. He established a close working relationship
with Arup Associates, whose building at Chatham became highly popular
with its users. Blackmore had great respect for the firm's multi-disciplinary
approach and its practical ways of solving problems. He valued the amicable
working relationship he had with Philip Dowson, Ronald Hobbs and Peter
Foggo and wanted to run the City project as he had run that at Chatham. Arup
Associates had served Lloyd's well and when it came to appointing architects
for the City site, they might have seemed the obvious choice.

Lloyd's did not want a standard City office block, either in layout or appearance. Since Heysham had completed his building in 1958, the City had whole-
heartedly embraced American-style commercial modernism. Most of the new
office buildings of the 1960s and early-1970s were desperately mediocre,
but there were exceptions. The firm of Gollins Melvin Ward had built the
Commercial Union tower, a creditable attempt at the Miesian ideal, just across
the road from Lloyd's. Richard Seifert's NatWest Tower, nearing completion at
the time Rogers came to Lloyd's, was expressive as well as tall. Many influential Lloyd's members felt, however, that Lloyd's needed a distinctive building
with a strong 'image' of quality – amongst them was Ian Findlay, deputy chairman and responsible for property matters. Findlay had taken a clear view on
Lloyd's accommodation problems. "We have to build a new Lloyd's: that can
be the only effective solution", he told the Committee.

Yet when, early in 1977, Lloyd's began the search for an architect, it
remained unclear exactly what that architect was being asked to do. The
notion of Lloyd's moving out of the City was quickly dismissed: its business
was based on personal contact and could not flourish beyond the Square
Mile. Could the 1928 building be satisfactorily remodelled? Or was a new
building the only answer? Lloyd's plans came to the notice of Gordon
Graham, recently elected as President of the Royal Institute of British
Architects, eager to see some of Britain's bright young practices get work
and well aware that Lloyd's could be the British commission of the decade.
Graham went to see Findlay and advised him that Lloyd's should look not for
a scheme but for a strategy – one priority was keeping Lloyd's in operation
during the rebuilding process. "I told Lloyd's to find an architect and work with

9 Lloyd's has a distinctive
presence on the London skyline,
contrasting with the bulky and
bland profiles of typical post-
1945 commercial buildings.
10 An early sketch by Richard
Rogers: Lloyd's as a medieval
castle, an open space
surrounded by towers.
11 GMW's Commercial Union
Tower was one of the most
admired of recent office
buildings at the time that the
Rogers scheme for Lloyd's was
commissioned.
12 The Lloyd's building reflects
the informal, 'medieval'
character of the City streets, a
context which inspired the
architects' approach.

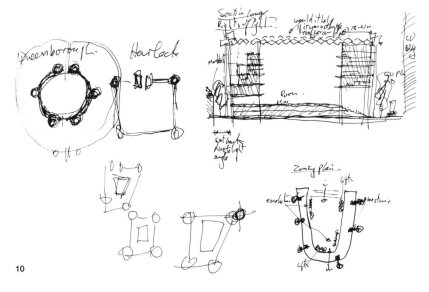

10

11

12

13 Lloyd's was determined to create a building of distinct character which stood out from the general run of City blocks.
14 The Rogers building grows out of the streets, filling its site and providing a series of visual incidents for the passer-by. It is a true London building.

13

14

15 The Lloyd's team (left to right): Geoff Ashworth (Monk Dunstone Associates), John Young (RRP), Sir Peter Green (Chairman of Lloyd's), Marco Goldschmied (RRP), Peter Rice (Ove Arup & Partners), Richard Rogers, Mike Davies (RRP), Courtenay Blackmore (Lloyd's), · Brian Pettifer (Bovis), Nick Ayres (MDA), John Smith (Bovis). Missing from this picture are John Bathgate (Lloyd's project coordinator) and Tom Barker (Ove Arup & Partners).

15

him on a development strategy before even thinking about designs", Graham recalls. Gordon Graham stressed the importance of a good brief as the basis for a competition. The competition should be by invitation and Graham helped to assemble a list of 'possibles'. A list of a dozen was drawn up and all were asked to submit examples of their work. Six were then selected to work up their ideas. The last six included (at the suggestion of Graham) Rogers as well as Norman Foster's Foster Associates, known for its stunning and recently completed Willis Faber & Dumas headquarters in Ipswich. Arup Associates was inevitably included. The other three finalists reflected Lloyd's desire to be seen as international in outlook. There was I.M. Pei, the Chinese–American architect who was then completing the masterly East Wing at the National Gallery in Washington DC; Webb Zarafa Menkes Housden, a very large Canadian firm with lots of commercial experience, but not a leader in design matters, and the French Serete practice, a more eccentric choice.

A Strategy for Growth

The chance of a big job at the heart of London could not have come at a better time for Rogers. He was still formally in partnership with Renzo Piano, whom he had met in 1970 and teamed up with to win the Pompidou Centre competition the following year. Getting the commission for a 1 million square foot building at the centre of Paris was a triumph for both men. Once the building was completed in 1977, however, Rogers found himself with little work. Piano was working in France and Italy. Rogers had an excellent team which had worked on the Pompidou Centre – including John Young, Marco Goldschmied, Mike Davies, Laurie Abbott and Alan Stanton, along with Richard Soundy, who was a recent recruit – but little for them to do. Rogers brought in John Young and Marco Goldschmied as partners in October 1977, but retained the title of Piano & Rogers. The recession had undermined the British development scene. John Young, who, like Abbott, had been with Rogers since the days of the Team 4 practice, was considering taking up cab driving to supplement his income. Rogers had found work teaching part-time at UCLA and spent a good deal of time in California. Goldschmied took time off to return to his studies.

Pompidou had made Rogers world-famous, but was as much a liability as an asset where Lloyd's was concerned. The building had been partly inspired by the work of Archigram, a group which had flourished at the Architectural Association school in London (where Rogers studied). Like Cedric Price's legendary but unexecuted Fun Palace, Beaubourg was envisaged as a centre of "self-participatory education and entertainment". Rogers had discovered further inspiration in the work of the Italian Futurists, the Russian Constructivists and the great British engineers of the 19th century, Joseph Paxton in particular. The Pompidou Centre was about fun, but it was also a building with a serious social message. It was not a message which went down especially well in the City of London. "If you are appointed", Marco Goldschmied was asked by Ian Findlay during a break in the interviews, "will we get another Pompidou Centre?" Goldschmied was taken off

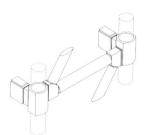

17

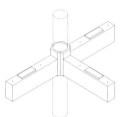

16 Axonometrics of the pre-cast concrete 'kit of parts' for the service towers.

17 The layers of structure, services and cladding articulate the elevation.

18 A concrete column and bracket assembly as built.

19 The services are carefully worked into the architecture of the exterior.

20 A plan of the concrete structure of the building.

21, opposite A detail of the concrete column and bracket assembly on the exterior.

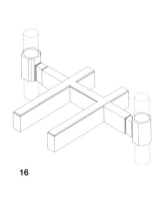

16

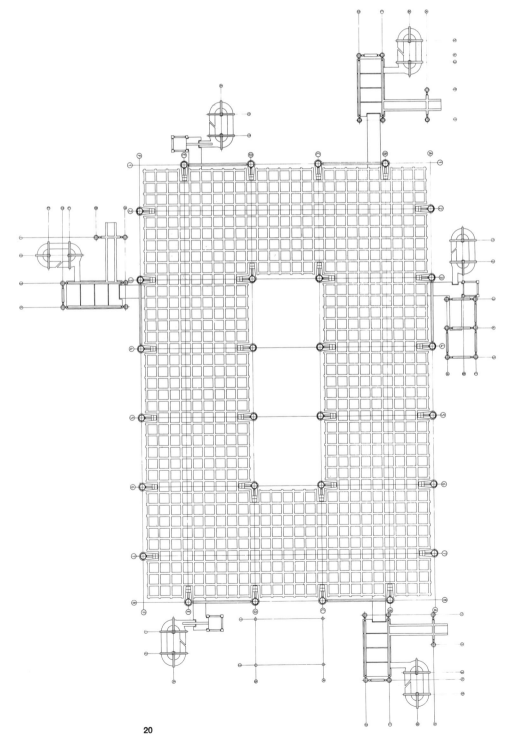

18

19

20

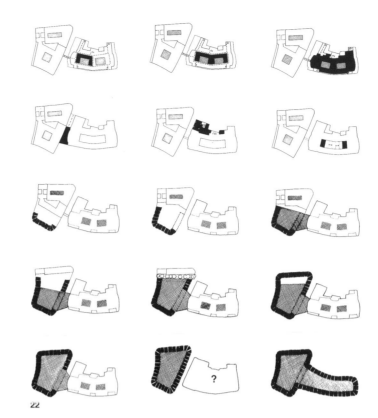

22

guard – "er, no", he replied. He explained that the Paris building had been a response to a brief and to a site: there would be no coloured ducts climbing the walls in Leadenhall Street.

Richard Rogers Partnership's victory in the Lloyd's competition was the outcome of the firm's response to Gordon Graham's formula – strategy first, scheme second. The first briefing at Lloyd's for the six short-listed firms was on 8th November 1977, Rogers being accompanied by Young and Goldschmied. There was a tour of the premises, a detailed explanation of Lloyd's special needs and a sociable lunch where the Lloyd's team met the contenders. Blackmore explained that "we wanted flexibility – with scope for the market to grow or contract". This requirement predisposed Lloyd's to accept a radically modern building. The six practices were asked to produce their initial ideas within four months. Two days after the briefing, the news came through that the 1928 building had been listed.

Rogers went immediately to one member of the Pompidou team whom he regarded as indispensable: Peter Rice. Rice (1935–92) was a member of the great engineering office Ove Arup & Partners, the parent organization of Arup Associates. He had established his reputation through his work on the Sydney Opera House. His contribution to the Pompidou Centre was of critical importance and he became a close associate of both Piano (with whom he worked on many projects) and Rogers (who saw him as "part of our inner cabinet"). Peter Rice told Rogers to "steer away from architecture" and think about giving Lloyd's not just space but time too. He endorsed Marco Goldschmied's clear view that the phasing of the rebuilding and the continuity of business was vital. It had been stressed in the initial briefing that Lloyd's wanted to see its problems solved for a good 50 years. A flexible place of work, rather than a one-off monument, was required. Rice worked with the Rogers team on a strategy for space. It was not immediately obvious that the 1928 building had to go. The range of possibilities would be presented and the client invited to work through them with the architects, who offered 26 distinct options, including one providing for conversion of the Cooper building.

The six short-listed practices returned to Lloyd's to expound their ideas in March 1978 and were interviewed by a newly established Redevelopment Committee. Neither the French nor the Canadians impressed the Committee – neither seemed to have given much thought to the vital issue of keeping Lloyd's in business during the rebuilding. According to Gordon Graham, Foster's presentation was "oddly half-hearted, as if he didn't want the job". Lloyd's was looking for commitment, "body and soul", according to Blackmore. Pei produced a fine model and spoke eloquently but there were doubts about appointing an architect based 4,000 miles away. Two firms impressed: Arup Associates and Rogers. The Committee felt that either could do the job very well. Arup were still the obvious choice. The Rogers team (Rogers, Young, Goldschmied and Rice) impressed greatly – partly because it was so obviously a team, not an individual – but the firm was relatively inexperienced. Although the practice was called Piano & Rogers, there was no sign of Piano. Where was the mysterious Piano?

23

24

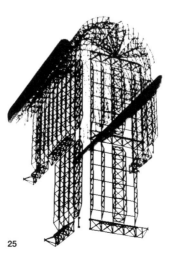

25

22 The architects offered Lloyd's a series of options for the site, ranging from adaptation of the existing buildings to total rebuilding.
23 A RRP drawing of 1980 showing the presence of the building on the street.
24 A pre-construction model shows relatively slim service towers.
25 A computer analysis by Arup of the atrium structure.

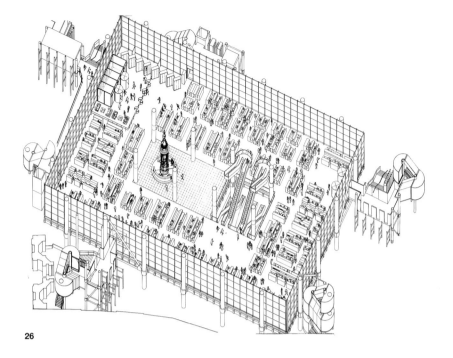

26

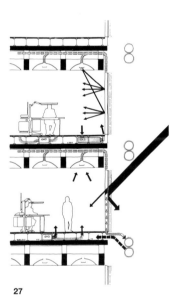

27

26 A 1985 axonometric
showing a draft layout plan for
the Room.
27 The Lloyd's high-
performance wall.
28 An early axonometric of the
exterior depicts very
understated service towers.
29 A rendered elevation
submitted as part of the Lloyd's
planning application.

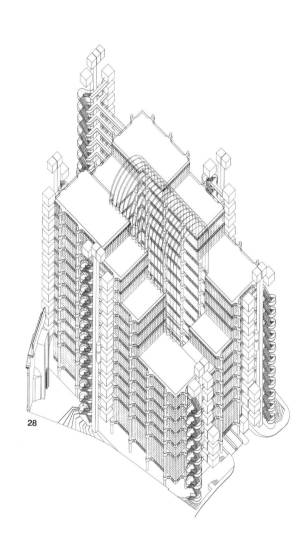

28

29

In the event, both Richard Rogers Partnership and Arup Associates were
asked to return for a 'run off' interview in April. Brilliantly restating the options
for Lloyd's, the Rogers team carried the day, helped by the presence of Mike
Davies, Jack (later Sir Jack) Zunz, a highly respected senior partner in Ove
Arup & Partners, and Renzo Piano (who had travelled specially from Italy).
The Committee was convinced that there was only one choice and even
Blackmore, loyal to Arup to the end, conceded the victory to Rogers. The reasons for the Rogers Partnership's victory were straightforward. The practice
seemed to offer the best hope that Lloyd's could achieve the kind of flexibility
it needed. Lloyd's was impressed too by the range of skills it demonstrated:
this was no one-man band.

Rogers learned of the appointment when Courtenay Blackmore called him
in the USA, where he had immediately returned to his teaching commitments.
He was soon on his way back to Britain, anxious to expand the team for the
new project. The Rogers office in the days of Lloyd's became the forcing
ground for new architectural talents, generating many of the new practices
who were to make their mark on the London scene during the 1980s.

The first step, Rogers felt, was to find out how Lloyd's worked – by talking
to the people who worked there and discovering their needs and aspirations.
Marco Goldschmied, the crucial strategist for the scheme, threw himself into
this task, spending day after day at Lloyd's. "I sat in a corner of the Room and
just observed", he recalls. "I got to like the atmosphere of the place – it was
oddly light-hearted." The Rogers team, Goldschmied says, "faced a steep
learning curve. We'd got used to French ways at Pompidou and had to begin
again from scratch". Talking to the people who worked at Lloyd's was a vital
part of the design process. The members, in particular, had to formally
approve the Committee's development plans. In November 1978, they did
so – overwhelmingly – after Ian Findlay, by now Chairman, had promised them
"a highly sophisticated roof under which we may develop our business for
decades to come". It was to be two and a half years before the construction
of the new Lloyd's began, a delay which seems extreme in the light of subsequent 'fast track' projects in the City but which reflects the strategy of design
agreed between architect and client and the determination of both to achieve
lasting success, not just a stop-gap solution. Lloyd's wanted continuity of
trading, the potential for expansion and contraction, and the retention of the
Room as a unified space, the historic heart of the institution. The architects
looked at the two previous purpose-built buildings and concluded that, while
built to last centuries, they suffered from an inability to accommodate change.
It should be possible, they argued, to distinguish between those parts of a
building which were permanent and unchanging and those areas which were
subject to obsolescence and deterioration. Richard Rogers' interest in prefabrication, in the impermanent monumentality of the Constructivists and
Archigram, and the dynamic visions of the Futurists (Antonio Sant'Elia especially) was reflected in Lloyd's but the project was also strongly influenced by
the work of Louis Kahn, which Rogers had discovered with enthusiasm during
his period as a student in America.

30

31

32

33

34

35

36

37

35–37 This fine model of the building – as executed – clearly shows the growth of the service towers. Compare with 24.
38 The detailed design of the atrium roof, a lightweight contrast to the concrete superstructure of the building.
39 Frank Lloyd Wright's Larkin Building – the ultimate model for Lloyd's?
40, opposite The soaring height of the atrium recalls Paxton's Crystal Palace, a 'progressive' monument of the Victorian age.

Kahn's buildings, Rogers feels, have a "quiet, almost Romanesque" approach to the integration of technology – in contrast to his own, more obviously expressive way. But it was Kahn's notion of 'served' and 'servant' spaces which impressed Rogers. At Pompidou, the perimeter walls had housed the services. In the case of Lloyd's, they were concentrated in towers in the manner of Kahn's Richards laboratories at the University of Pennsylvania. Kahn's own inspiration for the Richards laboratories was clearly that lost icon of 20th century architecture, Frank Lloyd Wright's Larkin Building at Buffalo, New York (1904–5), which contained a great central, top-lit workspace surrounded by galleries. Wright placed the staircases in corner towers, which also housed ventilation shafts. The plan of the Larkin Building, in fact, contained all the essential elements of Lloyd's, though Wright was not called on to provide any degree of flexibility and change. (The craggy, 'Gothic' quality of the Larkin Building also influenced, coincidentally, the design of Paul Rudolph's architecture school at Yale University, which was under construction while Rogers was a postgraduate student at Yale.)

The Best Concrete Building in Britain
John Young, who was to spend five years getting Lloyd's built, admits that "had we gone to Lloyd's with a model of the finished scheme, we would probably have been kicked right across the City. The concept emerged step by step: the visuals emerged later". The Rogers team's strategy offered Lloyd's a range of possible options, both for the treatment of the 1928 site and for the temporary adaptation of the 1958 building during the rebuilding operation. The need for more underwriting space had become desperate – at least 700 square metres was needed in the very near future. Rogers and his team had identified the rooftop of the 1958 building as temporary office space (provided in portacabins) and the spacious basement (containing car-parking and a telephone exchange) as a temporary home for displaced underwriters. This accommodation, central to the Rogers strategy, was carried out by a recent young recruit to the office, Jamie Troughton, and completed in the autumn of 1980. In view of its strident yellow colour scheme and location (underneath the main marine underwriting area), the basement area was nicknamed the 'Yellow Submarine'. There were, inevitably, some complaints from those who had to work there – location is a sensitive matter at Lloyd's – but the strategy meant that no Lloyd's member was displaced from the City during the whole course of the rebuilding.

Across the road, the various options were gradually whittled down. Although the 1928 building was listed – and it was by no means inevitable that consent to pull it down would be given – architect and client both came to the conclusion that retaining it, even in part, would be a poor investment; demolition and rebuilding would cost more but would represent far better value for money. A new building, Rogers believed, should take the form of a 'doughnut', with rings of underwriting space serviced from the perimeter encircling an atrium – in effect, the Larkin Building formula, though updated to take account of modern technical needs. Heysham's building made poor use of its site,

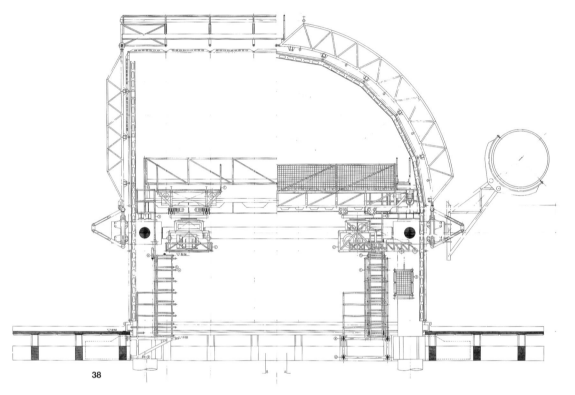

38

39

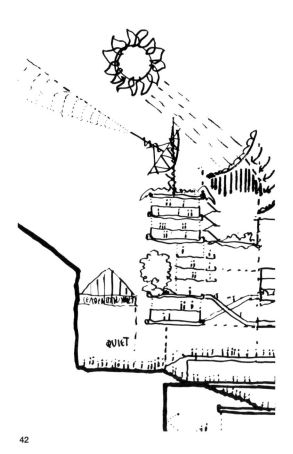

42

43

44

45

Marco Goldschmied concluded, after a detailed survey. The aim with the new building should be to ensure that at least 75 per cent of the total floor area was usable space. When Goldschmied and Blackmore met the City Planning Officer, however, the latter expressed the strong hope that the new home of Lloyd's would be located "behind the old façades". Lloyd's had kept close contact with the City Corporation since the idea of redevelopment had first been mooted and there were hopes that the Corporation would eventually back the plans – Lloyd's mattered a lot to the City.

These hopes were reinforced by the responses of the various amenity bodies who had been invited to visit Lloyd's in the spring of 1979. Surprisingly, none of them seemed especially anxious to defend Cooper's listed building and all appeared to concede, albeit reluctantly, that demolition was inevitable. (Cooper's work, in truth, was little regarded at this time.) The exception was the most recently founded and most dynamic of the conservationist groups, SAVE Britain's Heritage, which sprang to Cooper's defence. SAVE's eventual change of heart – it declared the Rogers proposals to be "novel and exciting" and a more than adequate recompense for the loss of the listed building – encouraged Rogers (who was subsequently to work with SAVE on its campaign to preserve Billingsgate Market) as did the comments of the Royal Fine Art Commission. "A most enlightened piece of architectural patronage", said the Commission. In September 1979, the City's Court of Common Council accepted the earlier recommendation of the planning committee and granted consent for the Cooper building to be demolished and an outline permission for a new block on the site. It was clear that the Environment Secretary would not intervene, since there had been no substantial objections. On 28 October 1979 demolition began. The interior of the Cooper building was stripped of anything of interest. The War Memorial and Library were to be reinstated in the new building, as was the historic Lutine Bell, the centre-piece of the Room. Much else – furniture, panelling, light fittings – was sold off to members. Such conservationist objections as arose were assuaged by the proposal that the grand arched portal on Leadenhall Street be retained as a memory of the old Lloyd's.

At this stage, the final scheme for the new building was beginning to emerge. Rogers' outline proposal report put to Lloyd's in June 1979 showed a building with all the essential elements of that eventually constructed. It was to total around 522,000 square feet gross (375,000 square feet nett), a 66 per cent increase over the Cooper buildings and implying a plot ratio of around 7.9:1. The Redevelopment Committee of Lloyd's, chaired by Sir Peter Green (later Chairman of Lloyd's and a consistent Rogers supporter), enthusiastically accepted Rogers' ideas, which centred on a central glazed atrium, surrounded by galleries, some of which would be lettable offices. The concept offered Lloyd's a building with greatly enhanced value, and the element of flexibility (present from the beginning) produced a building which could respond to change. (Should the densely populated market expand upwards, it was possible to add on more service towers to provide for the greater numbers of people.)

46

47

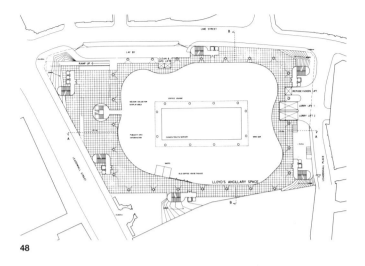

48

49

50

48 The architects envisaged the ground floor of Lloyd's as a largely public space. The reality was rather different.
49 Escalators are the key to circulation within the Room.
50 The completed building realizes the Rogers vision of Lloyd's as a flexible, multi-level market.

Peter Green, Lloyd's Chairman from January 1981 to December 1983, was (with Courtenay Blackmore) the key figure on the client side throughout the project, Green being the far-sighted patron and Blackmore his able manager and lieutenant. (The Redevelopment Committee met monthly, reporting back to the quarterly meetings of the main Committee.) There were key issues to be decided before a final design could be produced. First, would the new building contain just the Room and ancillary offices, or should it become the 'new' Lloyd's, with the Chairman's suite, committee room and Captains' Room transferred there? The Rogers team felt strongly that it should be exactly that and eventually managed to convince the client. The committee room took the form of a splendid Adam dining-room bodily transferred from the demolished Bowood House, Wiltshire, and relocated (in a badly cut-down form) in the Heysham building in 1957. It was now to move again. The Captains' Room, the architects proposed, should be sited on top of the new building, where members could enjoy fine views across the City. On this matter, Lloyd's disagreed, and the restaurant went to the ground floor. The character of the ground level was a second subject for prolonged discussion. Rogers felt strongly that it should be a public space, encouraging City workers and tourists. A wine bar, coffee house and display area for Lloyd's treasured Nelson Collection would open off a central court, an irregular, amoeba-shaped space. The Lloyd's Committee did accept this idea, but intensified security in recent years has effectively barred the public from Lloyd's, watering down the architect's vision of it as an extension of the City's streets, a retort to the hostile anonymity of most of its neighbours.

By early 1980 the detailed configuration of the new building had emerged, so that Rogers could present the scheme to the City in July of that year. The City finally approved the detailed plans in May of the following year, by which time demolition work (which had proved considerably more problematic than expected) was virtually complete. The basic 'doughnut' plan remained, but the building had emerged clearly as a forceful, dramatic new City monument. The most startling feature was clearly the external profile, punctuated by the servicing towers (modest, as it turned out, in comparison with those which were eventually built). Rogers initially envisaged Lloyd's as a steel structure, like Beaubourg. The main columns were to be of stainless steel. Arup Associates had actually completed a City office block, Bush Lane House, on an exposed steel frame, water-filled as at Pompidou. But in the case of Lloyd's the fire authorities were resolutely opposed to steel and not even Peter Rice was able to change their views. Rice advised against fighting for steel, since he felt the battle could be long and costly to the client. Rogers feared that a concrete building would be over-weighty and bulky, but in the event Lloyd's provided him with a chance to learn from the revered Kahn and, indeed, from American architects more generally. (The office of I.M. Pei, a contender for the Lloyd's commission, was particularly helpful.) John Young and Courtenay Blackmore, along with John Bathgate, Lloyd's project coordinator and Brian Pettifer of Bovis, recently appointed as management contractors for the scheme, went to the USA to study high-quality in situ concrete.

51 The concrete grid of the building, as initially conceived in pre-cast concrete.
52 In situ concrete was later substituted. U-beams transfer the loads of the floor grid to the columns via a bracket yoke assembly.
53, 54 The structure of the building is made clear in the atrium, which reflects Rogers' desire to make Lloyd's 'the best concrete building in Britain'.
55 Pre-cast concrete bracket and yoke assemblies.

53

54

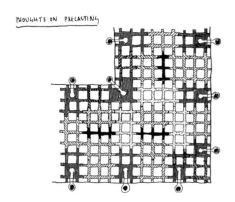

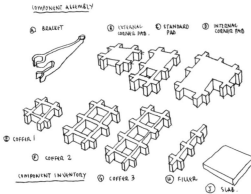

51

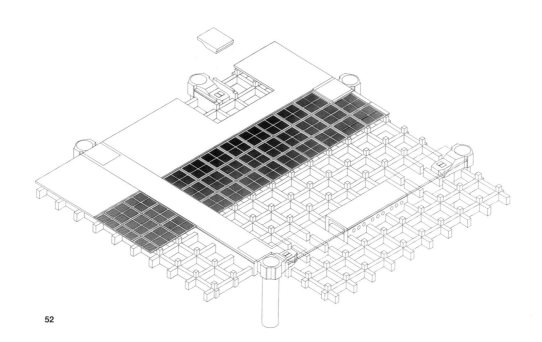

52

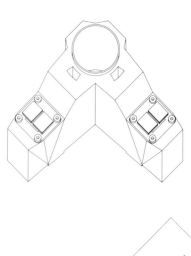

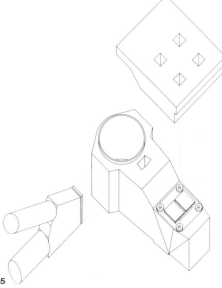

55

56 The Room in operation: the visions of Fritz Lang and Sant'Elia made real?
57 An early drawing by Mike Davies suggests the grandeur of the completed interior but not, perhaps, its great dynamism.

57

58

59

60

61

62

65

According to Young, the aim was to create "the best concrete building in Britain". If steel was rejected as a structural element, it was to be used for cladding the service towers – largely because of the fire officers' doubts about the safety of aluminium. The third element in the external look of Lloyd's was glass. Rogers' extensive use of translucent glazing on the building reflected his admiration for Pierre Chareau's Maison de Verre in Paris, a building which he had discovered in his student days. (At the Maison de Verre, the lighting was always external: by night, the house was lit by floodlights from the court-yard. This was impossible at Lloyd's and on dark winter days the interior of the Room can look a little gloomy.) Glass blocks in aluminium framing were proposed as the principal element in the cladding of the main block. In the finished building, triple glazing, with rolled glass to achieve 'sparkle', was used. More than Beaubourg, Lloyd's represented, for Rogers, the opportunity to bring together the themes which had preoccupied him since the days of his early partnership with Norman Foster. Given adequate funding, an enthusiastic and well-informed client and a distinct lack of obstacles ("there was a unique mood at the time: distinctly in favour of the new and radical", he says) Rogers was able to create a building which became (by the time of its completion) a defiant symbol of modern architecture under attack.

Test piling on the cleared site of the 1928 building had begun in March 1981, and work on the sub-structure began in June of that year. A 66 month programme was adopted. Even with additions to the brief (extra servicing and more meeting rooms, in particular) the job was completed with a month to spare. A formal ceremony at which the Queen Mother poured the concrete for one of the main columns of the new building followed in November. Before Christmas, the main tower crane had been erected at the southern end of the site. In June 1982, work began on the concrete super-structure of the building: it took 22 months, during which time the satellite towers were largely built and a start was made with the cladding. In the summer of 1984, work was well advanced on the steelwork of the atrium so that 'topping out' (again by the Queen Mother) could take place in July. By the end of 1984, the new Lloyd's was watertight. Easter 1986 was set as the date for the move from the 1958 building. Finally, at lunchtime on 23 May the 1958 Room was declared to be closed. Four days later, the new Room was formally opened by the Chairman of Lloyd's, Peter Miller, and Lloyd's entered a new age.

The commissioning and construction of the new Lloyd's, between 1977 and 1986, coincided with a period of rapid change in the way that financial dealings were conducted. (Later in 1986, the so-called 'Big Bang', the electronic-based revolution in financial operations, was to inaugurate the greatest office building boom in London's history and to create the new 'office cities' of Broadgate and Canary Wharf.) When Rogers won the commission, computers were scarce at Lloyd's (less than 4 per cent of underwriters used them) and many members, firmly attached to their traditional 'boxes' (a survival of coffee-house days) and to personal contact as the foundation of their business, expressed doubts that this situation would change. The Rogers team thought

63

64

58 Chareau & Bijvoet's Maison de Verre: Richard Rogers always admired this pioneering building.
59 The case-hardened steel dies from which the rollers were produced for the glass.
60 The first sheets of rolled, textured glass coming off the production line.
61–62, 63–64 Lloyd's under construction: the building was completed within the projected 66 month construction period.
65 Kit of parts formwork for the two-way floor structure.

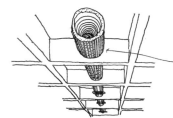

CAN A PERFORATED CLADDING
TO THE DUCTWORK PROVIDE
ALL THE ACOUSTIC ABSORPTION
REQUIRED AT HIGH LEVEL, SO
WE DON'T HAVE TO ADD ANYTHING
TO THE CONCRETE STRUCTURE.

FURTHER THOUGHTS ON
SERVICES STRATEGY

DIAGRAM DEFINITION.

SATELLITES 2, 3, 5, 6.
DISTRIBUTION FROM ROOF
ROOM HIGH LEVEL UPWARDS

SATELLITES 2, 5.
DISTRIBUTION FROM BASEMENT 2
ROOM LOW LEVEL ONLY.

SATELLITES 3, 6
DISTRIBUTION FROM BASEMENT 1
GENERAL AIR DISTRIBUTION
LOWER GROUND ONLY.

NON SATELLITE LINKED
SPECIAL SERVICES TO LOWER
GROUND - EG. CATERING

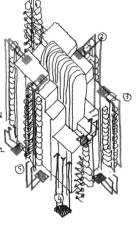

66

  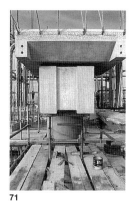

69　70　71

72

66　An early analysis of the
integrated structure and services
strategy for the building showing
the relationship between the
perimeter and core.
67　Cast steel brackets connect
the atrium structure to the main
frame of the building.
68　A large scale study model
of the concrete details for the
towers.

69　The pre-cast structural
elements of the towers being
assembled.
70　Cross-bracing for the end
bay of the atrium.
71　The pre-cast bracket and
yoke assembly.
72　Permanent formwork
steel trays spaced off the
concrete grid by cruciform
stub columns to create the
high level services zone.

67　68

otherwise – and was of course proved right. By 1981, with the building on site,
Lloyd's grasped the seriousness of the situation: the new building could (it
was suggested) end up gravely under-equipped. A specialist firm, Point
Consultants, had been brought in and their predictions of an almost universal
use of information technology and computer terminals would require a doubling of the anticipated power provision with a consequent dramatic impact
on cabling capacity and cooling. This had an inevitable impact on the look of
the building, with the six service towers gradually losing the emphatically slim
and expressive form which Rogers wanted and becoming bulkier and more
dominant. According to Tom Barker of Ove Arup & Partners, services engineer
at Pompidou and almost inevitably a member of the Lloyd's team, "the engineers always suspected that the towers might have to grow". Extra servicing
was vital to ensure flexibility and the scope for the Room to expand.

Structure and Services
The so-called 'energy crisis' which began with the Yom Kippur War in 1973
had a powerful (though sadly short-lived) impact on Western architecture.
'Energy' – by which was meant oil – suddenly acquired a new value. Rogers
responded to the new ethos decisively in the design of Lloyd's – the building
remains artificially-serviced – but there are elements which anticipate the
more radical exercises in servicing technology which the Richard Rogers
Partnership has pursued in the early-1990s in the face of a more widely perceived environmental crisis. The strategy document (produced in February
1978) which won the practice the Lloyd's job included a striking drawing,
showing the way in which the new building could make dynamic use of both
waste and natural energy.

　The essence of the Lloyd's servicing system is the use of the atrium form,
concrete structure and triple-glazed cladding as active elements. Conditioned
air is distributed through a sub-floor plenum into the offices, while stale air is
extracted from above through the luminaires. The extracted air is passed to
the perimeter of the building and forced through the triple-layered exterior
glazing – ensuring an almost zero heat loss from the offices during the winter
and reducing heat gain in summer. Heat from the return air is collected in the
basement sprinkler tanks and re-used. The internal concrete soffits and slabs
are 'heat sinks', absorbing heat during occupation and being cooled off
overnight using naturally chilled night air. This allows cooling to follow
a 24-hour cycle and reduces the peak cooling requirement. Air handling
equipment is located at basement level and in four service tower plant-rooms.
Lloyd's illustrates Rogers' pronouncement that "there is no such thing as high
technology or low technology – simply appropriate technology".

　Peter Rice said of Richard Rogers' architecture: "the structural solution
is the architecture – he approaches all his work through engineering". Lloyd's
is, like the Pompidou Centre, a vivid illustration of the fine balance between
technological determinism and a more conventional architectural instinct
which underlies all Rogers' major buildings. Some critics have alleged that
Lloyd's is 'a steel building executed in concrete'. The architects' preference

73 The sinuous ramp, fluid and inventive in form, provides a dramatic way into the building.
74 Plan of entrance canopy and structural details.

73

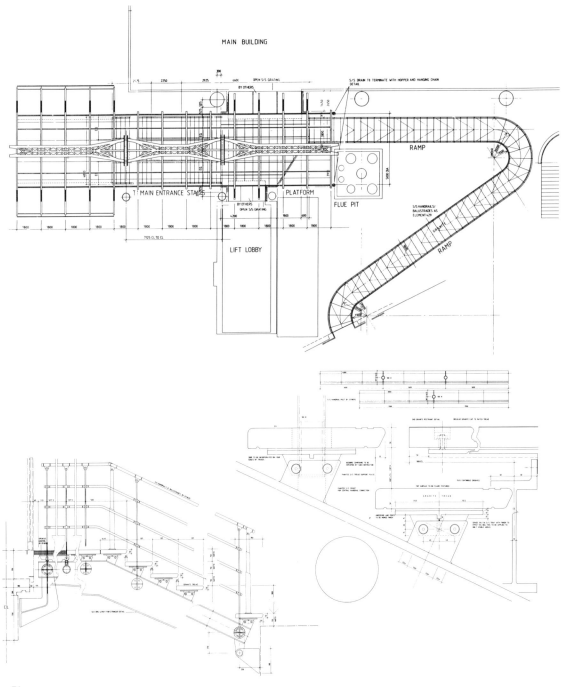

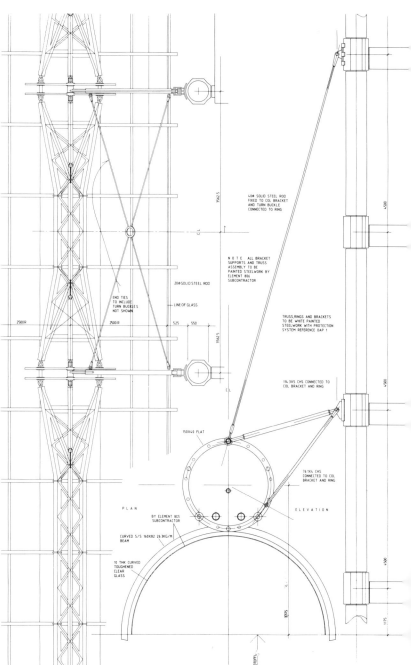

75

76

75, 76 The entrance canopy is an elegant and carefully-considered structure in its own right, an echo of the great roof of the atrium.
77 A section through the entrance canopy and details.

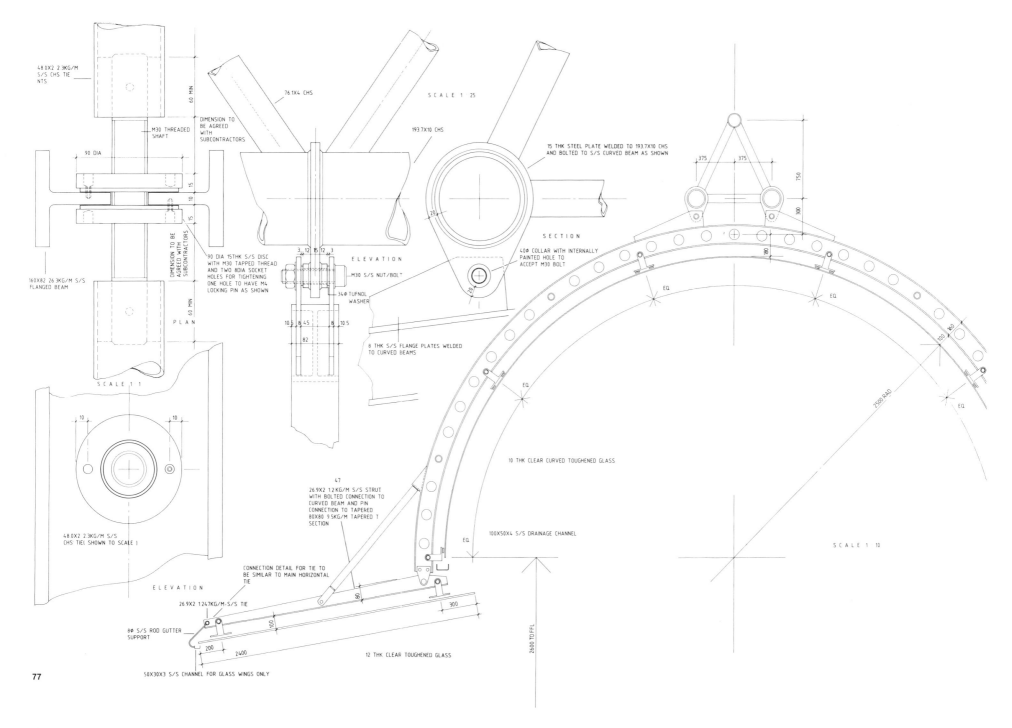

77

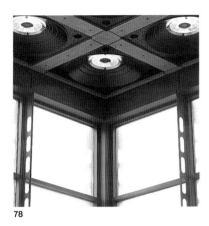

78

for steel was no secret, but, concrete being the inevitable choice, the Rogers approach was to make it a convincing exercise in concrete construction, using concrete in the expressive manner of Perret or late Corbusier. The basic form of the building is that of a large atrium, surmounted by a steel and glass arched roof, surrounded by galleries (12 levels of them on the north side) which contain the bulk of the underwriting space and a variable amount of lettable space, depending on the changing accommodational needs of the Lloyd's market itself. The floors intended to be let are glazed to the atrium, while those which are part of the Room are left open. The floors were constructed on a grid (which owes something in character to Kahn's Yale Art Gallery, the first major building which the American master had completed and one which Rogers much admired). By using beams with parallel sides and sharp arrises Rogers emphasizes that the floor is a grid and not a solid, coffered slab – great care was taken to secure this effect. To get it right, research was done into various types of formwork. That used owed a lot to Vince Kelly, an American consultant who had been retained to advise on concrete construction (he had worked extensively with Pei), to Bovis (the management contractor) and to Gleeson (responsible for the superstructure). The floors are supported on reinforced concrete columns on a 10.8 x 18 metre grid. The load is transferred between the columns and the floor beams by means of a precast bracket – an arrangement which inevitably recalls the steel 'gerberettes' of the Pompidou Centre. Pre-cast 'yokes' cast into inverted U-beams transmit the loads of the floor grid to the perimeter columns via the brackets. The great columns, both on the exterior of the building and within the atrium, stand proud of the cladding, increasing the highly-articulated 'Gothic' effect of Lloyd's. External cross-braces are actually made of steel tube concrete-cased for reasons of fire safety, which helped to maintain the spare slenderness of the exterior. It was proposed to leave the services within the concrete grid open to view, but the client demurred and the squares of the ceiling grid are filled with black metal panels which contain the light fittings.

The massiveness and weight of the interior of Lloyd's may come as a surprise after the predominantly metal and glass exterior, but the heaviness of the concrete superstructure (which really is reminiscent of the work of Louis Kahn) is successfully balanced by the airy and elegant lightness of the atrium roof, a startling re-enactment of the Victorian drama of The Crystal Palace and the great 19th century railway termini – though wrought iron is, of course, replaced by tubular steel. The roof sits, by means of steel brackets, on the main columns of the atrium. Its lattice steelwork is of painted, rather than stainless steel – an economy measure. The detailed design of the roof was modified as the project advanced – typical of the *ad hoc* approach of Rogers and Rice – and the welding of joints abandoned in favour of custom-made castings, which were, in such quantities, cheaper and looked better.

The service towers, three of them principally for firefighting and escape and the other three for lifts, lavatories and risers, are the visual expression of the Kahnian doctrine of 'served and servant spaces', the towers on the Gothic castle of Lloyd's. They provide access and escape routes by means of lifts and

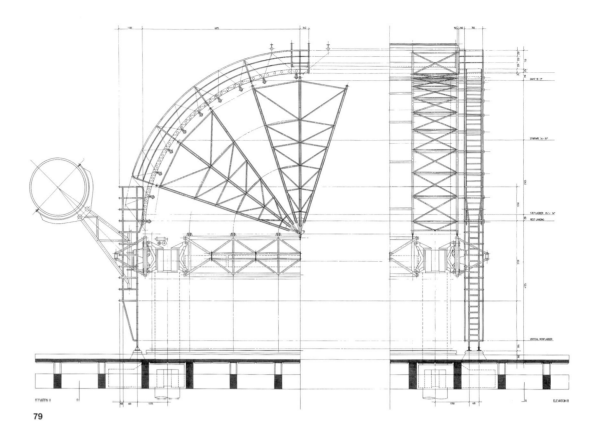

79

80

81

82

78 The multi-functional luminaire fills the module of the floor slab.
79 The contrast between the heavy coffered floor slab and the lightweight atrium roof is striking.
80–81 Lloyd's is a subtle balance of concrete and steel, in contrast to the lighter metallic aesthetic of the Pompidou Centre.
82 Fish-tail ducts fabricated from stainless-steel pressings drive air through the glazed façade.

83 The prefabricated lavatory pods were brought to the site on trucks and then hoisted into position prior to linking up to the service riser.

84 Lavatory pod interiors use stainless steel, ceramic tile and mirrors for wall and floor surfaces with solid white carrara marble vanitory units.

85 The plant rooms grew in size as a result of enhanced servicing requirements.

83

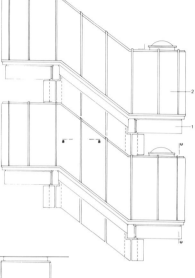

84

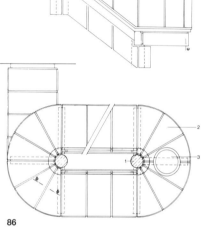

86

85

86 Cladding details of the staircases on the satellite towers.

87 The 'Airstream' trailer home inspired John Young's design for the lavatories.

88 The stainless-steel chassis for the prefabricated lavatory units were moved on pneumatic skates through the various production stages.

87

88

staircases – in an emergency the core building (which could have 6,000 people inside it) can be evacuated into the detached service towers within two and a half minutes. The precast concrete kit-of-parts of the service towers is not entirely independent of the main block of the building, as was proposed at one stage, but depends on a degree of restraint from the main building. (As Peter Rice explained: "it would be architecturally wrong for the towers to be independent; they were supposed to be subservient to the main building".) The towers form a flexible framework for the ventilation plant, lifts, service risers and lavatories (the replaceable, potentially obsolescent parts of the building) attached to them. The cladding of the towers is entirely stainless steel (for reasons already outlined). Four towers carry major plant-rooms, with mains services running vertically down the towers and connected into each level of the building. In contrast to the colour-coded service ducts of the Pompidou Centre, those at Lloyd's are cased in stainless steel, neutral in effect. The largest contain the air-conditioning, with lesser ducts for water, drains, power and electronics. On top of four of the six towers sit the plant-rooms, grown from the slender turrets Rogers initially envisaged into massive steel-clad boxes. Sometimes criticized as clumsy and over-dominant, they nonetheless underline the subordination of traditional architectural concerns to the all-important functional needs of the users. All the towers are topped by service cranes, painted a jaunty blue and intended to allow both maintenance and the easy replacement of obsolete or worn-out equipment.

Prefabrication of components has always been part of the agenda of high-tech architecture. The work of Buckminster Fuller and Jean Prouvé, for example, provided practical evidence of its relevance to 20th century needs. At Lloyd's, Richard Rogers sought to emphasize the distinction between the 'long life' core, the apparently permanent structure housing human beings, and the 'short life' perimeter, where the ever-changing technology was placed. The logical outcome of this formula is that the latter zone is given over to standardized, off-the-peg components, but this was not always the case. One of the prime tensions in the Lloyd's building (as in 'high-tech' architecture generally) is that between mass-production and craft methods. All of the 33 lavatory units in the building were manufactured and fitted out, ready for plumbing in, away from the site. According to John Young, the inspiration came not from Fuller or Prouvé but from the classic American 'Airstream' trailer home, the sort of unselfconscious mass-produced item which Young likes. Full-size mock-ups of the lavatories were made off-site and shown to the Redevelopment Committee – which immediately called for a rethink. Laminate-topped basin units and rubber flooring were simply 'not Lloyd's' – marble and ceramics had to be substituted, one of the numerous occasions when the client brief changed and costs rose. (This decision compromised the original concept – the addition of ceramic tiles meant that they could not be craned in without the risk of breakages. Some elements had to be fitted after they had been lifted into position.) Within a few years, ready-made modules of this sort were a common sight in the midst of the City's post-'Big Bang' building boom, though never as blatantly expressed as at Lloyd's. At Lloyd's in particular,

89, 90, opposite The main
entrance and a detail of the
entrance canopy.

89

91

91 The Pompidou Centre had dramatized the process of circulation by means of escalators snaking up the main façade.
92 At Lloyd's, the escalators are inside – but the drama remains.
93 Pre-cast lengths of one-piece aluminium tread and riser extrusions prior to assembly into stairflights.
94 The articulated form of the service towers creates a dynamic façade.
95 The interlocking tread and riser extrusions in a complete staircase.

pre-assembling elements of the building made sense because of the very confined nature of the site.

Staircases were another prefabricated item – one to which John Young (who was engaged virtually full-time on Lloyd's from 1981 onwards) gave much thought. The staircase system was based on one-piece (tread and riser) aluminium extrusions fixed to a steel carriage, with steel balustrade and glass infill. Young defines Lloyd's as "not a machine-produced building but one which makes use of machine-production methods, when they are appropriate". The notebooks he kept throughout the project provide vivid glimpses into the construction process and the degree to which important decisions had to be made as the building was rising. Yet there were few real crises – the system of consultation and creative dialogue, established by Courtenay Blackmore, worked well.

Blackmore was, says Rogers, closely involved in every important decision that had to be taken as the project progressed. He was the day-to-day link between the architects and the client – Sir Peter Green and the Committee. But Green's own involvement was close – "it was an exceptional client/architect relationship", recalls Rogers. A key part of the design strategy was that Lloyd's should be, like Pompidou, a place of movement. With the Room divided over a number of floors, it was vital that underwriters and brokers should be able to meet face to face without difficulty. Location had always been a contentious matter with Lloyd's members. A single-level room was impossible, but all parts of the Room had to be easily reached one from another. Rogers' strategy had always provided for the lifts to be located in the service towers, but the idea of external lifts ('wall-climbers') worried the client. Was this a practical idea, in view of the exposure of cars and mechanisms to the elements? Icing in winter might affect the operation of the lifts, while summer heat could make the glass-walled cars intolerable – especially if there were a power failure. A further fact-finding trip to the USA helped to assuage Lloyd's fears – here were external lifts which had worked well for years in a climate more extreme than that of Britain. The St Francis Hotel in San Francisco had depended on external lifts to serve 31 storeys of rooms, without problems. In the event, the lifts at Lloyd's incorporated a wide range of fail-safe measures – de-icing equipment for cold winter days, for example, and air-conditioning units attached to the bottom of each car.

The escalators snaking up the face of the Pompidou Centre remain the single most popular feature of Piano & Rogers' early masterpiece. At Lloyd's, escalators were used to connect the floors used for underwriting – at first, only two gallery levels were earmarked for this purpose but a third was subsequently added and the escalators in fact end at the fourth level. In 1991, the fourth floor was being used for underwriting, but was subsequently vacated and rapidly converted back to offices, a practical illustration of the Rogers strategy at work. Exposing the mechanism of the escalators behind clear glass panels was a way of 'celebrating' movement – like the glass lifts. Norman Foster had used a similar device at the Willis Faber & Dumas headquarters, a building Rogers much admired and took some inspiration from

92

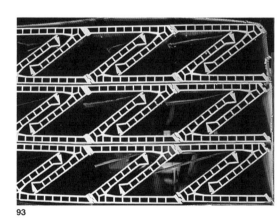
93

94

95

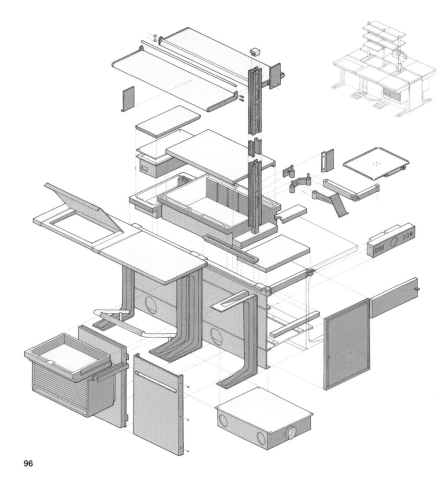

96

97

98

96 The kit of parts which make
up the underwriters' boxes, the
traditional workplace of Lloyd's
members.
97 The completed Room, fitted
out with the boxes.
98 The architects managed to
impose order on the potentially
chaotic operations of the Room.

in the design of Lloyd's (indeed, the first version of the Lloyd's atrium spread
amoeba-like in form, responding to the space in the manner of the Willis Faber
building). The effect of the escalators when the Room is at work, with people
hurrying from one floor to the next, is an essential ingredient of the character
of Lloyd's, a striking embodiment of the fantasies of a Sant'Elia (or, for that
matter, a Fritz Lang).

A Crisis of Confidence

The new building obliged the inherently conservative Lloyd's community to
accept change in the interests of survival. It was constructed at a time when
the character of Lloyd's was in flux. Yet there were aspects of Lloyd's which
resisted change obdurately. Underwriters had worked from 'boxes' since the
days of Edward Lloyd's coffee house near the Tower and had no intention
of abandoning them. Some wanted to simply transfer the boxes they were
already using. These varied in size – the largest seating 20 people. The
Redevelopment Committee and, of course, the architects, wanted a standard
model which could be adapted to individual needs. Mike Davies got approval
for an appropriate 'kit of parts' approach. At this point, Rogers brought in the
Czech-born architect Eva Jiricna to work on the interiors of Lloyd's after it
became clear that his ideas on furniture and fittings were somewhat at odds
with those of the client – there were members of the Lloyd's Committee
who wanted to take the interiors entirely out of the hands of the architects.
A chance meeting led to a two-year collaboration, with Jiricna working independently in the Rogers office.

It was in Sloane Street (where the two architects had met that day) that
Eva Jiricna had recently completed a shop for the fashion empire Kenzo.
The shop made ample use of wood. "I think that Richard Rogers saw the
use of wood as a way forward at Lloyd's", says Jiricna, whose first task was
to try to define the 'Lloyd's feeling'. Her experience of Lloyd's was not to be
entirely happy, but the matter of the boxes was resolved – although Rogers
and Young were never entirely happy with the compromise it represented.
Courtenay Blackmore insisted, however, that the boxes were "part of the
members' domain – a very personal area" where the opinion of the member-
ship had to prevail. John Young was not very happy with the use of teak as
a facing. Jiricna felt that there was a certain lack of co-ordination between
the structural grid of the building and the fit-out and concedes that the
boxes were a compromise, though not an entirely bad one. In use, they
seem to be a success.

A conflict of views over the interior of the building had been prefigured
by the matter of the lavatories. Courtenay Blackmore admitted that the majority view amongst members was that Lloyd's should be "clubbish – even
Heysham's interiors had been regarded by many as too modern". Little could
be done to alter the interior of the Room – where the architecture *was* the
decoration. Disagreement surfaced therefore over the ancillary interiors.
The members' restaurant, the Captains' Room, is an important part of the
Lloyd's scene. One long-standing member recalls the Captains' Room in

101

99, opposite A detail of the
escalator half landings.
100 Exposing the mechanism of
the escalators was a way of
celebrating movement.
101 Half landings on the escalator
route through the building provide a
good vantage point.

102

102 "Watch out which button you press for the lift!" ('Jak' in the *Evening Standard*). Lloyd's inspired cartoonists even before it was completed: few other modern London buildings are such recognizable landmarks.
103 The new Captains' Room as completed to the designs of Eva Jiricna, whose attempt to give Lloyd's a contemporary ethos was only partially successful.
104 Waiter stations in the Captains' Room.
105 The 'sails' evoked Lloyd's nautical origins.

the 1928 building as 'magnificent' and even Heysham's 1958 equivalent as 'pleasant'. Jiricna had the difficult task of designing a modern interior with reassuringly traditional associations. In an effort to get the design right, the Redevelopment Committee sanctioned the construction of a mock-up inside the half-completed building. A dinner was held there and comments were invited. One basic problem was the fact that the restaurant had to be fitted into a standard floor of the building, with its 10 foot floor-to-ceiling heights. The rigourous ceiling grid also had to be lived with. But Jiricna succeeded in creating an attractive space, through the use of light and elegant modern furniture and striking 'sails' covering the windows. She suspected, however, that there were those who would have preferred a very different ambience.

"I had a problem at Lloyd's", says Jiricna, "in being a woman, foreign, and a modernist – who maybe looked rather 'trendy' to the Committee. But the main problem was that I had been brought in by Richard Rogers and there were people who wanted to prevent him from having any further influence on the interiors." The crisis came with the matter of the two executive floors at the top of the building, containing the committee room and the offices of the Chairman and other senior officials of the Corporation of Lloyd's. "Eva Jiricna made a fatal error", recalled Courtenay Blackmore. "She proposed to give the Chairman a 100 per cent modern office." The chairmanship of Lloyd's had, at the end of 1983, passed to Peter Miller who did not share the enthusiasm of his predecessor, Sir Peter Green, for Rogers' building or for modern design more generally. Miller's wife (an interior designer) had equally strong views. Blackmore felt that the subsequent decision to go over Rogers' head, reject Jiricna's designs and employ another designer was "a great moment of loss of confidence". (He subsequently took the decision to retire as director of administration later in 1984, but he remained as redevelopment director on the building project until 1986.)

Gordon Graham, who had maintained an informal interest in the Lloyd's project from the time he had advised on the choice of an architect, tried hard to dissuade Lloyd's from changing direction, but to no avail. The Paris decorator, Jacques Grange, was appointed by Lloyd's and fitted out the executive floors in a 'traditional' manner, with lots of marble and heavy reproduction furniture – a failure of nerve which is all the more tragic in the light of Lloyd's unswerving support for Rogers over the previous six years. One particular loss was the 'jewel box' setting Rogers had proposed for the Adam room, with a glazed promenade around it, affording marvellous views of the City. Instead, Grange sank the room in a stodgy neo-Georgian corridor. The effect of these two floors is like a bad dream – it seems out of place and incongruous. Surely this can't really be happening – in a Richard Rogers building?

The last two years of the project saw growing resistance to Rogers' ideas for the interior and the intensification of a debate amongst Lloyd's members about the merits of the building which had started as soon as it began to take shape. Within a year of the building's opening, an opinion poll suggested that more than half its users would have liked to move back to the 1958 building – few seemed to recall the crisis of space which the Rogers building had been

103

104

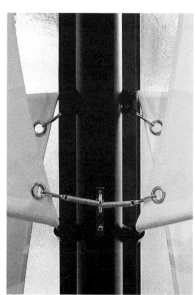

105

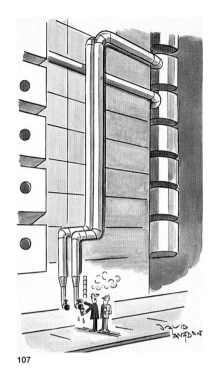

106 Basement lavatories serve the underwriting Room and use the same materials as the upper level prefabricated pods.

107 The building was compared to an Italian coffee machine – not necessarily a derogatory reference. "I'm glad we've preserved a little of the old coffee house tradition…" (Langdon's Lloyd's).

108 A public wine bar at lower ground level.

109 A lift landing in one of the satellite towers.

designed to resolve. Even as Lloyd's began to collect the first of a long series of design awards (the first from the Civic Trust for its contribution to the historic City scene) there were complaints that it was the wrong building at the wrong price. Accusations that Lloyd's was a particularly extravagant building, or that the cost 'ran out of control' have been made so frequently that the facts have been largely obscured. The projected cost when work started on site in 1981 was £75 million – excluding fit-out. The final 1986 account came to £143 million (including fit-out) – the equivalent of £107 million in 1981 prices, allowing for inflation. Lloyd's had, in fact, insisted on rigourous cost checks at crucial stages of the project. Added costs could be explained by the fact that Lloyd's got a notably larger building than it had originally commissioned. Additional meeting rooms, for example, had been added. More luxurious lavatories (at a cost of £1.5 million), the substitution of stainless steel for aluminium as external cladding, greatly increased servicing to cater for information technology, improvements to lighting and fire protection, and fitting out (including the underwriting boxes) easily accounted for the extra spending.

The debate about the merits of Lloyd's has hardly abated from the day of the building's completion. In the nine years which elapsed between Lloyd's initial decision to commission a new building and its opening, the climate of opinion in Britain changed. A few years later, consent to demolish Sir Edwin Cooper's Lloyd's might not have been obtained. The City of London had moved in a distinctly more conservationist direction – perhaps understandably in the light of the massive wave of destruction allowed in the 1960s and 1970s. The Prince of Wales' architectural campaigns had strengthened the hand of architectural traditionalists. When Rogers produced designs for a site next to Lloyd's it was made clear that they would not be approved. It was to be some years before he was to get another City commission for a new building.

A Great London Monument

In planning terms, in fact, Rogers had worked miracles. Although Lloyd's avoided the domineering arrogance of many recent City buildings, its plot ratio of 7.9:1 was, of course, far higher than the City norm. The secret lay in the way in which it put the open space inside, where it benefited users, rather than outside in the form of a bleak and (to London) alien 'piazza'. At the same time, the impervious walls of the Cooper building gave way to a mix of public and private space, with new public routes weaving under and around the new Lloyd's. The ratio of nett (usable) to gross space was also exceptionally favourable. These gains were the natural outcome of Rogers' radicalism, though the completed building had actually grown in comparison with the first plans. While the City planners had backed the project all along, there was hard bargaining to be done when it came to additional meeting rooms and augmented service towers – there were individual planning officers who seemed to have little sympathy for the scheme. "Suddenly, everything we wanted to do seemed to be made into a major issue and we had to fight

110, 111, 112, 113, opposite
Movement was the key theme of
Rogers' Lloyd's: the lifts are a
memorable feature, each fitted with
an air-conditioning unit.

110

111

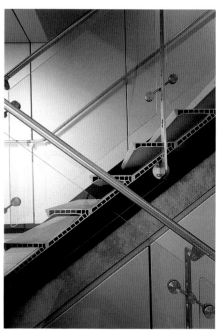

112

114

115

114 Richard Rogers compares Lloyd's to G.E.Street's Law Courts: both are varied in form and detail, drawing their inspiration from the street.
115 The Torre Velasca in Milan, designed by BBPR, is as 'Gothic' as the service towers of Lloyd's.
116 The vocabulary of Lloyd's survived in Rogers' National Gallery design – the most original (and controversial) of the proposals for the site.
117 The Coin Street scheme was Rogers' radical response to the wasteland of London's South Bank – but it fell foul of community objections.

for it", says John Young, while Richard Rogers sensed that there was a 'counter attack', part of a general swing against innovative design in the City which, he believes, encouraged developers to look towards Docklands. Rogers argues that the way in which the Lloyd's building maximizes the use of the site means a gain of around £40 million in its real value. It was not, he concedes, a cheap building: "Lloyd's wanted long life and high value and were sensibly prepared to invest in achieving those objectives". The value of Lloyd's in commercial terms derives from Rogers' architectural strategy – a dual-function building which is unique in London.

Richard Rogers' objectives in the building of the new Lloyd's were not, of course, purely commercial or purely functional. He was fortunate to find a client prepared to back him in his ambition to build a great commercial monument which also contributed to the enrichment of the public realm. Not that Lloyd's was spendthrift. As Courtenay Blackmore put it: "Lloyd's might have been seen as a big spender, but it wasn't really like that. You had to convince a lot of people of the need for every item of expenditure".

Seeking the origins of the building one is inevitably driven back beyond the earlier work of the Rogers practice (Beaubourg in particular) to the feverishly inventive world of the Architectural Association in the early-1960s. When Rogers looks back on the roots of the scheme, he quotes not just Wright's Larkin Building ("above everything else"), Kahn and Constructivism, but equally the influence of his sometime teacher, James Stirling (and of Stirling's Leicester engineering block, in particular), of the work of Rudolf Schindler (on whom he had written a thesis at Yale), of Naum Gabo (with whom he lodged for a time in the USA), and of Berthold Lubetkin. The 'bowellism' of early Archigram had impressed itself on his consciousness, but Rogers is the first to acknowledge his indebtness to his one-time partners Norman Foster and Renzo Piano. Lastly, Rogers recalls the work of his uncle, the romantic Italian modernist Ernesto Rogers. (Perhaps there is a hint in the great overhanging towers of Lloyd's of the famous Torre Velasca in Milan, designed by Ernesto Rogers' firm, BBPR.)

Richard Rogers has defined his aim at Lloyd's as being "to create poetry out of basic enclosure, by translating technology into form". He has compared the building to Street's Law Courts, a masterpiece of historicist street architecture in the hard Gothic style of the later 19th century. Lloyd's, says Rogers, "is richly detailed and layered in section. It cascades down towards the existing lower buildings and upwards to the higher ones". Rogers here makes analogies with very traditional architectural and urban values. Yet, he admits, the brief at Lloyd's implied "a responsive, indeterminate architecture". The building which resulted reflected Rogers' avowed search for "a balance between permanence and transformation".

It is this balance which is central to the character of the building, which is, in Rogers' view, "history-conscious, energy-conscious, functional, of course, like all our buildings, and more dynamic than Pompidou". Though some critics, most notably Martin Pawley, have argued that Lloyd's is not radical enough – that there ought to be provision for the entire building, core as

116

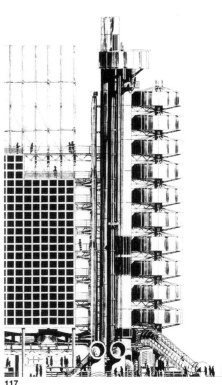

117

118

119

120

well as perimeter, to change – the building is clearly a precursor of the new office architecture of the later 1980s and 1990s. It provided a working model for the buildings spawned by London's 'Big Bang' in being essentially inward-looking and user-centred. In its flexibility, environmentalism and responsiveness to the changing shape of services, electronic and non-electronic, it is also a pioneer 'intelligent' building which Frank Duffy has described as "one of the most advanced technological edifices in the world". All of this depends on the basic strategy: core versus perimeter, 'served' and 'servant'.

If Lloyd's is a 'kit of parts', however, it is a kit of parts put together to impressive architectonic effect. Though Rogers has always looked longingly at the potential for an architecture of dematerialization (hence, for instance, his admiration for the work of Future Systems) Lloyd's expresses the 'controlled randomness' which typifies his own finest work. Out of Lloyd's come the Japanese projects, the National Gallery and Coin Street schemes and the sadly abortive Daiwa project in the City of London. Lloyd's is, far more than the classical building it replaced, a monument. The interior is, for all the activity going on, a place of overwhelming calm and order beneath the great columns and the soaring roof. The outside, for all the restless, mechanistic quality provided by the ducts, flues and lifts, has a grave permanence which is lacking in any of the post-war buildings in the vicinity.

Lloyd's transcends purely stylistic analysis. At one level the supreme monument, with Foster's Hong Kong Bank, of the high-tech, it is best understood as the response of a modern humanist to the City. Some of Rogers' ambitions for the building, notably for public access, have been partially thwarted: Lloyd's is a very private world. The precise, almost obsessive quality of the internal detailing is apparent only to those underwriters and brokers with the eye to see it. Like a medieval cathedral, Lloyd's is detailed beautifully even in those places which the eye cannot see. The medieval mason believed that God saw all. For Richard Rogers, detailing is part of the integrity and conviction which underlies good architecture.

The ghosts of Sant'Elia, Wright, Kahn, Chareau and others of Rogers' heroes haunt Lloyd's. Against all the odds, Rogers and his team gave conservative London a building which expresses the heroic age of modernism, a benchmark for everything built or proposed in the capital in the years that followed. Equally against the odds, Lloyd's is a real London building, big and monumental, yet full of the incident and variety which allow it to sit next to the Victorian market, in a streetplan which dates back to the days of Chaucer. To come across it suddenly and to comprehend the strength and conviction, the determination and the single-mindedness which made it, is an extraordinary experience. London may not see its like again.

122

123

124

121, opposite The glazed envelope acts as a translucent wall of sparkling light.
122 Lloyd's provides a calm, rational working environment for people who deal with crises daily.
123 Information towers summon people from all parts of the building.
124 Rogers' building is a benchmark for modern architecture in Britain, a heroic monument and a humane workplace.

Floor plans

Lower basement level

1 boiler
2 sub-station
3 generators
4 chillers
5 maintenance staff
6 air handling plant
7 strong room
8 goods lift
9 vehicle dock
10 vehicle lift
11 squash court

Upper basement level

1 staff mess room
2 mail room
3 female lavatories
4 male lavatories
5 maintenance
6 cleaners
7 liveried staff
8 telephone exchange
9 offices
10 cloakrooms
11 kitchens
12 black box park
13 old special dining room

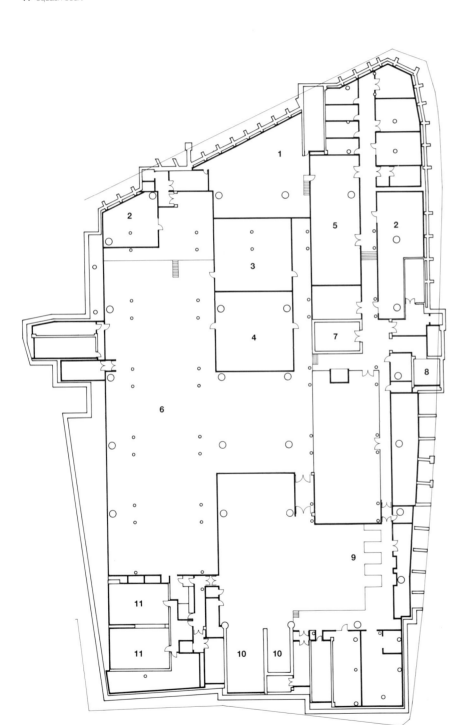

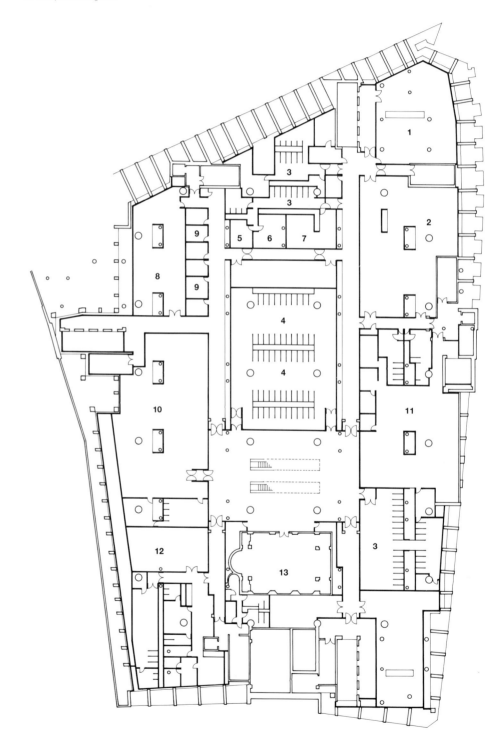

N

0 — 10m

0 — 30ft

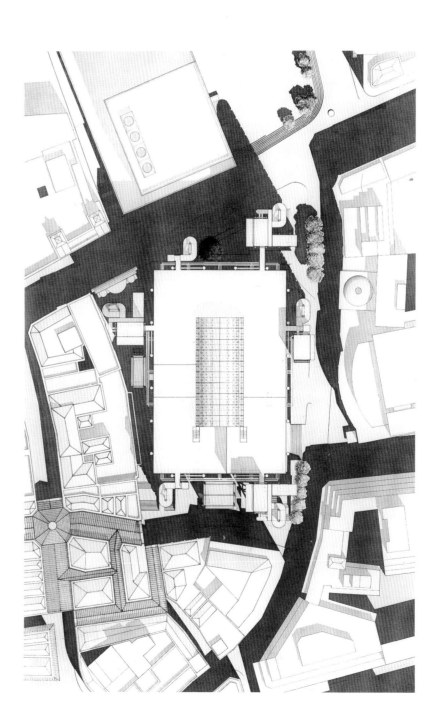

0   20m

0   60ft

Floor plans

Lower ground level

1 underwriters' entrance
2 restaurant
3 bar
4 kitchen
5 conference room
6 exhibition space
7 library

Ground floor level

1 main entrance
2 underwriters' Room

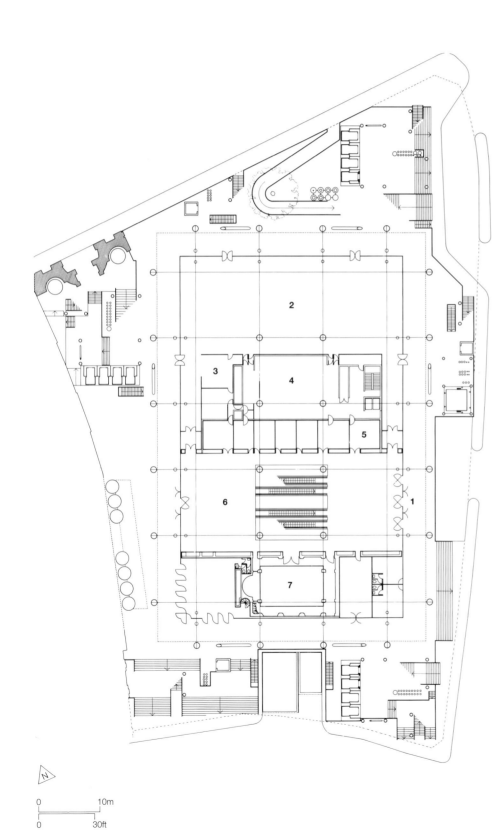

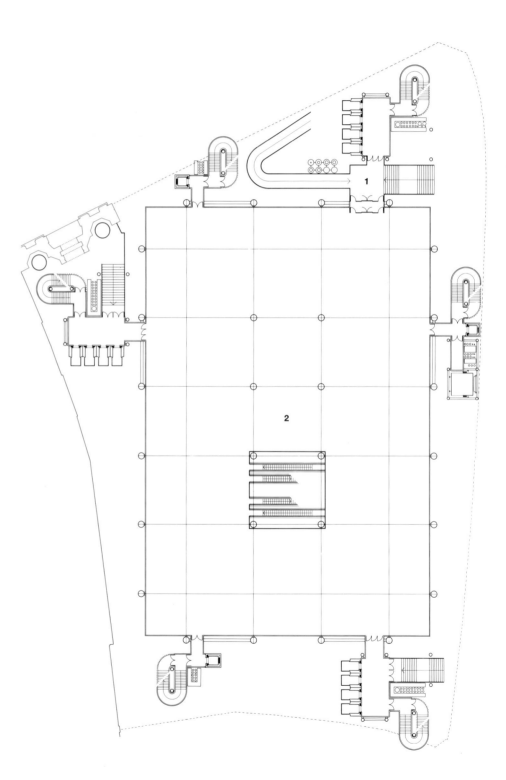

N

0   10m

0   30ft

Galleries 5 and 6

1 atrium
2 office space

Gallery 11

1 atrium
2 special dining room
3 Adam room

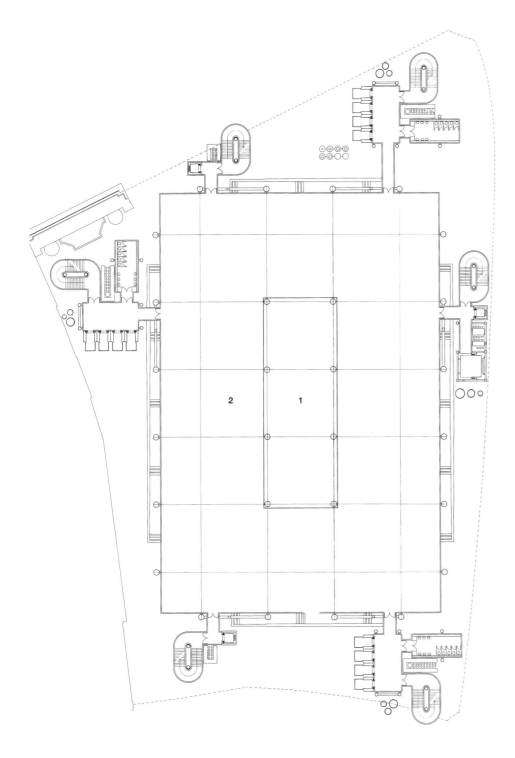

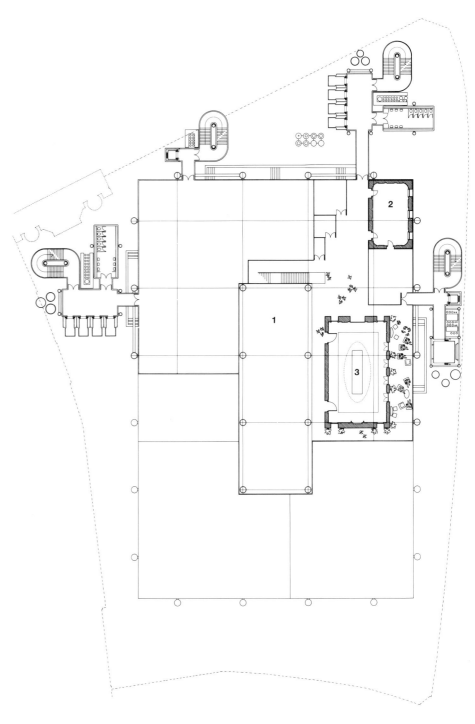

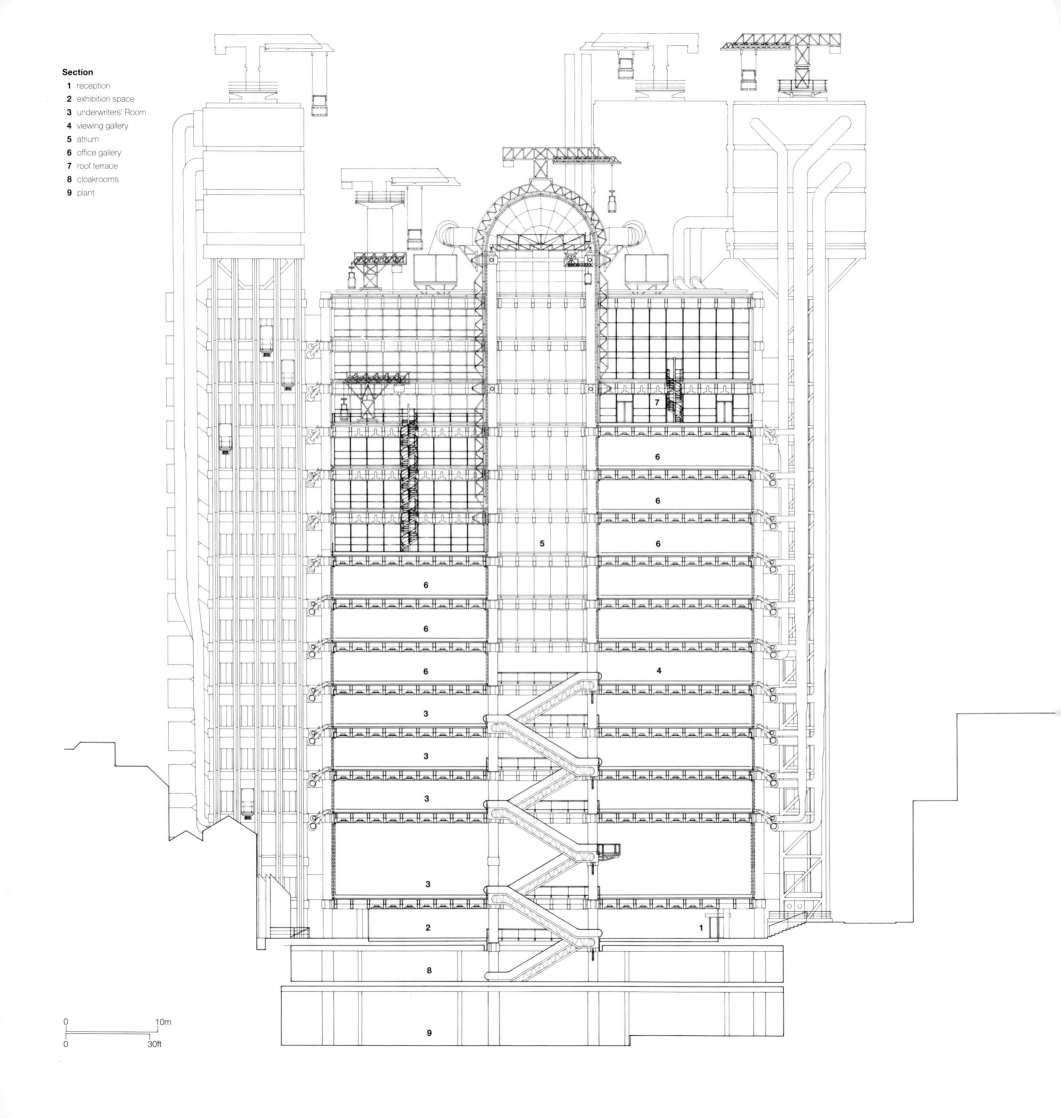

Section

1 reception
2 exhibition space
3 underwriters' Room
4 viewing gallery
5 atrium
6 office gallery
7 roof terrace
8 cloakrooms
9 plant

0   10m
0   30ft

Elevation detail

View showing the atrium
steelwork connected to the
concrete superstructure

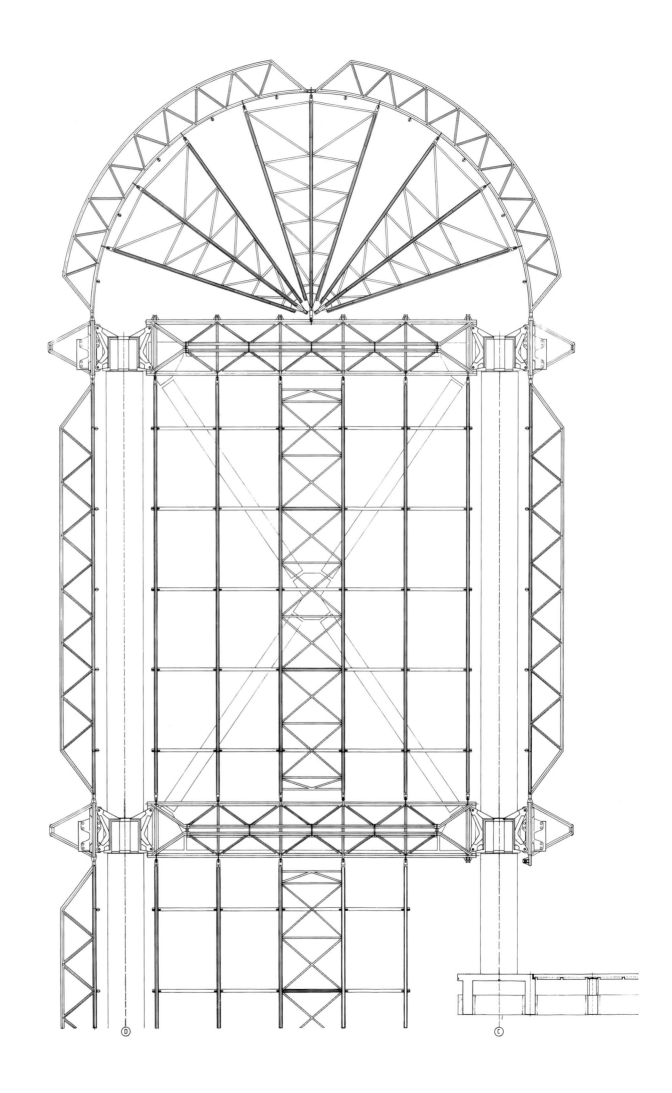

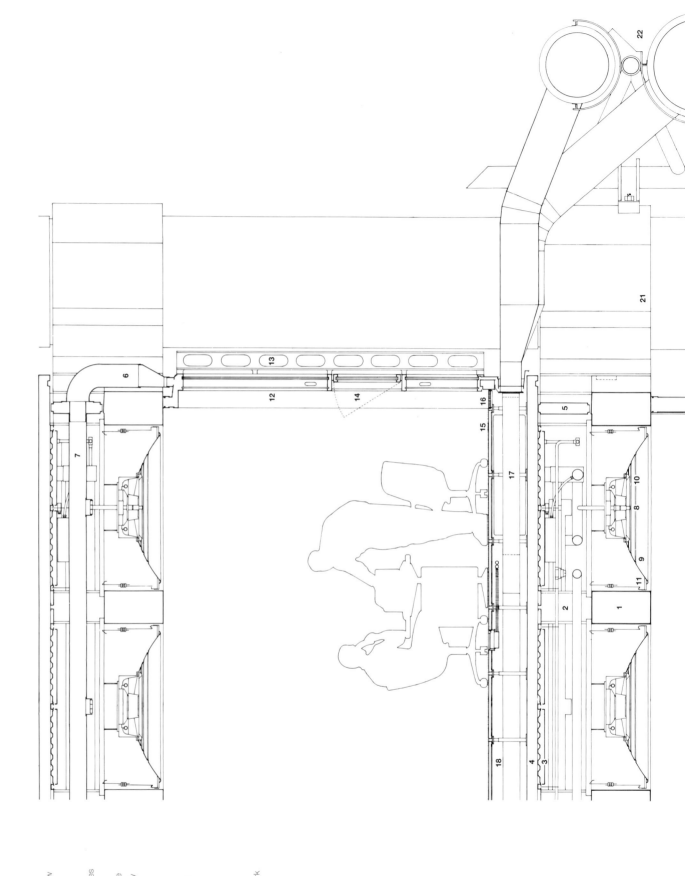

Detail section

1 in situ concrete beam
2 440mm deep services void
3 permanent steel formwork incorporating acoustic panel
4 100mm in situ concrete slab
5 anodized aluminium sandwich panel, 1 hour fire rated
6 insulated stainless steel 'fish tail' extract duct
7 ALUZINC duct extracting air through light fittings
8 sprinkler head
9 black painted spun aluminium luminaire shield
10 silver aluminium light spill ring
11 black painted perforated metal coffer infill panel
12 anodized aluminium cladding with triple glazing and ventilated cavity
13 anodized aluminium wind bracing fin
14 clear double glazed window openable at office levels
15 600 x 600mm lightweight concrete filled steel floor tiles on pedestals
16 extruded aluminium air grille
17 insulated galvanized supply air duct
18 350mm deep raised floor services plenum
19 unventilated double glazed cladding
20 in situ concrete column
21 pre-cast concrete column brackets
22 supply and extract ductwork
23 painted ductwork support bracket

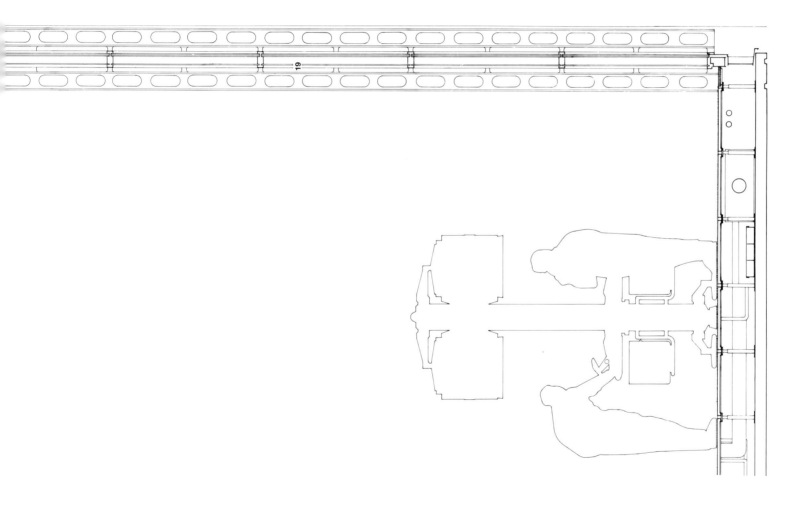

19

20

500mm

18in

0

0

Cutaway isometric
Staircase assembly

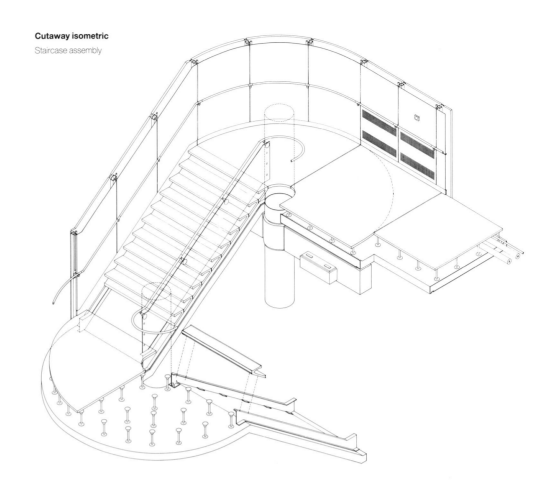

Stair section

1 extruded aluminium tread
   unit
2 threaded bolt welded to
   underside of tread unit
3 aluminium carriage
4 100mm glass fibre insulation
5 50mm glass fibre insulation
6 extruded aluminium nosing
7 studded rubber inset

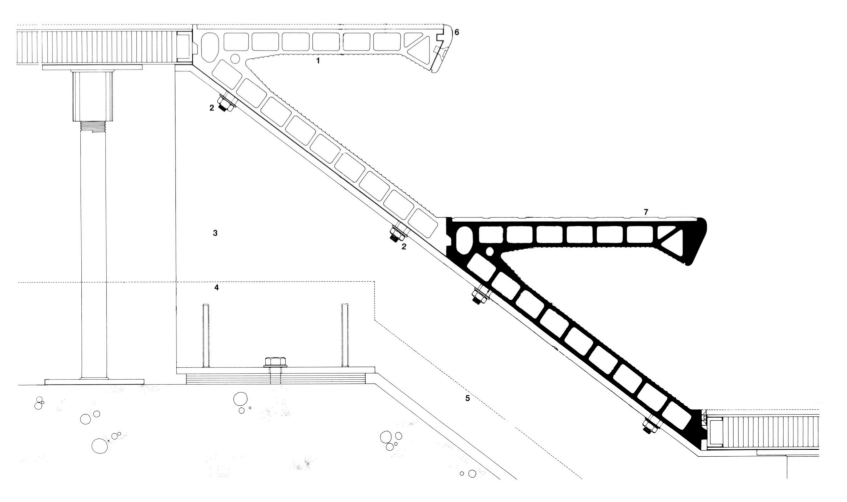

0   50mm

0   2in

Plan of satellite tower
Lift lobby, staircase, service riser
and lavatory pod

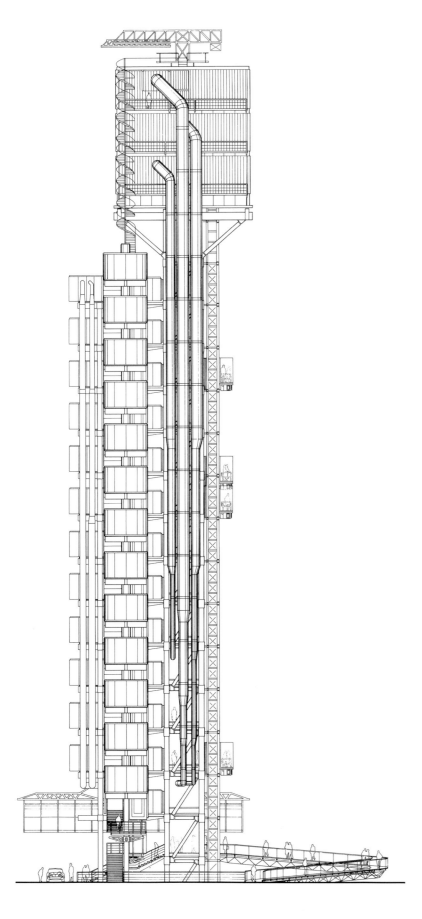

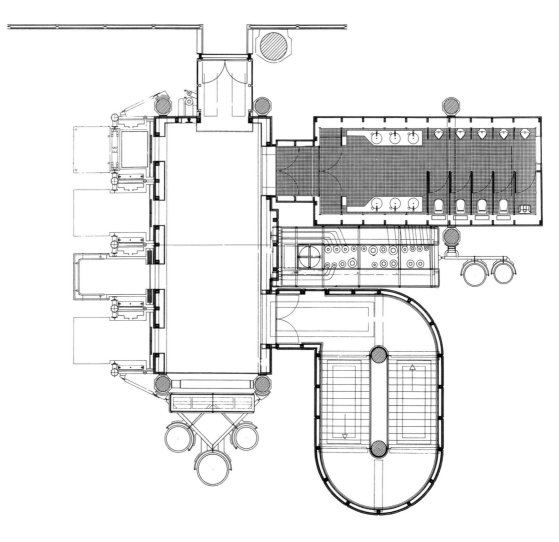

0   3m

0   10ft

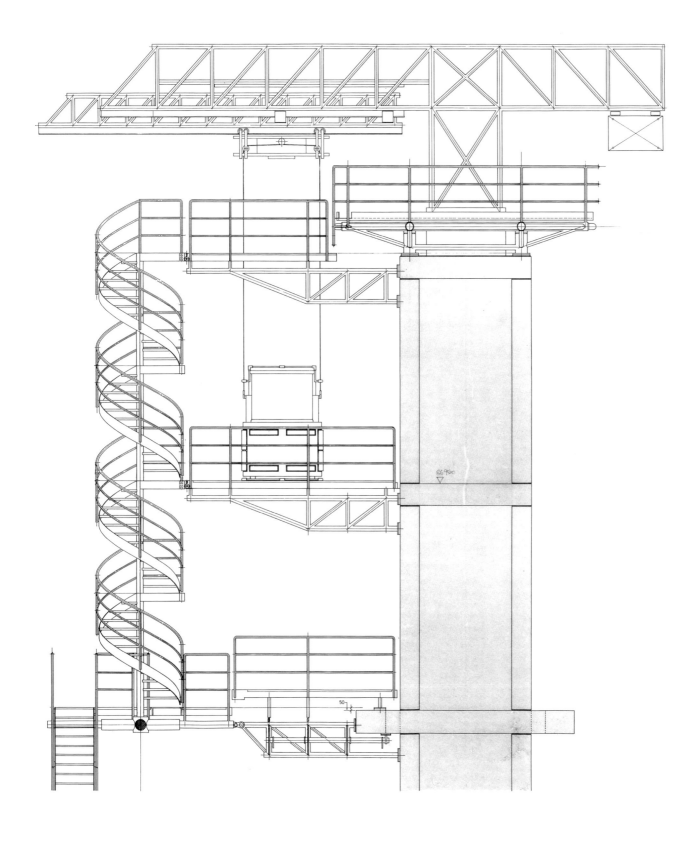

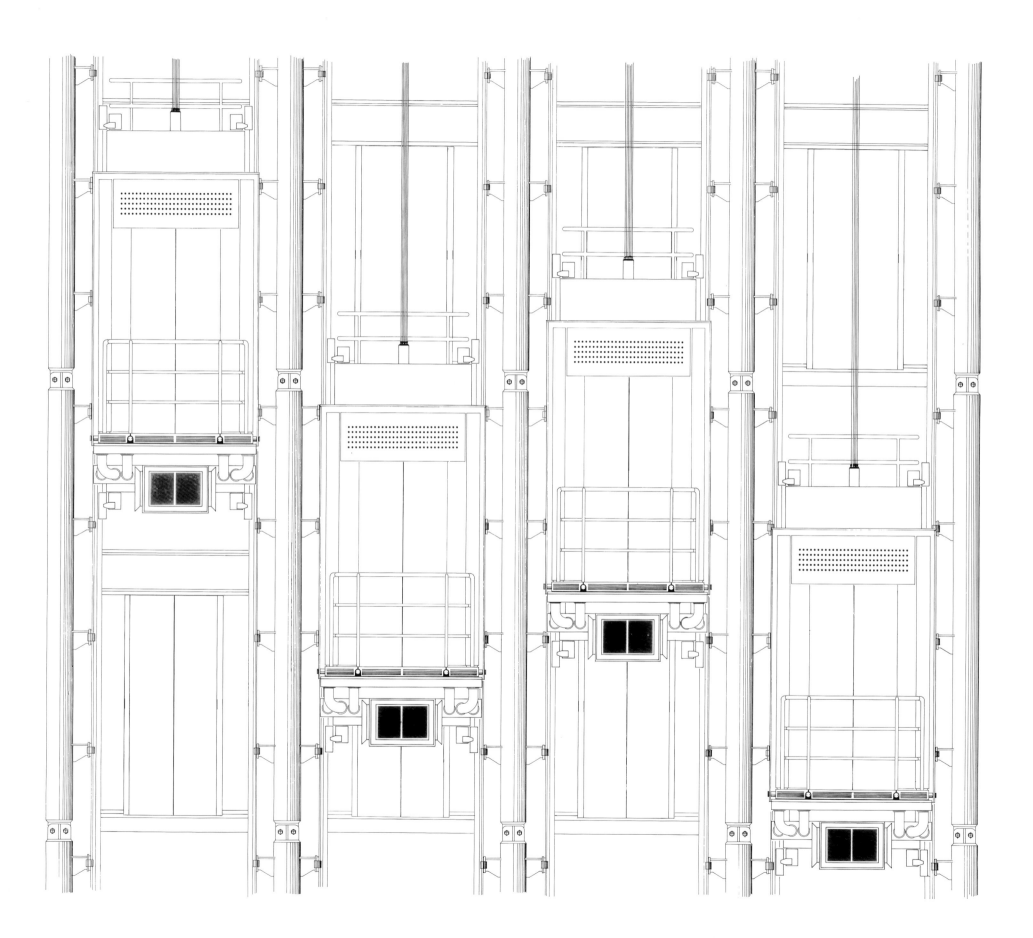

Location
City of London, England,
1978–1986

Client
Corporation of Lloyd's:
Sir Peter Green, Chairman of the
Redevelopment Committee;
Courtenay Blackmore, Director
of the Redevelopment
Committee; John Bathgate,
Project Co-ordinator

Architects
Richard Rogers Partnership:
Laurie Abbott, Graham Anthony,
Robert Barnes, Susan Blythe,
Kieran Breen, Julianne Coleman,
Ian Davidson, Mike Davies,
Maureen Diffley, Janet Dunsford,
Michael Elkan, Graham Fairley,
Marco Goldschmied, Mark
Guard, Philip Gumuchdjian, Ivan
Harbour, Roger Huntley, Eva
Jiricna, Andrew Jones, Wendy
Judd, Amarjit Kalsi, Kathy Kerr,
Stig Larsen, Malcolm Last,
Stephen Le Roith, Marcus Lee,
Colin MacKenzie, David Mark,
Richard Marzec, John McAslan,
Michael McGarry, Sue McMillan,
Peter McMunn, Andrew Morris,
Niki van Oosten, Frank Peacock,
Robert Peebles, Gennaro
Picardi, Elizabeth Post, Richard
Rogers, Henrietta Salvesen,
Georgina Savva, Kiyo Sawoaka,
Richard Soundy, Peter St John,
Alan Stanton, Graham Stirk,
Clare Strasser, Judy Taylor,
Peter Thomas, Jamie Troughton,
Stephen Tsang, Andrew Weston,
Chris Wilkinson, Joseph Wilson,
Yasu Yada, John Young

**Structural and Services
Engineers**
Ove Arup & Partners:
David Atling, Tom Barker,
Peter Bolingbroke, John
Burrows, Glen Calow, Richard
Cowell, Brian Duck, Paul
Duizend, Martin Hall, Martin
Harrold, Rob Kinch, Margaret
Law, John McGregor, Duncan
Michael, Turlogh O'Brian, Peter
Platt-Higgins, Geoff Powell,
Peter Rice, John Roberts, Harry
Saradjian, Andrew Sedgwick,
John Thornton, Paul Wellman,
Jack Zunz

Quantity Surveyors
Monk Dunstone Associates:
Geoffrey Ashworth, Nick Ayres

Other Consultants
Rights of Light: Anstey Horne
& Co.
Planning Consultants:
Montagu Evans & Sons
Lighting: Freidrich Wagner of
Lichttenchnische Planung
Acoustics: Sandy Brown
Associates
Catering: GWP Associates
Signs/Graphics: Pentagram
Design Ltd
Model Makers: Tetra Design
Services Ltd

Management Contractor
Bovis Construction Ltd:
Brian Pettifer, John Smith

Awards
Civic Trust Award 1987
Financial Times Architecture
at Work Award 1987
Eternit International prize
for Architecture: Special
Mention 1988
RIBA National Award 1988

Chronology

1977
July Lloyd's produces A case
for the Provision of Additional
Underwriting Space at Lloyd's
and concludes that an architect
must be appointed
August Gordon Graham,
President of the RIBA, meets
Lloyd's to discuss a new form of
competition to find an architect
20 October Six architects are
invited to compete, RRP (still
called Piano & Rogers), Foster
Associates, Arup Associates,
Serete, Webb Zarafa Menkes
Housden and I.M. Pei
8 November First meeting is
held at Lloyd's for the short-
listed competitors to discuss
the brief. Competitors are given
a four-month study period
to come up with a design
strategy for redevelopment
or refurbishment
10 November The 1928 building is listed

1978
February RRP produces
A Design Strategy for Lloyd's
March First presentations are
put to the Committee. The RRP
team is Richard Rogers, John
Young, Marco Goldschmied
and Peter Rice of Ove Arup
& Partners
April Final presentations are
made by Arup Associates and
RRP; Jack Zunz, Renzo Piano
and Mike Davies join the RRP
team; RRP is appointed
November Lloyd's members
vote for the proposed strategy
to redevelop the 1925 site by
a majority of 83 per cent

1979
January John Bathgate is
appointed project co-ordinator
March Royal Fine Arts
Commission complement
Lloyd's on 'a most enlightened
piece of architectural patronage'
May A planning application is
made
June RRP present their Outline
Proposals Report
July The Committee accepts
the outline proposals. Cost plan
and budget are established
21 September Outline planning permission and listed building consent are obtained
1 October Demolition begins

1980
13 May Bovis are appointed
as management contractor
June Scheme Design
Development Report is issued
An exhibition of designs is presented to the members of the
General Meeting
October Temporary accommodation in the 1958 building is
ready

1981
January Peter Green becomes
Chairman
3 February Demolition is complete; the site is handed over
to Bovis Construction
March Test piling begins
May Detailed planning permission is obtained, including an
extra level
June Work begins on the sub-
structure
October The Point report on
the implication of information
technology for the market is
published
November Foundation laying
ceremony at which the Queen
Mother pours concrete for one
of the main columns

1982
February Superstructure and
cladding contracts are awarded
June Work begins on the concrete superstructure
Lloyd's decide to commission
new underwriting boxes
Fire officers reject aluminium
cladding to satellites; stainless
steel is specified
September The RRP team is
appointed as interior designers

1983
May A decision is taken to
upgrade services on gallery 3 to
underwriting standard, in addition to galleries 1 and 2
July An underwriting box prototype is presented
7 September Gallery 7 is completed; 90 per cent of cladding is
manufactured
October Contracts for atrium
steel structure are let
December A full-course meal
is served in a mock-up of the
Captains' Room
Peter Miller is appointed
Chairman
French designer Jacques
Grange is appointed to do the
interiors of the Chairman's room
and levels 11/12

1984
January Underfloor services
installation begins
April The structure is complete
May A decision is taken to
upgrade services on gallery 4 for
more underwriting space
May The Queen Mother per-
forms the topping-out ceremony
August Room allocation is
agreed
September Ballots are held for
plots in each market area
October The building is watertight
Black lighting units are agreed
Courtenay Blackmore retires
from administration and returns
as redevelopment director to
work full time on the project

1985
February Tecno is contracted
to fabricate underwriting boxes
March Precise box allocations
are agreed
July Syndicates are interviewed
to establish Information
Technology requirements

1986
26/27 May Occupation over
Bank Holiday weekend

Select Bibliography

Financial Times, 'Bring down
Lloyd's', by Gordon Graham,
15 January 1979, letters page.
Architect's Journal, 'Lloyd's
Assured', 6 June 1979,
pp.1144–6.
RIBA Journal, 'The Frontiers
of Patronage', Vol. 86, No. 9,
September 1979, pp. 404–8.
International Architect,
'Architecture and the
Programme: Lloyd's of London',
Vol. 1, No. 3, Issue 3, 1980,
pp.25–39.
L'Architecture d'aujourd'hui,
'Projet d'immeuble de bureaux
pour le Lloyd's, Londres',
February 1980, pp.56–8.
Werk, Bauen + Wohnen,
'Projekt für die Lloyd's Versicher
in London', No. 4, April 1980,
pp.14–23.
The Architectural Review,
'Lloyd's', Vol. CLXXIX, No. 1011,
May 1981, pp.278–82.
The Arup Journal, 'Lloyd's
Redevelopment', by John
Thornton and Martin Hall,
June 1982, pp.2–7.
Concrete, 'Lloyd's room to last
for a hundred years', Vol. 17,
No. 4, April 1983, pp.36–41.
Building, 'Lloyd's Takes Shape',
Issue 18, 6 May 1983, pp.32–8.
Technique & Architecture,
'Richard Rogers – un décou-
vreur passioné', No. 350,
November 1983, pp.79–100.
Architect's Journal, 'Design
for Better Assembly – Case
Study, Rogers' and Arups, 5
September 1984, pp.87–94.
Building Magazine, 'A Year at
Lloyd's', by Brian Waters, Issue
38, 21 September 1984,
pp.30–37.
The Times, 'Lloyd's 21st
Century Coffee House', by
Charles Knevitt, 23 December
1985, p.8.
Lloyd's of London, Milan, 1986.
Blueprint, 'The Romance of the
Machine', No. 25, March 1986,
pp.34–7.
Architecture Interieure Cree,
'Contradictions in the City',
August/September 1986,
pp.74–89.
Designers' Journal, 'Beyond
the City Limits', No. 20,
September 1986, pp.40–53.
Architecture, 'England',
September 1986, pp.47–51.

Architect's Journal, Special
Issue, 'Lloyd's and the Bank',
Vol. 184, No. 43, 22 October
1986.
The Architectural Review,
Vol. CLXXX, No. 1076,
October 1986, pp.40–93.
Architectural Record, 'Lloyd's
of London', No. 11, November
1986, pp.104–17.
Baumeister, 'Lloyd's of
London', No. 11, November
1986, pp.14–21.
Vector, 'Lloyd's of London',
No. 01, 1987, pp.8–29.
Deutsche Bauzeitung,
'Lloyd's of London', No. 1,
January 1987, pp.23–8.
Architecture + Urbanism,
'Richard Rogers Partnership:
Lloyd's of London', No. 198,
March 1987.
AJ Focus, 'Insight – Glass at
Lloyd's', April 1987, pp.36–9.
Domus, 'Edificio Lloyd's,
Londra', No. 680, September
1987, pp.25–37.
Moebel Interior Design,
'Lloyd's of London setzt
Zeichen', December 1987,
pp.42–51.
The Client's Tale, Courtenay
Blackmore, London, 1990.

Acknowledgements
'Blue Cranes in the Sky' was first
published in *The Architectural
Review*, Vol. 180, No. 1076,
October 1986, pp.57–58.

Unless otherwise stated,
photographs and drawings are
courtesy of Richard Rogers
Partnership.

Mike Abrahams/Network: 15.
The Architectural Press: 39, 115
Richard Bryant: 9,13,14,17, 18,
30, 31, 32, 40, 43, 46, 49, 50,
53, 54, 73, 76, 78, 80, 85, 90,
92, 94, 99, 100, 101, 104, 105,
106, 108, 110, 112, 121, 122,
123, 124, page 8, page 9.
Martin Charles: 11, 12, 21, 34,
75, 81, 89, 91, 95, 97, 98, 103,
109, 111.
Peter Cook: 33, 44, 113.
Richard Davies: 35, 36, 37.
John Donat: 24, 47, 84, 116.
The Evening Standard: 102.
A.F. Kersting: 114.
Katsuhisa Kida: 120.
Ian Lambot, Foster Associates:
118, 119.
Lloyd's of London:
1,2,3,4,5,6,7,8,45, 107.
Ove Arup & Partners: 19, 61, 63,
64, 65.
Stephen Le Roith: 59, 60.
Harry Sowden: 62, 69, 70, 71,
72, 83.
Paul Wakefield: 56; page 5
Matthew Weinreb: 41
John Young: 67, 68, 82, 88, 93.

ARCHITECTURE 3s

PIONEERING BRITISH 'HIGH-TECH'

James S. Russell, AIA, is editor-at-large at *Architectural Record* magazine. He also writes for publications including *The New York Times*, the *Philadelphia Enquirer* and *Harvard Design Magazine*. He teaches at Columbia University, New York, and is the principal of a consulting firm, WorkDesign.

James Stirling and James Gowan
Leicester University Engineering Building

John McKean is a historian of postwar British architecture. He taught design and history in London and in Italy with Giancarlo De Carlo's ILAUD. He is currently head of interior design at the University of Brighton School of Architecture and Interior Design. He writes widely and is author of the *Architecture in Detail* monographs on the Royal Festival Hall and Crystal Palace.

Foster Associates
Willis Faber & Dumas Building

Gabriele Bramante is an architect who combines practice with a complex career as a teacher, writer and journalist. She guest edited a special issue of *The Architectural Review* devoted to the recent architecture of Japan and continues to contribute regularly to the magazine.

Acknowledgements A book like this is not produced in isolation. The author is grateful to everyone who contributed information. In particular she would like to thank: Maritz Vandenberg; Dr F. Thomas and Dr D.M. Ryle; John Simon Woodman and Colin Boyne for reading the text and making valuable suggestions; Massimo Scolari and George Finlay for their support and gives a special thank you to Clyde Malby for painstakingly proofreading the entire text. Illustrations are reproduced with the permission of the following: Malcolm Lewis (The Architectural Press) (3), Lucian Hervé (The Architectural Press) (15, top left), The Architectural Press (15, top right), Zoo Operations Limited (15, middle right), Wolfgang Volz (15, middle left), Martin Charles (15, bottom), Rupert Truman (33), The Architectural Press (36), East Anglian Daily Times & Associated Newspapers (37) and Alan Richards (The Architectural Press) (47).

Richard Rogers Partnership
Lloyd's Building

Kenneth Powell is an architectural writer and key figure in the Twentieth Century Society. He was formerly Architectural Editor of the *Daily Telegraph* and is the author of numerous books including *Grand Central Terminal*, *Graves Residence* and *Richard Rogers Complete Works: Volume One*, all published by Phaidon Press.

Acknowledgements This book is dedicated to the memory of two leading members of the team which built Lloyd's: Courtenay Blackmore and Peter Rice. Courtenay Blackmore was a painstaking and untiring supporter of the author's researches throughout, while Peter Rice explained the engineering of Lloyd's patiently and vividly. John Young has been my constant mainstay, always ready to advise and comment.

Among the many others who have helped me are: Nick Ayres, Tom Barker, Ian Davidson, Mike Davies, Ian Hay Davison, Jack Fielder, Marco Goldschmied, Gordon Graham, Sir Peter Green, Eva Jiricna, Martin Pawley, Richard Soundy, Jamie Troughton, Bob Woods and Sir Jack Zunz. David Coleridge, former Chairman of Lloyd's, and Alan Lord, Chief Executive, welcomed me to the building and answered my questions.

Richard Rogers suggested the idea of a book on Lloyd's and has given generously of his time to recount the story of the project and read my drafts.

In the Rogers office, Philip Gumuchdjian, Jo Murtagh and Harriet Watson were ever helpful.

Phaidon Press Limited
Regent's Wharf
All Saints Street
London N1 9PA

Pioneering British 'High-Tech' first published 1999
© 1999 Phaidon Press Limited
ISBN 0 7148 3880 2

A CIP catalogue record for this book is available
from the British Library.

Printed in Hong Kong

Leicester University Engineering Building originally
published in Architecture in Detail series 1994
© 1994 Phaidon Press Limited
Willis Faber & Dumas Building originally published
in Architecture in Detail series 1993
© 1993 Phaidon Press Limited
Photographs © 1993 John Donat and Ken
Kirkwood unless otherwise stated
Lloyd's Building originally published in
Architecture in Detail series 1994
© 1994 Phaidon Press Limited